Rise Up and Walk

Volume I

Rise Up and Walk

A Journey Through Divorce Recovery

Ann Hazard

Writers Club Press

San Jose New York Lincoln Shanghai

Rise Up and Walk
A Journey Through Divorce Recovery

Writers Club Press
an imprint of iUniverse.com, Inc.

For information address:
iUniverse.com, Inc.
5220 S 16th, Ste. 200
Lincoln, NE 68512
www.iuniverse.com

All Bible quotations, unless otherwise indicated, are from the NIV (New International Version).

ISBN: 0-595-20326-4

Printed in the United States of America

DEDICATION

This book is dedicated to everyone who has journeyed through Divorce, and who is contemplating that journey now. May you find comfort and healing here.

Contents

INTRODUCTION

Humpty Dumpty sat on a wall,
Humpty Dumpty had a great fall.
All the king's horses and all the king's men
Couldn't put Humpty together again.

Can you relate? Do you feel so shattered that nobody could ever put you back together again? Rev. Joseph M. Scerbo, S.A., Ph.D., academic dean of Trinity College of Graduate Studies in Orange County, California, offers these words of hope: "When we experience trauma, pain and perceived rejection, we fragment emotionally. If our spiritual lives are focused on Jesus, the healer, we allow him to gather the fragments of ourselves so that nothing is lost."

If you are like 70 percent of newly separated Americans who seek help with divorce recovery, you didn't make the decision to get divorced. Your marriage was put on trial and sentenced to death by your spouse. You probably didn't attend the trial, and the verdict caught you by surprise. What you now realize is that although two people decide to get married, if one person wants a divorce, the other one has no choice but to consent. And oh, that hurts. It hurts. It hurts so bad.

Or maybe you're part of the other 30 percent who seek divorce recovery—the people who walked out on their marriages because it was too painful to stay another day. While you may feel that exhilarating rush of freedom that comes when you've first escaped tyranny, the next minute you may well be miserable and racked with guilt. You left. You have committed a major, perhaps unpardonable, sin. And, yes, that hurts too.

So what are you going to do? You may or may not be a Christian. Even though this book is written from a Christian point of view, God loves all of us equally, and offers equal help to everyone. If you are a Christian, you *know* that God hates divorce. You've read all the Bible passages about it, and you stand thoroughly convicted. Your family, friends, and pastor are encouraging you to work toward reconciliation, whether you were the one who left or the one who was left. What do you do? How long should you keep on praying, hoping, begging God to bring your mate home to you? How do you know if and when he or she is gone for good? Or how do you reconcile with someone who refuses to accept any responsibility for the sickness within your marriage, someone who blames you entirely and says that if *you* change, everything will be OK? Just the thought of it chokes the breath out of you. Wherever you stand in regard to these questions, how can you ever hold your head up in church again?

You know what? Christians divorce at nearly the same rate as non-Christians. It isn't supposed to be that way, but it is. And you know what else? I hate divorce. You hate divorce. Your mother hates divorce, especially if she went through one herself. No one hates divorce more than those who have crawled along its pitted and muddy back roads on their bloody hands and knees. I'd bet anything you didn't approach the altar at your wedding thinking, *I don't believe in all this "till death us do part" stuff. If it doesn't work out, no sweat. I'll survive. My spouse will survive. If we have kids, they'll be fine. Piece of cake!* Hardly! You got married with your eyes shining with love's radiance and your heart overflowing with its happily-ever-afters.

Yet by the time you have picked up this book, your divorce may already be in the works or looming like a fearsome tornado on the horizon. What do you do? Here are a few suggestions:

- Ask your spouse if he or she is willing to get a third party involved to help you confront and work on the problems in your marriage and help you learn to communicate more effectively and lovingly with each other. This could be a therapist, a pastor, an elder in your church.

- Get good legal help. If you have children, this is crucial, for their well-being and your own. If you and your spouse own property or have other assets, you also need to protect yourself.
- Surround yourself with supportive, loving people—friends and family who will offer you kindness and understanding without clobbering you over the head with their opinions and criticisms. Don't isolate! You need others now.
- Read your Bible, or any other inspirational book you have that helps you feel connected to a Higher Power. Reach out to God, the spirit of love, truth and healing. Pray your heart out. It doesn't matter what you say, or even if you get mad and scream and yell. The shoulders of the Almighty are big enough to handle any emotion you have. And to heal all your hurts ... in time.

Even if you do everything I've suggested here, please remember this: Reconciliation is a goal but not a guarantee. It takes two people to make a marriage. Both you and your spouse have to be willing to do the hard, painful, and frustrating work required to get your marriage out of the "sick" category and into the "healthy" category. That's why you need the help of a loving and neutral third party. Can it be done? Oh yes! *But it takes two.*

At some point in the not-too-distant future, one of two things will become clear to you: Your marriage is going to survive, or it's not. This decision may be your spouse's; it may be yours. No matter who makes the call, God will be there with you, every second of every day. With him as your comforter and guide you can and will move forward, resting in the knowledge that he loves you unconditionally, *no matter which fork in the road you end up taking.*

I got divorced in 1990 when my children were three and five. I struggled, I agonized, I berated myself, I got berated, I wallowed and I struggled some more. That first year I inflicted incredible damage on myself. Then, in desperation, I turned to God. As I worked my way through the dark back roads of what my friend, Jim Smoke calls "Divorce Country," I assure you, I would have never made it through without him. Nor would I have made it without the people who stood by me and loved me through the *really icky parts*.

If divorce has become a reality for you, I am grateful that this book has found its way into your hands. Read it and do the exercises every day. If you're still hungry for help, visit the Divorce section of your local bookstore. Or visit Amazon.com. Find a divorce recovery support group or workshop and get involved. It will help! But you can expect to feel like Humpty Dumpty for a while. After all, what God brought together is now somehow being pulled asunder.

I liken the experience of being pulled asunder to that ancient form of torture where one's arms and legs are tied to four barely restrained stallions. The horses are released and race off in separate directions, ripping the person to pieces in the process. Gruesome metaphor, for sure. But I know you will agree with me that *the pain can be that severe.* The difference here is that while you may be all torn up inside, you still look OK on the outside. It may be impossible for those closest to you to discern the depth of your suffering. But you can trust in God. *He understands your pain and he will heal you in time. If you let him.*

Divorce is a crisis of awesome proportions, and it's been best described using the two-sided Chinese symbol for crisis. One side of this symbol represents "catastrophe" and the other "opportunity." Let's look at a few words associated with each:

- **Catastrophe.** Disaster, tragedy, failure, despair, terror, remorse, guilt, misery, shame, unworthiness, desperation, isolation, depression, horror, rage.

- **Opportunity.** Newness, growth, awareness, understanding, accountability, repentance, compassion, courage, perseverance, patience, acceptance, empathy, forgiveness, healing, excitement, trust, hope, faith.

Allow *Rise Up and Walk* to be your companion for this season. It doesn't follow a chronological, calendar format, so you can begin right now. Each day starts with a biblical or an inspirational quotation, followed by a few thoughts and observations on a subject associated with divorce. Some of the stories are composites, gleaned from my years of experience working with other divorced people as a divorce recovery leader, program director, and program creator. In some stories names and details have been changed.

Before you start, go to an office supply store and pick up a three-ring binder, a six-pack of subject dividers, and some lined paper. Feel as if you're going to school? You are! I challenge you, as you read, to write about something each day. Do that and pretty soon you'll be able to look back and see God working each day in your life, giving you strength and answering your prayers.

One last, important thought. We all experience grief in stages, and you can expect to struggle on many different levels. In most cases it takes *a minimum of two years* to work your way through this grieving process after a marriage ends.

So commit right now to *give yourself the gift of time.* Allow yourself at least two years to get through this. Be aware that the national average of times a person goes through recovery is *three.* So, if you want to read this book two or three times, you certainly won't be doing yourself a disservice! Now, take a deep breath and then take that first step, friend. May the Lord hold you tightly today and every day from now on. And may you feel the comfort of his arm around you and his hand in yours, every step of the way. Remember these words of the apostle Paul:

Praise be to the God and Father of our Lord Jesus Christ, the Father of compassion and the God of all comfort, who comforts us in all our troubles, so that we can comfort those in any trouble with the comfort we ourselves have received from God.

2 Corinthians 1:3-4

WEEK ONE

WEEK ONE: SUNDAY
SHOCK AND THE WAKE-UP CALL

> You're blessed when you feel you've lost what is most dear to you.
> Only then can you be embraced by the One most dear to you.
> From Matthew 5, The Message

It was my first night alone in my "new" house. I roamed through half-assembled rooms, the dog at my heels. The silence howled at me, a hopeless, dismal wail. I turned on the radio, tried to sing along. Every song seemed to be about falling in or out of love. I could deal with neither, so I switched it off. I went to the refrigerator and opened it. Ugh. Leftovers and lunch-box fare. How unappetizing! I shut the door and went back to pacing. Numb. I was numb. I tried to think of someone to call. Couldn't. I tried to dredge up a memory that would make me mad or sad—anything. Couldn't. I pinched myself. Was I still alive? Barely. A shadow of pain greeted the white nail prints on my forearm. I felt as see-through and ethereal as a ghost. And so alone.

It wasn't supposed to be this way, I reminded myself. I was supposed to rejoice in my freedom. I'd promised myself I wouldn't mope around. No pity parties for me. I would have my new life up and running in record time. Six months max. I was a mover and shaker, a survivor. Wasn't I?

Yeah, right, whispered a nasty little voice inside my head. *You blew it at marriage, Ann. Now you can't even make it through a night alone.* Desperation crashed in on me and I ran into my room, flung myself on the mattress, and cried. I'd been so busy planning, moving, and taking care of details that the shock of my impending divorce had not penetrated.

When it hits us—whenever that happens—its impact is swift, piercing, and stunning. We aren't sure who we are today or who we were yesterday, and we're utterly uncertain about who we're supposed to be tomorrow. Our feet are no longer planted on *terra firma,* and we feel as if we are spinning out of control, through the cosmos. This is incredibly scary, but it passes; I promise.

Your first assignment is to pray the following prayer, then open your journal and let yourself express your feelings about ending your marriage and starting over. Have you faced a night (or many) alone yet? How was it for you?

> *Father, I feel as if you're so far away right now. I feel so empty, so lost and so alone. Please put your comforting arms around me and allow me to feel your presence. Thank you for loving me, for promising to love me no matter what.*
>
> *Amen*

WEEK ONE: MONDAY
JUST WHAT IS THE GRIEVING PROCESS?

> God whispers to us in our pleasures…but shouts in our pain. It is his megaphone to rouse a deaf world.
>
> C. S. Lewis, *The Problem of Pain*

When our marriages die, we grieve. What exactly does that mean and how is it supposed to feel? Well, first off, it feels pretty bad. It's disorienting. Crazy. It can feel as if you're stuck on Mr. Toad's Wild Ride—blindfolded. It's as scary as being alone and broke in a crowded city where you don't speak the local language. It makes you so mad you want to murder and so ashamed and depressed that you want to die. And often you ask yourself, *Will this ever end?!*

It will. Grief is definitely not an event; it's a process. Elisabeth Kübler-Ross identified it as having five stages: denial, anger, bargaining, depression, and acceptance. The Christian divorce recovery movement has added a sixth: forgiveness, which precedes acceptance. I learned about the grieving process at the first divorce recovery workshop I attended. As the speaker described these stages and the feelings that accompanied them, I jumped to the quick and easy solution: Voila! I had worked my way through the entire process *before* my separation. I was free! I was in acceptance! I could move on and avoid the whole embarrassing, time-wasting mess called suffering. (I was in denial.)

How do you view grief? Look it up in the dictionary and write the definition in your journal. What feelings and images come to mind? How do you feel about suffering? Shame? Depression?

Lord, I'm afraid of what the future holds. Help me to trust you, to know that you are with me always, and to remember that you will see me through this process.   Amen

WEEK ONE: TUESDAY
DENIAL—I AM OKAY! OKAY?!

When I was a child, I used denial to protect myself...from seeing things too painful to see and feelings too overwhelming to feel....Denial protected me from pain, but it also rendered me blind to my feelings, my needs, myself. It was...a thick blanket that covered and smothered me.

Melodie Beattie, *The Language of Letting Go*

I've learned that when an unpleasant surprise comes my way, it takes awhile for it to penetrate my personal denial blanket. I used to revel in my strength and impenetrability, only to find that a day or two after the fact my facade would shatter. Yes, previously I'd been calm and in control, but then I'd be shivering in fear or seething with rage. What happened? Reality had penetrated my denial blanket.

That denial blanket protects us from feeling pain until we're ready to deal with it. When I first became single-again, my blanket was as thick and tough as a rhinoceros hide. It took at least six months for life to strip it off of me. You can expect to go through a period of suspended animation where numbness, disbelief, or wishful thinking are more real to you than the reality staring you in the face. In denial, some people think they can catapult over the grieving process; some think they can pray their marriages back into existence.

Do you find yourself reacting to unpleasant situations by checking out emotionally? Do you deny your feelings of anger and frustration so you can dodge arguments? Do you consider yourself to be on top of things, confused, miserable, or just plain old neutral? Explore these thoughts in your journal.

Dear Father, I may not understand my feelings right now, but I trust that you will bring them to my awareness when I am strong enough to face them.   Amen

WEEK ONE: WEDNESDAY
ANGER—WHAT IS THIS AWFUL FEELING?

My God, my God, why have you forsaken me? Why are you so far from saving me, so far from the words of my groaning?

Psalm 22:1

When our sense of disbelief is dispelled and reality sets in, we get furious. We blame ourselves. Our former spouses. Our families. God. The anger associated with divorce comes at us unexpectedly and explodes hard, heavy, and hot like a volcano erupting from deep within our souls. It is at least as intense as the intimacy that once characterized the marriage. It is born of broken dreams, dashed hopes, and shattered trust. And its roar is mighty.

I've led divorce recovery support groups for years. The subject of anger always comes up by the second or third meeting. "Are you upset?" I ask. I remember two women who sat side by side on my couch. The first was trying so hard to be a model of Christian propriety.

"Absolutely not," she assured me, her hands twisting in her lap. "Even though I'm pretty sure he has a girlfriend, I have faith that, if I stay close to the Lord, he'll bring my husband to his senses and send him back home to me. For our son's sake, at least." Her mouth curved in a hopeful smile, but there was terror in her eyes.

The woman next to her burst out, "What? Are you nuts?" She practically levitated off the coach. Her eyes spit fire. What followed was a litany against men in general and her man in particular. She gave us a run down of all the horrible and unforgivable things he had done to her before, during, and after their separation.

Several weeks later, after receiving divorce papers and being forced to send her one-year-old away for the weekend, the first woman was slapped in the face by reality. God had let her down. And then her anger surfaced. Big time.

Which response was normal? Both were. We are all unique; we express our emotions in different ways. But we are all alike in that we all need a safe place to vent our anger. Anger is part of our humanity. We need to listen to what it's telling us. Today, open your journal and write down five (or more) things that really, really tick you off. If you don't feel angry, then try writing five things that scare you, frustrate you, or hurt you.

Dearest Lord, please give me the words to put my feelings on paper. Help me to feel your hand on my shoulder as I let it pour out of me. Help me to know that you are my forever Father, Friend, and Comforter.   Amen

WEEK ONE: THURSDAY
WHAT IN THE WORLD DO I TELL MY KIDS?

Speaking the truth in love, we will in all things grow up into him who is the Head, that is, Christ.   Ephesians 4:15

Children possess a clear-eyed innocence that allows them to see through many of our adult charades. Do you remember as a child asking your parents a serious question and being told you weren't old enough to know about that subject? Or worse yet, getting a bogus answer? Kids know when they're being talked down to, and they know when they're being lied to. My kids have called my bluff so many times I no longer underestimate them!

Whether they're four or forty-four, your children deserve to be told the truth about an impending divorce, from both of their parents. Otherwise, they may blame themselves. Or they may resent one or both of you. Either way, they'll have a big, aching question mark in their hearts that cries out for understanding—and for truth. They don't need a two-hour Mom- or Dad-bashing session, but neither do they need false levity. They need a few solid reasons as to why the family is splitting apart. They need something credible to hang on to.

Being able to "speak the truth in love" is a sign of Christian maturity. It's a sign of knowing how much to say to a four-year-old, when to say it, and whether to do it alone or with your soon-to-be-former spouse. If the thought of telling your children is completely overwhelming to you, seek wise counsel from a person (or several people) whom you respect. Pick up one of the books listed in the Reading List. Your children need to know that you love them and that you'll be there for them, no matter what. Today, write a tentative script between you and your children. What do they need to hear from you? What kind of help do you need? Pray this prayer and ask help from God's people.

O Father, thank you so much for the incredible gift of my children. Help me to find the right words to answer their questions about this divorce. Give me the courage to speak the truth in love and to help them feel secure, not only in my love for them, but in yours, too, which is the greatest love of all.
Amen

WEEK ONE: FRIDAY
BARGAINING—SHORT CUTS THAT DON'T WORK

Trust in the Lord with all your heart and lean not on your own understanding; in all your ways acknowledge him, and he will make your paths straight.   Proverbs 3:5-6

I've known people who believe God will never forgive them or love them again because their spouses left them. These men and women are so mortified by the idea of divorce that they say they'll do *anything* to avoid the disgrace of divorce. Sure that they've committed *the unpardonable sin* and disconsolate at the idea of being on their own, they're willing to do *anything* to get their mates back. *Anything.* They pray to God with gut-wrenching desperation. "Please God, please God, please! I promise to be the perfect wife. I promise never to yell at him. I'll quite complaining, running up the Visa bill...."

We bargain with our spouses, and when we get really desperate, we bargain with God. We become willing to twist ourselves into psychological, emotional, and spiritual pretzels to avoid getting divorced. But what we're really doing is *setting ourselves up to fail and then to endure even more rejection.* Bargaining isn't a functional way of negotiating through conflicts. It's a power play and a quick fix, which stinks of one upmanship and dishonesty. It is manipulation—pure and simple. Surprisingly, it's more about the bargainer's needs, hopes, and desires than anyone else's. It doesn't take into consideration God's will. And it doesn't take into consideration the spouse's will. If you've ever gone on a diet to please someone else, only to gain all the weight back later on and be mocked for your failure, you know that bargaining doesn't work. It's an attempt to find a quick and easy solution for a complex problem.

I'm not saying you shouldn't pray for reconciliation. You should. Absolutely! But *remember this sad truth:* If your spouse is dead-set on the divorce and is unwilling to consider reconciliation, you're going to have to make a decision to move forward in your life, alone. Otherwise you will be lost in limbo, living in the past and going nowhere.

God doesn't want you to waste your life. He wants you to keep growing in love, courage, and perseverance. Think back to the time since your separation. Have you bargained with your former spouse? Have you bargained with God? What results did you get from it? Have you tried to recreate yourself, either wholly or partially into the *perfect mate?* How did it make you feel? Is your spouse truly open to reconciliation, or is she or he finished?

> *Father, help me to stop trying to force things to go my way. Please show me your will and give me the strength to obey it. Amen*

WEEK ONE: SATURDAY
HELLO?! WHERE HAVE MY FRIENDS GONE?

For the Lord God will help Me; Therefore I will not be disgraced; Therefore I have set My face like a flint, And I know that I will not be ashamed.   Isaiah 50:7, NKJV

Rejection. Just looking at the word on a piece of paper makes my stomach churn. When we divorce, we are divested of our citizenship in couples' country. We become incomplete units socially and diminished units economically, because we lack partners and we also are unable to maintain our former standard of living. And that can feel pretty disgraceful.

Jim Smoke's research concludes that in the first year following a divorce, it's not unusual to lose up to 90 percent of your friends. When I first heard that statistic, my jaw dropped. *Ninety percent?!* But then I thought back. When I expected to have my life all put back together within six months, I was mirroring the expectations of my friends and family. They were mirroring the expectations prevalent in late twentieth-century America. But then, after the six-month mark passed and I was more lost than I'd been in the very beginning, my married friends began to bail. Some drifted away so quietly I barely noticed. One friend sent me a letter: "You brought this on yourself," she wrote. "Stop wallowing and get on with your life." The sting of it lingered for years.

Open your journal and tell God about the friends who have left you and those who are still around but whose impatience scares you. Share your pain and fear with him.

> *O heavenly Father, please help me to forgive those friends who have left me. I know they don't understand how they've hurt me. Keep me close to you today, Lord, and saturate me with your strength-giving words of encouragement.*   *Amen*

WEEK TWO

WEEK TWO: SUNDAY
DEPRESSION—O DARK NIGHT OF MY SOUL

> The wounds of the past continue festering. The warping effects...keep us from seeing reality clearly; we make the same errors, the same mistakes over and over, all the while believing what we think we see and not what is.... Deep grieving purges.
>
> Robert Hemfelt, Frank Minirth, and Paul Meier, *Love Is a Choice*

In divorce recovery we call it the black hole. The pit. The toilet bowl. You get my drift. Depression. It grips you by the throat, threatens to choke the life out of you, and tosses you into a dark dungeon of despair. Yet it's a normal part of the grieving process. It's also the most painful stage, by far. Like unexpected outbursts of anger, it can catch us unawares. We wake up in the morning and before our eyes open, we just *know*. It's going to be one of those days. One of those black days. O God, we cry out. Not again!

Our culture doesn't like suffering. It's so, well, unbecoming! When I felt the black cloud of depression descend over my spirit, I used to throw myself into a frenzy of activity. I figured, the busier I was, the less chance I had of being sucked down that porcelain tube. Besides, I believed that depression was a sign of self-pity, and I was raised to loathe self-pity. So what did I end up doing? I ran in circles, repeating behavior that quickly became self-destructive. That, in turn, fueled up the fires of my self-loathing and deepened the depression. Not too effective, huh?

Where do we hide from our pain? Work is an excellent diversion. It's even respectable. Partying is a great escape, except that it's full of obvious pitfalls. Romantic attachments are extremely effective. They're intoxicating beyond belief, but they can tie us up in knots that take months or *years* to untie.

So what should we do? With God's help we can face the depression, and with his grace we can work through it. Try it. In your journal tell God how you've tried to disguise your pain. Open your heart and let it pour out onto the paper.

> *O blessed Father, please help me to stop trying to run from this pain. Please open my eyes so that I can see what it is you are trying to show me. I thank you and praise you for being the my master Physician. Heal me with your love.*
> *Amen*

WEEK TWO: MONDAY
REACHING OUT—ASKING FOR HELP

> Do for others what you would like them to do for you. This is a summary of all that is taught in the law and the prophets.
> Matthew 7:12, NLT

It was a training session for group leaders for a divorce recovery workshop. Twenty of us sat around a conference table and introduced ourselves. Everyone had been through a divorce and had previously attended the workshop. What motivated the others to give up seven Monday nights to be volunteers in this emergency room called divorce recovery? I wondered. One man summed it up. "I went through the workshop last fall. I remember where I was then. I was a mess. It helped me so much. My group met for months afterward; in fact, we're all still good friends. I don't know what I would have done without this. It changed my life." He looked around the table and smiled. "And now I want to give something back."

When we become single-again, we need to find a new community. As non-divorced people come to understand more about divorce and the many losses associated with it, perhaps we won't be faced with so much rejection. But in the meantime we need to find a safe place where we'll be accepted and loved, right where we are today. If you haven't participated in a divorce recovery group, or if you don't know where to find one, I suggest you call the churches around you. Ask if they have or know of any groups. Here, in the spiritual and emotional ER, you'll meet people with whom you have much in common. Here you'll find empathy, support, and companionship. And healing.

Today's assignment is to research divorce recovery programs in your area. Write what you find out in your journal. Ask God to point you to the right one. Also make a list of those people who have *not* vanished from your life. And thank God for them.

> *God, please help me to reach out. Direct me toward people who will understand and accept me, who will walk with me through this painful place.*   *Amen*

WEEK TWO: TUESDAY
REDISCOVERING AND REDEFINING FRIENDSHIP

> Be joyful in hope, patient in affliction, faithful in prayer. Share with God's people who are in need. Practice hospitality.
>   Romans 12:12-13

When I became single-again, my kids and I moved into a new neighborhood. My first Saturday there, I tiptoed outside in my bathrobe to pick up the newspaper, hoping no one would see me. No such luck! There, across the street, was a woman with long dark hair picking up her newspaper *in her bathrobe*. We struck up a conversation, and she invited me over for coffee. Her name was Kathy, and she was a single mom.

A friendship was kindled that morning that has lasted eight years so far. We've been through ups, downs, sideways, and backwards together. Her friendship has been an amazing gift to me, as she would tell you mine has been to her.

For a single parent who's home alone night after night with small children, the lack of adult company can get overwhelming in a hurry. That's what drew Kathy and me together initially. Our loneliness, isolation, and situational similarities. I'm nothing like her, and she's nothing like me, although we're less dissimilar now than we used to be. When we met, she was cautious, low key, and uncomfortable with change. She gave people the benefit of the doubt, sometimes long after they deserved it. I, on the other hand, was impulsive, high energy, and hooked on change. I became disillusioned with people easily, and after they disappointed me a few times, I was history. There were times when I considered her a plodder and was certain that my way of doing things was far superior to hers. Not anymore.

Kathy and I have learned much from each other. For years she was the only person who was there for me, unconditionally, and vice versa. I broadened my vision as I came to respect and absorb some of her values. Most of all, I learned to trust her and connect with her emotionally.

Is there anyone on the periphery of your life whom you might consider getting to know? Someone different from your usual choice of a same-sex friend, but someone by whom you feel encouraged and with whom you feel intrigued? Pray about it. Then jot down a few names. Don't pick up the phone unless you feel the immediate urge to do so.

Just let the thought of a new friendship drift around in your mind for now.

> *Father, thank you for being the God of new beginnings. I ask today that you send a new friend to me or that you open my eyes to see someone I already know who needs an understanding friend as much as I do.*   *Amen*

WEEK TWO: WEDNESDAY
"HOW WILL I EVER?"—THOSE THREE A.M. ANXIETY ATTACKS

> Look at the birds of the air; they do not sow or reap or store away in barns, and yet your heavenly Father feeds them. Are you not much more valuable than they? Who of you by worrying can add a single hour to his life?   Matthew 6:26-27

Oh, those obnoxious, gut-wrenching, heinous 3 A.M. anxiety attacks! Have you ever bolted straight up in bed, eyes wild, heart racing, adrenalin pumping? The events of the previous day, week, or month careen across the video screen of your brain. The volume is on full blast, and all the players are larger than life, their faces distorted and angry. You hit the stop button. Breathe easy now. OK. Let's replay those scenes, making them come out better. You are caught in an "if only…" nightmare. Then the worrying starts. That court date is coming up. You have to get all your financial stuff together by Friday. What if you don't get enough child support to live on? How will you ever make ends meet? Or what if your ex-wife gets awarded a huge chunk of child support, *plus* spousal support? She thinks you really have the money. You know you don't! How will you live? What if, what if, what if ?

Been there before? We all have. Wide-awake brain, exhausted body. Paranoid brain, captive body. Total insanity. I've tried lots of different things to ward off those late-night meanies. I tried counting my blessings, but those blessings would dance across my mind like sheep jumping over a fence. And, like those sheep, they danced right over the fence and evaporated into thin air. My mind raced back to the "what ifs." I tried reading. I tried writing. I tried calling someone (once). I even tried exercising (twice).

How about trying to pray? Instead of dreading the insomnia, we can make it our special time to be alone with God. (There certainly isn't anyone else around to talk to!) It will become, over time, a *sacred* time instead of a *scared* time. Recapture, in your journal, some of your late-night terrors. What did you try to do to get back to sleep? What would you do tonight? Can you dedicate that time to God?

Father, I cast my worries upon you and ask for the comforting presence of your Holy Spirit in the darkest hours of the night when I feel the most afraid. I dedicate that time to you, and I trust that you will always care for me.   *Amen*

WEEK TWO: THURSDAY
MOVING INTO A BETTER PLACE

The Lord is good, a stronghold in the day of trouble; and He knows those who trust in Him.   Nahum1:7, NKJV

This journey through divorce country reminds me of that line the Alcoholics Anonymous folks use so often: "One day at a time." It also reminds me of taking "baby steps" or of taking two steps forward, one step back.

Today we're going to practice taking a step forward. It can be a baby step or a giant step, whichever you feel up to. First, take yourself out for coffee or sit yourself down in a sunny window. Find a place that makes you feel better.

You're there? Now pull out your journal and write: "The Worst!" Then describe the most *negative* thing that happened to you this past week. Write as much as you want to about it. Let it all hang out! Now get ready to shift gears. Dramatically. Turn the page and write: "The Best!" Describe the best thing that happened this week.

Now go to a third page: "Helping Others." Think for a few minutes. Do you long to adopt a child or bring foster children into your home? Have you secretly wished you could help out the homeless or assist at a home for abused women or children? How about a rape crisis center or an unplanned pregnancy clinic? What about assisting in a prison ministry or volunteering at a senior center? Have you read about Habitat for Humanity and wondered how to get involved? Or have you dreamed about taking a trip to a third-world country and helping to build an orphanage?

Make a list of things that you could do to help others. Commit right now to doing one thing on the list within twenty-four hours. Do it. When you're finished, describe the shift in your emotional state.

O heavenly Father, thank you for offering me the opportunity to feel better simply by following the example set by your Son and allowing myself to be used as a servant. Use me, Lord. Show me where I'm needed.   *Amen*

WEEK TWO: FRIDAY
JUST WHAT IS THIS THING CALLED FORGIVENESS?

If we claim to be without sin, we deceive ourselves and the truth is not in us. If we confess our sins, he is faithful and just and will forgive us our sins and purify us from all unrighteousness.

1 John 1:8-9

The fifth stage of divorce recovery is forgiveness. "What?" you shriek. If you looked in the mirror right now, your face would undoubtedly radiate disbelief, disgust, and fear. Come on! How in the world can we ever forgive our former spouses? I mean, after all, aren't they the ones who have become our legal, emotional, and spiritual enemies? Instead of saying, *Father, forgive them, for they don't know what they're doing,* what's running through our heads is more like, *Father, kill the lousy, lying, cheating skunk; will you please?* (I always get a laugh out of divorce recovery groups by calling *forgiveness* an "F word.")

Even though it feels pretty good to be hateful and bitter, and it's unavoidable right now (and you probably have every right to feel that way), eventually, to get better, you're going to have to deal with this forgiveness thing. There isn't one person on this planet who is without sin. Jesus died for every single one of us. So who among us has the right to judge which sins are more heinous than others? We all need God's grace.

The whole concept of forgiveness is mind-boggling. It is the simplest act God performed for us, yet it required that he sacrifice his only Son, a sacrifice that was undoubtedly the most painful ever experienced, anywhere. Forgiveness starts with God. He forgives us. We forgive ourselves. We ask for forgiveness from others. One hopes they forgive us and ask our forgiveness in return. Which, ideally, we give. Sound easy? Sometimes it is; often it is not. Forgiveness is complex and paradoxical. It's usually a slow, agonizing journey with lots of struggling and plenty of backsliding; it's a journey that doesn't always result in a restored relationship. But God calls us to forgive. He calls us to work toward letting go of our need to get even—to stop lashing out at the person who hurt us and to forego the temptation to hurt that person back. Forgiving your ex doesn't happen overnight. So don't feel you have to do it today, OK?

Try this instead. Think of someone else who wronged you in a minor way but with whom you were able to patch things up. Write that name down and what that person did. How long did it take before things got better? How did the two of you work through your differences and how has forgiveness affected your relationship? Do you understand the boundaries that separate you more clearly? How is the level of trust between you now?

Father, thank you so very much for sending Jesus to earth so that we can experience the miracle of your forgiveness every day. Help me to understand it, Lord, and to work through my bitterness and need for revenge.   *Amen*

WEEK TWO: SATURDAY
GOD HATES DIVORCE, BUT HE LOVES ME, ANYWAY

For all have sinned and fall short of the glory of God, and are justified freely by his grace through the redemption that came by Christ Jesus.   Romans 3:23-24

In divorce recovery groups, someone nearly always brings up the subject I call the "unforgivable sin." Even though we read in the Bible that God forgives our sins, deep down inside we're absolutely convinced that God will never, ever, ever forgive us for failing at marriage. After all, who among us has not been attacked by a well-meaning Christian for getting a divorce?

I remember one Sunday when I was sipping coffee after church. A woman came up to me and said, "Aren't you the one who leads that *divorce* group?" Yes. I was. She moved her face to within two inches of mine and said, "How could the pastor of this church allow such a thing? This can't possibly be a biblically based church! If any of you ever read the Bible, you'd certainly know that Jesus said you *cannot* get divorced. Not under any circumstances!" And she stormed off.

God does hate divorce. He hates sin, period. But Jesus forgave the woman at the well who'd been married and divorced repeatedly (John 4:7-16). He forgave sinner after sinner after sinner, and then he willingly died for all sinners. So you can be sure he can forgive you for getting a divorce. Yes, you've sinned. And he won't spare you the consequences of your sin. You will suffer. (You are suffering.) But you'll grow through this, and he can use this difficult experience to make you a better person.

Make a note in your journal. Next time someone shoots you with a blast from the "unforgivable sin" gun, try turning your cheek from the angry accusation and answering in peace. Try this: "Yes, I know God hates divorce. So do I, believe me. It's awful and I understand that it is a sin. But Jesus came to forgive sinners, all of us." And walk away.

Dear Lord, thank you again for your grace, your mercy, and the incredible gift of your forgiveness. Please forgive me for getting a divorce. Amen

WEEK THREE

In a divorce you get custody of yourself. Jim Smoke

After leading divorce support groups for several years, I went to work for Jim Smoke, who founded the divorce recovery movement twenty-something years ago. One wise piece of advice he gives to people in his workshops is to memorize these few lines and to repeat them at least once a day standing in front of a mirror:

"I now have custody of myself. I am the project. I want to focus on learning and rebuilding right now. I need a narrow flashlight to shine on myself or I will lug all my baggage with me from this divorce into my next marriage."

Don't get hung up with the last two words: *next marriage.* The vast majority of divorced people remarry, and the divorce rate for second marriages is higher than that for first marriages. Why? Because most people subscribe to the theory I call "Don't face; replace!" They don't take the time and energy to focus that flashlight on themselves. After all, it can catapult you into that black hole of depression for a while. It's much easier to shove the baggage up into the attic where no one can find it and rush out to meet someone new. Once the magic of infatuation sets in, all that baggage gets forgotten, anyway. Until the next honeymoon is over.

You're alone now, yes. That's not fun. But God has given you the gift of time. Try drawing this sequence of pictures. Jesus is with you, handing you a flashlight. He walks with you into the attic. Your beam of light finds a moldy old suitcase covered with cobwebs in a corner. He nudges you to go to it and pry the lid open. You do. Suddenly the light flares up, illuminating the contents. What's in there? How do you feel? Turn to Jesus and tell him. He will, in time, bring you understanding, wisdom, and healing. You have the opportunity to experience tremendous growth right now. Accept the gift. Take the flashlight.

Father, thank you for loving me enough to stand by me and guide me through this time of building and rebuilding. Help me to keep the light focused on myself and give me the courage to open those moldy old suitcases. Amen

WEEK THREE: MONDAY
AH YES (SIGH), ROMANCE!

In the midst of pain and doubt—you're not clear how it happens—just when you least expect it, you fall desperately in love. It's the classic "coup de foudre"—bolt of lightning romance and you are swept away. It's just like being a teenager again.... You've been dead so long in marriage, it's time to be born again!
Abigail Trafford, *Crazy Time—Surviving Divorce*

One of the most difficult things to discuss in Christian divorce recovery groups is dating. Why? Because romance and sex are so inter-related. The conventional wisdom warns loudly and clearly against both. No! Don't be tempted into an affair! Moral assertions aside, let's face it. You're not ready for a serious relationship. You'll end up having an emotional collision with another hurting person and find yourself even more broken and battered than before!

But when that bolt of lightning strikes, you are sure that *you are the exception*. You have found your own little slice of heaven. You have been spared all that messy grieving and been given Mr. or Ms. Right instead. And then your reasoning slides further.

Unfortunately, the conventional wisdom is correct. Though most of us will learn this lesson the hard way, you can be sure that your passion for the new person is, as Trafford states, an "avoidance strategy...a temporary way to put your depression, anger and ambivalence on emotional ice—not to mention the welcome break you feel from mortgage payments...and sticky Christmas plans."

The bolt-of-lightning romance is a shortcut that becomes a detour— a detour that is like slogging your way through a dark swamp with low branches that tear at your face and arms and slimy mud that oozes up between your toes. Alligators? Snakes? It's a fearsome detour to take. My heart was so fragile after my divorce, and I was so vulnerable. Yet I was totally impervious to my own vulnerability. The new person broke my heart. Big time.

> *Lord, please protect me from bolt-of-lightning relationships. Give me the discernment and wisdom to see the temptation for what it is and provide me with the strength to stay on the course you've charted for me.   Amen*

WEEK THREE: TUESDAY
GOLD MINE OF GRACE

Gratitude unlocks the fullness of life. It turns what we have into enough, and more. It turns denial into acceptance, chaos to order, confusion to clarity. It can turn a meal into a feast, a house into a home, a stranger into a friend. Gratitude makes sense of our past, brings peace for today and creates a vision for tomorrow.

Melody Beattie, *The Language of Letting Go*

Having a grateful heart changes one's view of the world. It transforms ugliness into beauty, lack into abundance. But if our hearts are hurting, if we're sure the world is out to get us (or at least the ex-spouse, the bill collectors, the boss, and the IRS), then how on earth are we supposed to feel *grateful?*

In a Bible study I attended, we kept track of our prayer requests. Every week we'd go back to see what God had been up to. "Hey! Wow! Check this out!" one of us would say. "Three prayers off last week's list were answered! Two off the list from three weeks ago!"

Another person would chime in, "Look what God did! Never, in my wildest dreams, would I have imagined that he'd do *this* for me!" Or, "Well, at least now I know I was on the wrong track. It's a good thing I didn't rush into...." Our next step was to write a thank-you note to God. We kept track of our blessings and didn't forget to thank him for his creative, amazing answers to our prayers.

A grateful heart can be developed. It's sort of like getting in shape. First we commit to a regime, then we have to stick to it, and pretty soon our stamina increases. Not only do we look better, but we feel lots better too. But stop working out and what happens? We get flabby and lethargic again. Too soon we forget how good it felt to be in shape.

God asks us to bring our requests to him. A pastor once told me, "God always answer our prayers, with a yes, a no, or a not now." No matter what his answer, I know that the Lord is infinitely wiser than I am, so I do my best to accept his answer. And I am so grateful that he cares enough to answer!

Today, take one of those index tabs I asked you to buy and label it "Thank-You Notes to God." Label another tab "Prayer Requests" and make a commitment to document your requests to God. Keep track of when, where, and how he answers your prayers. When he does, turn to your Thank-You Notes and tell him of your gratitude. This works! A grateful heart *is* a gift from God. All we have to do is accept it and develop it. Do this and you'll discover a gold mine of grace.

God, I want to develop a grateful heart. Please help me to remember all the incredible things you've done for me and to take the time to thank you.   Amen

WEEK THREE: WEDNESDAY
DEVELOPING PATIENCE

But they that wait upon the Lord shall renew their strength. They shall mount up with wings like eagles; they shall run and not be weary; they shall walk and not grow faint.

Isaiah 40:31, TLB

I do not come from a patient family and one of my biggest lessons has been waiting. I did not learn it gracefully, and I still don't find it easy. When my daughter entered fourth grade, her teacher distributed a handout for parents: "Ten Rules for Being Human." One sentence caught my attention: "A lesson will be presented to you in various forms until you have learned it."

About this time I was probably on my seventy-fifth lesson on patience. Being as stubborn as I was impatient, I still didn't get it. But God stuck that "rule" in my face like a banner. *Hello?! Anyone home here? Do you get it yet?* I got it.

Open your journal. Are you still resisting some lesson that is being presented to you over and over? What are some things that keep going wrong in your life? List them. Is there something you desperately want that keeps eluding you? See any patterns?

Dear God, we live in such an impatient, instant-gratification world. Please open my eyes and allow me to see what lesson you are trying to teach me. Help me to trust that you'll give me what's best for me and that I will soar like an eagle when I wait on you. Amen

WEEK THREE: THURSDAY
SPIRITUAL CRISIS

Be still, and know that I am God. Psalm 46:10

"I'm totally frustrated," I whined to my group leader about six months after my divorce was final. "How can I know what God's will is? He hasn't exactly called to me out of any burning bushes lately.

She smiled. "Slow down," she said. "You're running in too many different directions at once. Your life is way too full of background noise. You need to be quiet; then you'll be able to hear what God is saying to you."

"What?" How could I slow down? I mean, I was on the fast track to spiritual maturity, trying to cram a lifetime of biblical learning into a year or two. I'd become so pious my sister called me Susie Sunday School. Yet I felt God was eluding me, that somehow he didn't consider me important enough to talk to. And that was beginning to really bug me.

While I was scrambling to outgrow the label "Baby Christian," another person in the group was undergoing another type of spiritual crisis. "God has forgotten me," he complained. "I spend lots of time alone with him. I've been a Christian for twenty years. But he's just not there for me since my divorce. I don't see how a God who loves me could have let this happen to me! How could he let my family break up?"

Divorce leads many people to God, but it causes others to turn away from him in anger and despair. Even people like me, who found him in the midst of my chaos, can feel horribly disappointed when they perceive him as silent. *Is he going to reject us too?* we wonder.

Where are you spiritually right now? Are you growing at a pace with which you're comfortable? Or do you feel that your prayers are falling on deaf ears? Are you angry at God? Do you feel that he's abandoned you? Explore these questions in your journal. Then open your Bible to two or three these passages and paraphrase them: Genesis 18:1-15; Exodus 4:1-17; Judges 6; Matthew 14:22-32; Mark 9:14-29; Luke 7:18-23; John 20:24-31.

> *Father, thank you for your Word. Please quiet my heart and still my mind. Let my doubting be eased as I feel your comforting arms around me.*   *Amen*

WEEK THREE: FRIDAY
THE FINAL STAGE OF GRIEF—ACCEPTANCE

> I have learned the secret of being content in any and every situation, whether well fed or hungry, whether living in plenty or in want. I can do everything through him who gives me strength.
> Philippians 4:12-13

The final stage of grief is acceptance. It is the goal of the recovery process. We have to shed that blanket of denial, work through truck loads of anger, and develop the discernment to see through the bargaining (our own and others'), and work at learning healthier ways to negotiate. We have to visit the black hole of despair plenty of times, but we struggle and struggle and try to look for the lessons. Every lesson learned becomes the rainbow after a storm; the silver lining in each dark cloud. As our hearts soften and we become better at being grateful, we will find forgiveness not such an impossible feat. And then, when we have opened up so many moldy suitcases and worked through so much *stuff,* we will amazingly, miraculously one day find that we have reached the point of acceptance.

We learn, as the apostle Paul did, to find contentment in the here and now. We accept our circumstances. We may not have chosen them, but we are surviving in spite of them. In fact, we may even see an extra glimmer of light on the horizon. What does it mean? Hey! We are not only surviving the divorce, but we are growing. Getting better. Thriving. We can laugh at our weaknesses and celebrate our strengths. We realize that we are exactly where God wants us to be this minute. We realize he is with us.

Take out your journal and write down the word *acceptance.* What does it mean to you now? What pieces of your new life are you OK with today? What things do you still resist? What bugs you?

> *God, help me to accept myself, those around me and my circumstances and to be grateful for them, as impossible as that may seem to me right now.*   *Amen*

WEEK THREE: SATURDAY
BOTTOMING OUT

> Hit bottom and cry your eyes out. The fun and games are over. Get serious, really serious. Get down on your knees before the Master; it's the only way you'll get on your feet.
>
> From James 4, The Message

"Why can't I go to the movies this weekend?" a boy asked his mother. A flush spread over her cheeks. "I...I don't have any money. Maybe next weekend."

He picked up a can of Pringles and flung it across the room. "I hate my life! You never let me do what I want! All you ever do is work, work, work! I hate you! I want to go live with my dad!" He ran into his room and slammed the door.

"What do I do?" his mom asked me. "How can I tell him the truth? He idolizes his dad." He maintained a "Disneyland Dad" presence in his kids' lives and showered them with gifts when they visited him. But he didn't pay his child support. Being self-employed and quite clever, he'd managed to outmaneuver the legal system so far.

"Your son is ten. You have to tell him, or he'll keep on blaming you." I advised. "He senses that you're covering something up. You have to let him know that what he senses is real. Otherwise, he won't trust his own feelings. He needs to hear the truth, unpleasant as it is."

"I can't," she cried. "I just can't tell him the truth. It will turn him against his dad."

"Then you're going to take the fall for it," I said. "By hiding the truth, you're validating his opinion of you as a selfish drone and Dad as a generous do-gooder."

We all walk such a tightrope when discussing our exes with our kids. It's so hard to know what to say! When was the last time one of your children (or anyone) asked you a question that stabbed you in the heart? Did you dodge it, lie outright, or answer truthfully? What was the result? With the benefit of hindsight, what would you have said or done differently?

> *Father, please help me when I bottom out. Give me the courage to speak the truth in love so that I will teach my children courage and honesty by my example.*   Amen

WEEK FOUR

WEEK FOUR: SUNDAY
THE WAR ZONE

> Act. Don't react. If you can't get through a conversation with your ex with your sanity intact, then hide in a closet when he or she comes over. You have the right to make some choices about boundaries to protect yourself.   Jim Smoke

"A closet?!" she exclaimed. "How do I hide? It seems to me like every encounter with my former husband is a close encounter of the very worst kind. I hate this! Marriage may not be forever, but divorce sure is! When you have kids you don't get a clean break. You just exchange one set of crummy circumstances for another!"

This woman had just heard Jim speak. She went on to explain to our small group that she and her ex-husband couldn't have any kind of conversation without pushing each other's buttons. Full-on red alert, four alarm fire.

"So how," someone else asked, "do we learn to keep those alarm bells from going off? How do we neutralize those buttons?"

The hurts and anger of divorce are overpowering. He withholds child support. She withholds visitation. He sends the kids home with filthy clothes. She forgets to tell him about the third grade class play. He files for custody. She submits a 27 page declaration to the court detailing his sins in blaring, exaggerated color. Divorce at its worst becomes a bloody free-for-all that drags everyone we know into it. The war takes on a life of its own. It's pathos and high drama. It forces people to take sides and it claims many victims—including our sanity and our children's sense of security.

It's an extreme form of the blame game. I heard Scott Peck speak about that once. He said: "The only way to stop a game is to stop." Jim says: " Growth begins where blaming ends." And again: "Act. Don't React." We have a choice. Write those sentences down and meditate on them. Let your thoughts flow freely into your journal. Who do you know who has survived or bypassed the divorce wars? Write their name(s) down and contact at least one of them.

Oh Heavenly Father, please bring people alongside me who will help me learn to act and not react. Please help me to do my part to stop this game before it escalates into a full-scale war.
Amen

WEEK FOUR: MONDAY
A CLOSET FOR THE MEMORIES

So be truly glad! There is wonderful joy ahead, even though it is necessary for you to endure many trials for a while.

1 Peter 1:6, NLT

I moved last year after living almost six years in the same house. Before I packed up the boxes, I sorted things into two piles: things to go with us into our new life and things to be jettisoned. Into each room I went, sorting, downsizing. I noticed, eventually, that a third pile emerged in each room. The nonessential, possibly impractical, but sentimentally important items that defined my life in nuances and afterthoughts. Would I ever use my college typewriter again? What about my son's first-grade papers? My wedding pictures? The family videos?

It dawned on me then that rearranged families need to start fresh without denying the past. The typewriter left; the rest of the stuff in the third piles stayed. I packed, that day, a special box that evolved into a whole closet in our new house. I have given my children ownership of that closet. It's their nonessential, special moments closet. In it they can explore "life before the divorce." They can also touch and reflect upon mementos from our more recent past.

Divorce always results in downsizing. If you moved, have you unpacked your boxes? If you have children, have you allowed them a special place to visit with things that belonged to their previous life? There were some good memories in there, right? You don't want to make a shrine to the past, but memories do need to be preserved. Your old wedding photo doesn't belong on the mantle anymore, but it is good for the kids to have a picture of Dad or Mom on their dresser. Do they?

> *Father, as I rearrange my life and my home, please help me to*
> *make a special place for good memories. Once I have done that,*
> *Lord, please help me to move forward and entrust them to you.*
> *Amen*

WEEK FOUR: TUESDAY
SHAME AND SELF-LOATHING

Shame springs from the lie that the normal condition for human beings is perfection and absence of problems. If we believe this lie, we feel uniquely flawed.

Sandra Wilson, Ph.D.

Maybe you were raised on a diet of "Ozzie and Harriet" and "Leave It to Beaver"—TV shows peopled with folks who lived without crises, even serious interpersonal conflict.

How did they do it? They didn't. They were make-believe people. Real people have problems and real people struggle. A lot. Life isn't easy, and it isn't pain free. When we pretend that we don't make mistakes, or that we aren't hurting or frustrated or afraid, we are buying into the lie that good people lead trouble-free, hassle-free, pain-free lives. We believe there is something truly *wrong* with us because we make mistakes.

Shame causes us to loathe ourselves at a deep level. The tapes running through our heads may be *I'm not good enough. I can never get it right.* Life is very black and white, because there are only two scenarios for us: all right or all wrong. No middle ground. Hey, guess what? *Jesus Christ was the only person who walked this earth who could ever claim perfection.* None of the rest of us can even come close to it!

I know this on a cognitive level. Yet whenever I'm stymied by a crisis or a recurring problem (read that unlearned lesson) in my life, this nasty little voice in my head starts blasting me. I call it, the viper voice. It says things like *What's wrong with you? You can't feel that way! You should have learned this lesson by now. You are such a loser!*

Does any of this sound familiar? Is there a voice in your head that treats you like a stupid, incompetent child? That puts you down and makes you feel worthless? Open your journal and explore the concept of shame. You don't need to affix blame on any one person for planting this lie in your heart; just bring it out into the light.

> *O Lord, I know that I am a person of inestimable value to you. Please help me to turn off this demeaning, shameful voice in my head and replace it with your voice, offering me love, kindness, forgiveness, and encouragement.   Amen*

WEEK FOUR: WEDNESDAY
THE SEEKING POWER OF LOVE

> Ask and it will be given to you; seek and you will find; knock
> and the door will be opened to you. For everyone who asks
> receives; he who seeks finds; and to him who knocks, the door
> will be opened.   Luke 11:9-10

Current psychological research tells us that we have three basic
emotions that parallel the three primary colors: love, anger, and fear. In
the next three reflections, let's look at the power of these emotions,
starting with love.

Can you think back to the last time you saw a newborn baby with its
mother? Didn't she pick him up when he cried and cuddle him? Didn't
she gaze at him with unveiled adoration? Didn't she feed him and
change him when he soiled his diapers? Didn't she tickle him, bathe
him, coo at him, shower him with kisses? The baby has just been thrust
from the Eden-like perfection of the womb into the cold, painful,
bright, and noisy world. Yet when Mom holds him, he is safe once more.
By the time the child is three or four months old, he's reaching his arms
out to Mom, smiling and cooing back his pleasure. He has learned that
he can trust her. Trust is a key element of love.

When you love someone, don't you crave that person's presence?
Don't you seek that person out and spend as much time with him or her
as possible? If you (like me) love hot, spicy food, don't you find yourself
longing for it periodically? When that craving hits, don't you figure out
a way to get yourself to a suitable restaurant as soon as possible? I sure
do!

In the same way, God loves us. He seeks us by putting those gnawing
feelings of longing in our hearts. *He craves our love, and he wants us to
love him.* What he's really asking is for us to seek his presence with a

burning and a yearning in our hearts. He wants us to seek him, and he wants us to believe that he loves us—even when we're at our most unlovable. He wants us to trust him, above everyone and everything else. God loves us with action-oriented, unconditional agape love. To him, love is far more than an emotion. It's a very conscious choice that is mirrored in his actions. He wants us to choose to act lovingly, too.

Whom do you love? How do you seek them? How do you show your love? Whom do you trust? What did they do to earn your trust? What things do you love? How do you seek them? Have you ever been able to love someone who did something really raunchy to you? Describe it. How did it feel?

> *Heavenly Father, thank you for loving me no matter what I do or say. Help me to remember that the greatest of all gifts you've given me is your love. Teach me agape love.*   *Amen*

WEEK FOUR: THURSDAY
THE IN-YOUR-FACE POWER OF ANGER

> Do not take revenge, my friends, but leave room for God's wrath, for it is written: "It is mine to avenge; I will repay," says the Lord.   Romans 12:19-20

Many of us didn't learn to manage our anger very well. We may even think that good Christians don't get angry, so we stuff our anger and pretend it doesn't exist. We've found that intense expressions of emotions have earned us nothing but criticism. Or they have scared people away. More reasons to stuff our feelings. Unfortunately, repressed anger erupts in unexpected outbursts of rage, or it turns inward and causes depression and a whole myriad of illnesses. We have to learn to accept and deal with our strong and difficult emotions. Or they'll deal with us.

Guess what? God created anger. In fact, in the Old Testament, the word *anger* is used more than 450 times. And guess what else? More than three-quarters of these refer to God's anger. Remember Jesus' anger when he tore into the Pharisees, calling them snakes, blind guides, and hypocrites? How about when he overturned the booths in front of the temple? On the human side of things, do you remember how mad Moses got when he found out the Israelites had built the golden calf?

Anger can lead us to sin. It can make us cruel, vicious, vindictive, warring, hateful, and bitter. Its fire fuels revenge, and that's where it gets dangerous. In your journal explore your attitudes toward anger. How did your parents treat you when you got angry? How did they treat each other? How do you usually act when you're upset? Do you stuff your feelings, lash out in fury, run out the door and head for the gym? Or do you take a time out until you and the other party cool off and talk it through? Can you give examples from your own life of each way of dealing with anger?

> *Dear Lord, I know I don't handle anger as well as I should, especially now during this divorce. Please help me to understand what's behind my anger so I can learn to deal with it more effectively.*   *Amen*

WEEK FOUR: FRIDAY
THE I-WANT-TO-GO-HIDE POWER OF FEAR

> If a ruler's anger rises against you, don't leave your post; calmness
> can lay great errors to rest.   Ecclesiastes 10:4

Fear is movement away from someone or something. Something happens, a button goes off, and suddenly we're scared out of our wits. All we want to do is run and hide. Whether we physically leave the scene of our discomfort or mentally vacate the premises, we essentially check out when we're lost in our fear.

What wigs me out? I asked myself that recently. As I looked back on the years since I became single-again, I saw that for years I was afraid of being alone—and afraid I'd always be alone. I was afraid of being an inadequate parent. I was terrified of criticism in general and paralyzed with fear when faced with the demands, commands and disapproval of others. I was sure I had to be the perfect mother. I turned myself into a martyr, always putting myself in last place. I was more concerned with trying to avoid pain and conflict than I was with being true to myself.

When I failed to live up to the unrealistic expectations I set for myself, I was just sure everyone I knew was putting me down behind my back. And how did I feel then? Like hiding. I felt awful, defeated, deflated. I felt angry and defensive too and I wanted to strike out at them. I was locked into a seemingly endless cycle of despair, hopelessness and depression.

Yuck! Now, if you ask me, that's a pretty scary way to live. But that's how I lived. It took a lot of work for me to own up to the fact that *I had to take responsibility for my fears.* I had to listen to them, accept their existence (as bizarre as some of them were) and examine them. It took a whole a lot of courage for me to say no to unreasonable demands. Sometimes I was put down. Sometimes people did bad-mouth me behind my back. A few people did walk out of my life. But eventually, as I came to value and respect myself more, the criticism diminished. So did the rejection. And those fears ceased to be my primary motivators.

Fear is primal. But, as the Bible tells us in 1 John 4, God's perfect love casts out fear. It brings us back into balance. Can you put a name to some of your fears? Write as much as you can on the subject.

Father, help me to name to my fears. Help me to express them to you so they stop controlling my life. Please help me to see that there is no fear in love and that your perfect love drives out fear. Amen

WEEK FOUR: SATURDAY
HOW DO WE SPLIT EVERYTHING, EVEN THE KIDS, EQUALLY?

O God, you are my God; I earnestly search for you. My soul thirsts for you; my whole body longs for you in this parched and weary land where there is no water.

Psalm 63:1, NLT

David penned these lines when he was alone in the wilderness. I can empathize with his craving for the renewed hope and strength that comes with God's comforting touch. We need to search for God when we're in the midst of that tearing asunder that comes with the ending of a marriage. We thirst for him, ache for him, yearn for his peace that surpasses understanding. We need to know that God is always there, even in the darkest, deepest valleys when we're certain we're never going to see daylight again. He will pull us through—even though we all doubt it sometimes.

What do we have to split up when we go through a divorce? Although I am not an attorney, these are a few of the things I've learned over the years:

1. All the property and possessions acquired during the marriage. Down to the can opener and the refrigerator magnets.
2. All the money we have and all the money we owe.
3. Legal custody of our children, if we have them. Most (not all) states award parents joint legal custody, which means they are to share equally in all major decisions regarding their children. Sole custody, where one parent makes all major decisions without input from the other, is rare.
4. Physical custody of our children. Historically, especially for younger children, the most common child-sharing arrangement is a seventy-thirty split, with the mom acting as the primary

custodial parent. A seventy-thirty split works something like this: The kids live with Mom and spend Wednesday nights and every other weekend at Dad's, plus a couple of weeks' vacation time during the year. A fifty-fifty split could be half the week at Mom's, every other week at Dad's, or every other month at Dad's. More and more judges automatically assign fifty-fifty custody when both parents work outside the home.

5.   Spousal support isn't awarded to everyone. It depends on your circumstances.

6.   Child support is determined based on the information on Mom's and Dad's income and expense statements.

If you haven't already, make a list of what you have to divide between you. Make a list specifying everything you want. Then list everything you think your ex wants. Last, make a compromise list, which is somewhere in between. Then read all of Psalm 63.

> *Father, I see clearly why you hate divorce. This is so hard and so ugly. I ache for you, Lord. I need you like I've never needed you before. Comfort me with your Holy Spirit and help me see that I'll get through this.   Amen*

WEEK FIVE

WEEK FIVE: SUNDAY
THE BIG NOODLE

> Be merciful to me, O Lord, for I am in distress; my eyes grow
> weak with sorrow, my soul and my body with grief.
>
> Psalm 31:9

She didn't want him to leave. But he was leaving anyway. They'd slept
in separate bedrooms for over a month, living together but barely
speaking. Her heart was broken.

She called me. "He packed up his car and left this morning. Asked me
to hang around while the movers loaded up his stuff. They're three
hours late! I'm so mad I could spit! There are boxes everywhere. I can
hardly walk through the living room! Oh, no. He's back." Her voice
dropped to a whisper. "He's back," she repeated, referring to her
husband. "Now what do I do? I'm afraid I'll bite his head off!"

"Do you have your Noodle?" I asked her.

She actually laughed. "Yes."

"Go in your bedroom and lock the door. *Use it.*"

She'd told me earlier about her Noodle. You know, one of those long,
skinny bendable toys that kids goof around with in swimming pools. A
friend had given her one and instructed her on how to use it. It was for
when the anger hit hard and heavy. She could go into her room and

whack the wall as hard as she could with her noodle, releasing that anger. It worked she said. She swore it helped.

I checked in with her later. "So? Is he gone? Are you better now?" I asked.

"You better believe it. He saw me take the Noodle and head for my room. He *knows* about my

Noodle. So he was smart enough to stay away from me until I calmed down some." She sighed. "Yeah. He's all moved out. I'm moving furniture, rehanging pictures." Her voice caught. "Bawling my head off. Trying to make this place my own."

Do you feel a lot of anger? Or a truckload of sadness and despair? You should have a Noodle. Everyone should. Although I've never used mine, this friend bought me one not too long ago. My kids use it in the pool, and I know where it is. Just in case.

Father, help me to channel my anger and hurt in nondestructive ways. Amen.

WEEK FIVE: MONDAY
CAN WE MAKE JOINT CUSTODY WORK?

> I pray that out of his glorious riches he may strengthen you with power through his Spirit in your inner being, so that Christ may dwell in your hearts through faith.   Ephesians 3:16-17

More and more frequently fathers are petitioning the court for 50 percent custody of their children. "Does it work?" I asked a lawyer friend of mine. "Sometimes," he answered. He scratched his head. "I'd say it works maybe half the time. It requires exceptional parents who can put their kids first. They absolutely have to understand that the kids rights are superior here, that they have priority over both Mom's and Dad's."

"So why are the courts awarding this fifty-fifty custody if it isn't always in the kids' best interests?"

"It's the new thing in family court, especially when both parents work. It was originally designed to give fathers a greater say in the way their children are raised. But when kids are shuttled back and forth between warring parents, it is definitely *not* good for them. All the experts agree on that. The kids are caught in the cross fire. When there's shooting going on, they're likely to take a bullet.

In her landmark book *Second Chances: Men, Women, and Children a Decade after Divorce,* Judith Wallerstein devotes an entire chapter to joint custody. If you have questions and doubts about your ability to coparent effectively in a joint custody situation, go to the library and find this book. You'll see how this form of shared child rearing belongs to parents who can cooperate and communicate with each other in a respectful and kind manner. Bullying and other forms of nasty behavior will only hurt the children. Dr. Wallerstein says that parents who can't manage that level of civility should consider other options.

If you have children, what kind of time split are you living with right now? Is it working? How are you and your ex communicating? What are your strengths now as parents? What areas between you need to be improved? How can you do your part so that your children's rights are paramount?

> *Father, strengthen me in my innermost being. Fill me with your presence, so that I may reflect Jesus in my dealings not only with my ex-spouse, but also with my children. Amen*

WEEK FIVE: TUESDAY
THE KIDS ARE HURTING TOO

Then little children were brought to Jesus for him to place his hands on them and pray for them. But the disciples rebuked those who brought them. Jesus said, "Let the little children come to me, and do not

hinder them, for the kingdom of heaven belongs to such as these."
Matthew 19:13-14

Speaking at the divorce recovery program at a large Southern California church, I asked how many of the participants had kids. Out of one hundred, I think ninety-three raised their hands. Most of us in divorce country do have children. If you don't, you're bound to meet plenty of single parents. They'll become your friends. You may date some of them, and even marry one someday. So the better understanding you have of the single-parent scene, the better.

A few years ago I did research to put together a program for children of divorce. Here are a few things I learned:

1. We have a responsibility to help our children understand the divorce.
2. We have a responsibility to hold their hands and help them through the grieving process. Sharing our feelings with them can help us heal, too.
3. We have a responsibility to provide a stable home environment for our kids, even though our circumstances may have changed dramatically.
4. We owe it to God, ourselves, and our kids to rebuild. Our family structure will be different for sure, but we can and must create a strong, loving bond of respect and affection between ourselves and those children he entrusted us to raise.

Are you wondering how to know what your kids are going through? Do you wonder what they need? First of all, they need to know what happened. What went wrong? Will all the yelling stop now? If Dad moved out, when will they see him? They may be in shock or denial, in which case they may be sullen and withdraw from you, or they may be ultra cheerful and pretend everything's just fine. Create the opportunity for communication. Take your child on a long walk. Find a private place where it's OK not only to share feelings, but also to throw a serious tantrum, if need be. Afterward, pray together. It will do you both good!

Turn to the Reading List in the back of this book. Pick at least one of the titles for helping kids cope with divorce. Commit to reading it.

Lord, I need a lot of help in getting my kids through this divorce. Please give me the wisdom, courage, and strength to be there for them right now.   *Amen*

WEEK FIVE: WEDNESDAY
WHY DO I HIDE OUT WHEN I'M FEELING BAD?

Our world is full of disillusioned and broken people. God still uses the scars of those who have been wounded to comfort the hurting. In order for the wounded to believe, they must see our scars.   Bill Brandt, *Single-Parent Family Magazine*

When I am in a less-than-centered state, I tend to hibernate. Why? I'm afraid of being interrogated. I'm afraid of being told what to do, say, think, and feel. I'm afraid of being put down and stomped on when I'm vulnerable and weak.

My friend Leslie always busts me. She's tenacious and doesn't mince words. "OK," she'll say when a week has gone by and I haven't returned her phone call. "You're hiding again. What gives?"

At first I didn't tell her. I was used to people close to me who disapproved of my disappearing acts. They thought I was weird—out there. And my "out there" wasn't anywhere they wanted me to go. No thank you! They wanted me to snap out of it, and the best way they knew of to do that was to deliver to me one or two swift kicks in the pants!

But Leslie doesn't kick, criticize, or lecture. She listens, she understands, and she loves. She's no stranger to grief, so it doesn't intimidate her. She's been through a divorce and a series of nearly crippling back surgeries. Death has claimed her father and two of her closest friends. Is she bitter? No. She's wise, gentle, and kind. She is a beautiful example of a wounded healer.

In the early divorced days, I was so lonely I opened my arms wide to nearly every single person I came across. I got burned a few times, and then I slammed my arms shut. It took the understanding of a friend like Leslie to help me learn to trust again. And to learn whom to trust—and whom not to trust with my wounded parts.

Do you find yourself retreating from people when you're going through difficult times—or turning to people who can't help? Are you comfortable or uncomfortable with your solitude? Do you feel in your heart that you are too much alone? To whom do you feel safe reaching out? Make an inventory of the people in your life. Ask God to bring a wounded healer into your circle.

> *Dear Lord, thank you that you use our wounds to minister to others. Please bring such a person into my life. And when I'm ready, please use me too.*   Amen

WEEK FIVE: THURSDAY
MY BELIEFS CREATE MY ATTITUDES?

> He will have no fear of bad news; his heart is steadfast, trusting in the Lord. His heart is secure, he will have no fear; in the end he will look in triumph on his foes.   Psalm 112:7-8

I used to believe that my reactions to life were determined by what happened to me. I thought an event triggered a response and that was that. In reality, I was putting my faith in blind reactions that didn't allow any room for me to make choices and exercise my God-given free will. That type of thinking rendered me powerless, because, to follow my logic all the way through, it could only mean that I was a victim of my circumstances *and* my emotions. That kind of thinking created a fearful, bitter attitude of expecting the worst and blaming others for my unhappiness. I was short circuiting. I wasn't taking responsibility for my life!

What was missing? In his book *Self-Talk*, Dave Stoop offers us an equation for our attitudes. He says that most of us assume that our circumstances dictate our attitudes. So if life treats us well, we say, "Hey! All right!" We're delighted. But when we get thrown some curve balls, we're enraged, disappointed, and demoralized. We beat ourselves up; we lash out at others; we can't even pray, because we're too mad at God to speak to him.

I've learned that there is a missing variable in this equation. What happens to us *combined with our basic beliefs* determines the way we respond. I remember an old saying: Life is 5 percent what happens to us and 95 percent what we make of it. That 95 percent is attitude, which is defined by our belief systems. So how did I go about improving my attitude? I began by listening to my inner voice. It was more of a critical parent than an affirming, loving encourager. It was mean and demeaning, far more so than any person in my life had ever been. I wondered where it had come from. I wanted to pin it on someone. Then suddenly I saw that I didn't need to blame anyone for it. I just needed to hear it out and see for myself how irrational and self-defeating it was.

How would you describe your attitude? Do you feel like a victim of your circumstances? Your feelings? What does your inner voice tell you about your belief system? Let it speak freely.

Dearest Father, I feel so out of control sometimes. Help me to understand that it is my attitude that determines my joy in life, not my circumstances.   Amen

WEEK FIVE: FRIDAY
HELPING KIDS WORK THROUGH SHOCK AND DENIAL

A father to the fatherless, a defender of widows, is God in his holy dwelling.   Psalm 68:5

I know a thirty-eight-year-old woman whose parents are going through a divorce. Being opposed to airing their dirty linens in public (although how she qualified as "public," I couldn't figure out), neither of them would talk with her about it. She was frustrated and angry. "Why now?!" she asked me. "Who will take care of them when they're sick? Have they always hated each other? They never fought much. What in the world happened? *Why won't they ever even acknowledge anything messy or painful?*"

No matter how old your kids are when you get divorced, they're going to be full of questions, and they're going to go through the stages of shock and denial, anger, bargaining, depression, and acceptance. One hopes they will be able to process their feelings and get to a place of forgiveness.

What do kids act like when they're in the early stages of grief? Well, a normally effervescent child may retreat and snarl at you like a cornered bear. Like us, fear can numb kids out. They worry that because one parent has left, the other will disappear too. They may panic. They may not sleep or eat well, or they may overeat or get sick a lot. If they fall deeply into denial, they may pretend that their missing parent will return. They may create an extended fantasy-family in their minds. They may also become temporarily hyperactive, unable to focus on anything, running in several disconnected directions at once.

While all these behaviors are normal and to be expected, they are difficult to deal with, especially when Mom and Dad are themselves emotionally distraught. At times like this, it's best to turn to a trusted friend who understands the pain and chaos of divorce. Get support! Get help! Pray! Give your children as much time, love, and understanding as you can. Remember that God is always there, an ever-present source of strength. Lean on him! Lean on his people too!

Today, write about your kids. How are they behaving? Continue reading your chosen book about kids and divorce. Find out if there's a single-parents' group in your church or community. Take some positive steps to build yourself and your kids a supportive network.

Father, thank you that you are a Father to the fatherless. Please fill my children with your presence. Let them feel your love. Lead me to other Christians who will help them get through this difficult time.   Amen

WEEK FIVE: SATURDAY
SHAMEFUL SECRETS

O Lord, you have searched me and you know me. You know when I sit and when I rise; you perceive my thoughts from afar. You discern my going out and my lying down; you are familiar with all my ways. Before a word is on my tongue you know it completely, O Lord.   Psalm 139:1-4

Secrets. We all have them. Those things we do when no one is looking. Those things we enjoy but hope no one ever finds out about. We're ashamed of them, so we hide them and lie about them, pretending they don't exist. Shame and lying isolate us. They grab us by the throat, toss us into jail, and keep us their prisoners.

Here are some secret diversions common to people going through divorce: smoking cigarettes; drinking too much (or smoking pot or doing other drugs); obsessing about sex; having sex; binging on food; purging; running up credit card bills; ignoring our kids; raging about our ex-spouses in front of our kids; using our kids as emotional crutches because our friends are sick of us; obsessing on sins from our past.

Are you surprised I wrote these down? Let me confess to you: I've committed more of those secret sins than I'd care to admit. I was clean on the outside but dirty on the inside. We all sin! We all have our slimy little secrets. During the crisis and subsequent isolation of divorce, we are particularly susceptible to finding these secret diversions comforting. And to drown ourselves in a cesspool of secret shame.

There are no secrets from God. Make a list of your secret sins. No one ever has to see it. Own them before God. Now close your eyes and see yourself carrying them, one at a time, to the foot of the cross. Look into the eyes of Jesus as you lay each burden at his feet. Know that he will cleanse you and free you from the bondage of these secret sins—either one by one or all at once, if we let him. Then pray this prayer from Psalm 139:23-24:

> *"Search me, O God, and know my heart; test me and know my anxious thoughts. See if there is any offensive way in me, and lead me in the way everlasting."* Amen

WEEK SIX

WEEK SIX: SUNDAY
THE MANY SCARY FACES OF FEAR

> There is no fear in love. But perfect love drives out fear, because
> fear has to do with punishment. The one who fears is not made
> perfect in love.　　　　　　　　　　　　　　　　1 John 4:18

It was Fear Night. The night in divorce recovery when we got down and dirty and put some names and faces to our fears. "OK," I started. "We're playing school tonight. Everyone take out a piece of paper and pen and write down ten things that absolutely terrify you right now. When you're finished, number them in order of most to least scary."

Ten minutes later we went around the room sharing our number-one fears. By the time the evening was over, we all had a pretty good handle on what we were afraid of. We sorted through them and came up with this list as a group:

1.　No one will ever love me again.
2.　I'll never trust anyone enough to love again.
3.　God will never forgive me.
4.　I've failed myself, my kids, my family, God—everyone.
5.　I'll never be able to make it on my own.
6.　I'm going to starve to death.
7.　I've ruined my kids.
8.　My ex is going to destroy me.

9.   I'll never find my way out of this dark tunnel.

10.   I'll be all alone for the holidays.

I've kept up with some of the people from my groups. Two, three, and even five and six years later, when we get together and the subject of those fear lists comes up, we invariably have a good laugh over them. Why? *Because none of those things ever happened to any of us!* They all seemed horribly real when we wrote them down, but as time passed and God healed people's lives, things got progressively less crazy. Faith and hope resurfaced and the fears receded.

Write down a list of your top ten fears and leave a few blank lines between each one. Then number them in order of most to least scary. Can you identify things in your past that make you accentuate those particular fears? Reread the Bible passage for today. What would Jesus tell you about each of your fears?

Lord Jesus, I know you said that perfect love drives out fear. Please bathe me in your perfect love and drive away my fears. Amen

WEEK SIX: MONDAY
THAT BRUTAL VOICE IN MY HEAD

People can tame all kinds of animals and birds and reptiles and fish, but no one can tame the tongue. It is an uncontrollable evil, full of deadly poison. Sometimes it praises our Lord and Father, and sometimes it breaks into curses against those who have been made in the image of God.   James 3:7-9, NLT

Do you have a persistent, pessimistic, mean little voice in your head? Does it whine, complain, criticize, and judge? Does it warn you not to hope, not to trust, not to believe that things will ever get better? Does it tell you that *life is not fair and neither is God?* Does it demand to know why someone hasn't come along yet to make things better for you? This brutal little voice craves an easier existence where its abilities and accomplishments will meet with praise and, yes, even adulation. It wants to be heard at all costs, to be appreciated and taken care of. It gets furious when it doesn't get its way. Then it wants to curse, plot revenge, or run to a dark, safe, lonely cave where it can cry bitter tears.

Hey wait a minute! You mean you have one of those nasty little viper voices in your head too? We all do! It's always there, but its voice seems to get louder during times of crisis.

This is the voice that feeds your fear, fuels your anger, and threatens to send you off the deep end at least every other day lately. It is the voice of agony and depression. It sees everything in shades of black and white, and when someone hurts you or lets you down, it commands you to react. Immediately. No second chances. You can't risk another betrayal. This poor little voice longs for Eden. It wants life to be perfect. Life hasn't been paradise since the serpent showed up and convinced Eve to bite into that apple, but that little voice sure wishes it were.

For today, give that sad, brutal little voice within yourself free rein. What does it have to say to you? Listen to it as though you were a detached, neutral, third party. Observe who it's ticked off at. Is it angry at you? What are its list of grievances? What is it scared of? Put this voice down in writing. If all it has to say is bad stuff, that's OK. This is between you and God. No one else. It'll let off some pressure. And you won't wake up tomorrow morning feeling like a jerk, because you spewed venom all over someone you shouldn't have....

Father, please give me the courage to give voice to my fears, my sorrow, my anger, and my feelings of betrayal—knowing that you'll comfort me, understand me, and love me no matter what I'm feeling right now.   Amen

WEEK SIX: TUESDAY
WHAT IS GOD'S PLAN FOR MY LIFE?

> You're here to be light, bringing out the God-colors in the world.
> God is not a secret to be kept. We're going public with this, as
> public as a city on a hill.
>
> From Matthew 5, The Message

When my career within the construction industry became obsolete in the early nineties and I was laid off, I took it as a not-too-subtle clue that it was time to do something different with my life. Although I'd enjoyed the salary and prestige of my job, I had to admit that I was burned out. When I went to work I felt as if I were going into battle. It wasn't much fun anymore.

I was ready to do something a lot gentler. I wanted to be somewhere that made me feel a lot closer to God, but I sure didn't know where that was supposed to be. So I began to read, to ask questions. I became a student again. I began to take long talks with God, pouring my heart out to him in a rambling, disjointed, flow-of-consciousness sort of way. I listened for his voice, and I followed him as best I could. I started working on "my issues." I delved into my past, into my heart and mind, and listened to my own inner voice as I revisited the wounded places inside me.

And I explored other options. I began to write. I went to work in divorce recovery. I wanted to get on the path that was right for me. I wanted to unearth my spiritual gifts and build upon them. At church I found the acronym DARE as a way to accomplish this:

1. *Dream.* Throw aside all restraints and dream before God.
2. *Attitude.* It's everything. To stay positive.
3. *Research.* Explore who you are before God.
4. *Exercise.* Let yourself stretch in new directions.

Jot these down on a piece of note paper and post it on your refrigerator. Then answer these questions: What do you enjoy doing most? What makes you overflow with delight? Which of your talents, abilities, and personality traits, when expressed, make you feel exhilarated just to be you? What are the five most important principles in your life? Who are the five most important people in your life? Why?

Father, I want to find out your plan for my life. Please help me to unearth my gifts, and lead me to people who will help me to use them for your glory.   Amen

WEEK SIX: WEDNESDAY
WHO HAS JERKED ME AROUND LATELY?

Therefore, if you are offering your gift at the altar and there remember that your brother has something against you, leave your gift there in front of the altar. First go and be reconciled to your brother; then come and offer your gift.

Matthew 5:23-24

Are you one of those people who insists that life be fair? Do you keep a running list in your head of whom you owe what to, and who owes you? Are you always acutely aware of who's ahead and who's behind? Are you meticulous about keeping your accounts straight? How do you feel when someone doesn't do the fair and just thing and the accounts get out of balance? What about the people who seldom, if ever, play fair? Do you just hate them? Or are you devastated by their wickedness? Maybe your feelings fluctuate from outrage to disappointment and fear.

Remember the parable of the ungrateful servant, in Matthew 15? He owed the king a bigger debt than he could ever repay. He asked for mercy and the king canceled his debt. But for some reason, he didn't believe he'd been forgiven. In his heart, he felt he still owed. So what did he do? He ran to all the people who owed him and demanded repayment.

Somehow word got out that the king had forgiven this servant his debts, so the people he was harassing figured he was just being a greedy pig. They turned him in. They told the king what he was doing. The king was furious. He threw the ungrateful servant into the torture chamber.

By the same token, when we've been forgiven and God has canceled our debts, he insists that we do the same to others. I think of that line from the Lord's Prayer: "Forgive us our debts as we forgive our debtors." Life isn't fair. It just isn't. People will always disappoint us. We will always disappoint others. It's that old no-one-is-perfect thing. Keeping a record of someone else's wrongs just locks us into a prison of bitterness.

Who owes you right now? Who has hurt you, disappointed you, rejected you, or cheated you? List your grievances against them. Now ask yourself : Whom have you hurt? How? Have you asked God's forgiveness? If you have, can you cancel the debt of the person or people who owe you? If you can't right now, can you see that it needs to happen eventually?

> *Father, this forgiveness stuff is really tricky. I'm hanging onto my scorecard because I want life to be fair! Help me to understand debt canceling, Lord, so that I may walk the path of righteousness, not the path of desolation.   Amen*

WEEK SIX: THURSDAY
NAMING MY PAIN

Even though I walk through the valley of the shadow of death, I will fear no evil, for you are with me; your rod and your staff, they comfort me. You prepare a table before me in the presence of my enemies. You anoint my head with oil; my cup overflows.

Psalm 23:4-5

Divorce tosses us into the pit of grief. So does the death of a loved one, being laid off, fired, or downsized out of a job. Even retirement causes grief. So does losing our church. Or moving. Losing a friendship is like a death. And so is giving up on a dream. Even if it was someone else's dream for you and not your own.

Most of us have things in our pasts that we haven't allowed ourselves to grieve over. Maybe you never went to medical school and wish that you had. Maybe you had or participated in an abortion. Maybe you got all hung up in the drugs, sex and rock and roll scene, and deep inside you feel tainted. Maybe you never got your parents' blessing, and you've spent your entire adult life hungering for it—begging for it—and failing to get it.

We need to put a name to the things that cause us to hurt. Until we name that pain, we can't grieve it. We'll be stuck in it. It will own us and we won't be able to grow through it. Can you put a name to your pain? Aside from your divorce, is there something you've never grieved? Can you name it and acknowledge it now before God, in your journal? Can you grieve for it now, so it won't hold you captive any longer?

O heavenly Father, please help me to name and face my pain. Walk with me through the dark valleys until I am healed and my cup overflows. Amen

WEEK SIX: FRIDAY
HELPING KIDS THROUGH THE NITTY GRITTY OF GRIEF

For the Lord your God is God of gods and Lord of lords, the great God, mighty and awesome, who shows no partiality and accepts no bribes. He defends the cause of the fatherless and the widow, and loves the alien, giving him food and clothing.

Deuteronomy 10:17-18

Just as we have to face the feelings churned up by the loss of divorce, so do our children. It's the only way to heal. Children may yearn for the security and comfort of the past. They may want to drive by the old house and reminisce about all the great barbecues you had in the backyard. They may want to peek over the fence and see if the new people kept their swing set. While these activities may tear you apart, they're healthy. While you don't want to push, when your children begin remembering, when they begin to feel the sadness, encourage them to express themselves. Talk it out. No matter how old they are, hold them. Cry along with them.

Once, when I knew my kids were harboring a lot of bottled up anger, I took them on a hike. I told them in advance that we were going to go somewhere where we could take turns yelling at the top of our lungs. No matter who they were mad it, it was OK to let it out. We went to a deserted hillside. There wasn't anyone within hearing range. Although he'd been a little skeptical about the whole thing, my son made the first move. He picked up rocks and heaved them down the hill. He shoved; he screamed; he cried; he fell on the ground and beat it with his fists. My daughter and I followed his lead. By the time we finished, our faces were powdered with dust and lined with tear trails. We were panting. But we were hugging, laughing, and crying all at the same time. We have never forgotten that day. It helped us to release our anger, and it deepened the trust and affection among us.

The deepest part of grief is made up of that kind of anger, along with profound sorrow and disappointment. Acknowledging those feelings to and with our children is an affirming gift of love and courage. Today, if you can't take your children somewhere where it's safe to be very angry, then try helping them write a letter to Jesus. They can share their sadness, fear, and fury with him, while resting in the assurance that he won't punish them.

> *Jesus, my children need you. Help them draw close to you. Help them through their grief and feel not only my love for them, but yours too. Always.*   *Amen*

WEEK SIX: SATURDAY
PICKING MYSELF UP AND DUSTING MYSELF OFF

Come with me by yourselves to a quiet place and get some rest.
Mark 6:31

One morning, soon after I became single-again, I woke up with hope and joy bursting forth from within me. I was ready to leap out of bed and seize the day. Then all of a sudden I remembered. And all the good feelings vanished into thin air, replaced by a heavy black cloud of sadness. Ugh.

Been there? One of the best things we can say (out loud) to ourselves after our marriages end is this: *I am somewhere I never intended to be. I'm traveling down a road I never wanted to take. I don't like it. I wish it weren't happening. But it is, and I will be given the strength to deal with it. I will make it through. God may have to carry me a good portion of the way, but he's promised me that he won't drop me off by the side of the road to rot in the gutter. He's promised to hang in there with me every single day. No matter how empty, lonely, and miserable I feel. He'll be with me, and he'll help me get back on my feet again.*

In Mark 6 Jesus' disciples had just returned from their first big road trip. On their own, without him there to guide and comfort them. They were hungry. They were physically exhausted and also devastated by the news that Herod had beheaded John the Baptist. Jesus took the disciples in a boat to a remote, solitary place to rest. But what happened? The hungry crowd followed them. And Jesus fed five thousand people from five loaves and two fishes.

Read Mark 6:7-44. What does this story say to you? Do you see that even when the darkest of the doldrums hit and you're physically, emotionally, and spiritually depleted, Jesus will carry you off to a quiet place where he will provide an abundance of whatever it is that you need? I think that's pretty amazing. What is it that you need from him right now? Write him a letter and ask. Just pour your aching heart out. But before you do, read the second paragraph in this meditation out loud.

> *Lord Jesus, I need you to take me away to a quiet place where you can restore my soul, ease the pain in my heart, and turn my fearful, angry thoughts into loving, grateful ones. I can't do this alone, Lord. Please help me.   Amen*

WEEK SEVEN

WEEK SEVEN: SUNDAY
FACING THOSE UNCOMFORTABLE FEELINGS

> Since mentally healthy human beings must grow, and since
> giving up or loss of the old self is an integral part of the process
> of mental and spiritual growth, depression is a normal and
> basically healthy phenomenon.
>
> M. Scott Peck, *The Road Less Traveled*

Depression isn't fun. In fact, it's dark and greasy, like an oil spill. It smears itself all over us, covering our eyes with an opaque film that feels as if it will never wash off. It slithers around the nooks and crannies of our hearts and gums them all up. It gets into our minds and convinces us that spring will never come again. Depression is death.

We are bound to experience depression when we have to let go of parts of ourselves. It doesn't matter if they're healthy or unhealthy parts. The letting go feels like an amputation and that hurts!

But to grow, we have to let certain parts of our former selves die. We have to clear out the attic and get rid of the stuff that doesn't work anymore. We have to learn new, healthier attitudes and behaviors. This is hard. It's scary, and at this point many of us realize we need some help. So we get into therapy.

For me, depression has been the most difficult part of the recovery process. I'm a summer person. I live in Southern California, and even our hint of winter is too much winter for me! I've always felt the same way about depression. No thanks! I prefer laughter, hope, and playfulness.

As much as I fought him, God kept taking me back to depression. To get my attention. To get me to face up to the things I needed to change in myself. To say good-bye to them, to mourn them, and to move on. To ignore and try to outrun the loud *"hello!"* of depression is to invite it back again and again. It will keep coming at us until we sit down and work through it.

Today, write the word *depression* in your journal. What feelings does that word conjure up? What depresses you? How much of the time are you depressed these days? What do you think God is trying to teach you through the depression?

> *Father, please help me to see what things I need to change, what deaths I need to grieve in my life and within myself, and give me the courage to face them. Amen*

WEEK SEVEN: MONDAY
WHEN FEELINGS ERUPT IN OFF-THE-WALL WAYS

> Let not those gloat over me who are my enemies without cause;
> let not those who hate me without reason maliciously wink the
> eye.   Psalm 35:19

Have you ever been talking with someone when, unexpectedly, a hot button is activated? Her smile disappears. Her eyes darken. Her nostrils flare. Her entire countenance stiffens. All of a sudden she's a volcano, spewing molten lava all over you. While the rage scorches you and threatens to bury you alive, you wonder, *Gee, what did I say?*

That's an off-the-wall eruption of feelings. It can easily trigger an equally off-the-wall reaction in us. And then, without really knowing what happened or how we got there, we're engulfed in a furious battle of the wills. Have you ever later realized that the button you pushed in the other person *really had nothing to do with you?* Say the person had been put down for being ungrateful as a child. You ask if she got the book and card you left on her doorstep last week, and bingo! Red alert! Immediately she's eight, ten, or thirteen years old again. In a nanosecond she's replayed all those messages about being rude, forgetful, selfish, and ungrateful. She's on the defensive. It's volcano time!

Has anyone caught you off guard with an eruption of emotion lately? How did you react? How did you feel about it later? As you relive the incident, what are your thoughts now? When was the last time you went ballistic like that? What event triggered it? What root do you think it had in your childhood?

> *Heavenly Father, please help me to be more understanding and empathic when others go off on me. Teach me to recognize my own buttons and to understand them, so that they won't run my life anymore.   Amen*

WEEK SEVEN: TUESDAY
WHAT'S WITH THESE CUSTODY BATTLES ANYWAY?

> The wicked are trapped by their own words, but the godly escape such trouble.   Proverbs 12:13, NLT

I accompanied her to court. Two years after their divorce, she and her ex-husband faced off in front of a judge. He wanted to change the custody arrangement from eighty-twenty to fifty-fifty. She didn't. They'd never achieved a workable peace. All attempts at negotiating had failed. They'd ended up hiring lawyers and going through months of attack, delay, attack, dodge and attack again before they ended up in court. The monetary cost was high. The emotional cost to both was incalculable, as it was to their daughters. When the dust settled, the original custody split remained. So where did it leave them? Exactly where they'd started — but a lot poorer!!

Sadly, their story is typical. The incidence of custody battles is rising. They've transported divorce with children to a new level of monstrosity as ex-spouses do their best to annihilate the character of this person they once loved. It becomes The Deadbeat versus Super Mom. Or Darling Daddy versus the Irresponsible Witch from Hell. Flaws are exaggerated and virtues extolled as the exes ready themselves to give an overloaded judge a Polaroid snapshot of their situation. Judges hate this stuff. Their concern isn't with two immature adults—it's with the children they chose to bring into the world.

A custody battle is like a wild fire—what seems at first like a tiny, containable blaze is soon raging out of control, consuming everything and everybody in its path. Remember, fifty-fifty custody works well only when Mom and Dad can get along. If you're gearing up for a custody fight, pick up Judith Wallerstein's book, *Second Chances*. The woman I went to court with, read it *after* the battle was over. "How I wish I'd read that book a couple years ago! The money I would've saved! The heartbreak! It should be required reading!"

Have you faced a custody/visitation dispute with your ex? Do you know other

people who have weathered this storm? If you don't, ask the Singles Director in your church to put you in touch with someone who has not only survived a custody battle, but has emerged from it wiser and more compassionate. What is your philosophy on co-parenting? How can you improve your relationship so that you don't inflict serious, lasting damage on everyone, especially your kids?

Lord, help me to act with wisdom, maturity and kindness as the new parenting roles evolve. Protect me from evil, Father and protect my children too. They are truly the innocent victims here. Put a hedge of angels around them to watch over them through this difficult time.   Amen

WEEK SEVEN: WEDNESDAY
THE STRUGGLE WITH SIN

I do not understand what I do. For what I want to do I do not do, but what I hate I do. And if I do what I do not want to do, I agree that the law is good. As it is, it is no longer I myself who do it, but it is sin living in me.   Romans 7:15-17

Current psychology often tells us that we are all addicts. The line I remember from Sunday school so long ago, "Thou shalt have no other gods before me," rings in my ears when I think about addiction. Why? Because addiction is idolatry; it's putting something or someone ahead of God. And we all do it. There are the particularly destructive toxic chemical addictions. Add sexual addiction, love and romance addiction, compulsive behaviors, overeating, anorexia, bulimia, and gambling. These are all shame-based addictions that will end up making us hate ourselves as well as those around us who try to get us to stop. But there are more subtle forms of addiction that take us away from ourselves and our families and separate us from God. They can be addictions to exercise, work, TV, romance novels, religion, and so forth. Because they aren't so obviously toxic, we convince ourselves that they're harmless.

Why do we get hooked on things? Well, we're all born with a hole in our souls, an innate sense of emptiness, a hungering for completeness that can be satisfied only by God. But we can't see God or touch him, so we look for substitutes. And our addictions take our minds off our pain. They give us a little vacation from suffering.

During the crisis of divorce, we are in so much pain that often our brains scream, *Stop this pain! Now! Give me my meds.* And we are more vulnerable to addiction because of the severity of the pain. The problem with addictions is that they don't work—for long. Toxins build up— physically, emotionally, mentally, and spiritually when we use "idols" to take away our pain. Not only do the "meds" wear off, but they leave us in worse shape than before.

The only cure for pain is God. But how does he cure us? First we have to admit that we hurt. We have to tell ourselves the truth. Then we tell God. Maybe we can trust someone else with it too, someone who will be gentle with us. Whether it's a support group, a good friend, a pastor, or therapist, we need to share our burdens with someone who can help.

What is it that you do that you don't want to do? Write it down. Whom in your world do you trust to help you work on freeing yourself from this problem? Are you comfortable with the idea of sharing your burden, or do you feel too ashamed of it?

Lord Jesus, thank you for showing me that all of us struggle with idolatry. Please help me to let go of my crutches and to turn to you to ease my pain.   Amen

WEEK SEVEN: THURSDAY
ON THE ALERT FOR SEXUAL PREDATORS

You are my hiding place; you will protect me from trouble and surround me with songs of deliverance.   Psalm 32:7

A Christian woman accepted a new job in a community where she knew no one. Right before she left, she and her husband had a big blow-up, and she filed for divorce. Almost everyone she met in this new town was married. Lost, lonely, afraid, and hurting more than she even knew, this woman was engulfed in an identity crisis of major proportions. Her entire support system of twenty-five years was gone. She was a sitting duck for a sexual predator.

We always assume that it's the men who do the preying on vulnerable women, particularly single moms. And this is usually true. There was a man in this community who was known for having a progression of lovers. Where he found them all was a subject the local gossips loved to ponder. When this new woman rolled into town, he'd been alone for a while. She was desperate for companionship, and there was no one else. Within a few days of her arrival, he was at her front door with a potted plant. A week later they were having dinner together, as friends, almost every night. Soon they were having sex.

This woman, like all of us at times, had her way of rationalizing things. Having sex with this man was like popping a pain pill; it quieted her spirit and made things hurt less for a while.

A month or two later, this woman's husband came seeking forgiveness and possible reconciliation. Anesthetized by her liaison, she was frozen. In her heart she *knew* she still loved her husband, but she was afraid to try again with him. She was afraid of getting hurt, afraid of failing. She sent him away.

When I later saw this woman, she was destitute. The new man had left her for someone newer. Her divorce had become final, and she felt hopeless to reach out to the ex-husband she still loved. "How could I have been so stupid?" she lamented. "I let myself be seduced. Heck! I wanted to be seduced. I wanted to numb out to avoid the pain. Now it's worse than ever. What do I do? *I screwed up! I love my husband!*"

"You tell me. What do you do now?"

She started to cry. "I need to get right with God, don't I? Like down-on-my-knees, flat-on-my-face right with him, huh?"

I nodded. "And when the time is right, God will prod you. Don't call your ex-husband till then. But afterwards, when you do, try saying: 'I love you. I was wrong. I'm more sorry than you'll ever know. Please forgive me.' And see what happens."

What good and not-so-good habits have you developed to avoid the pain of loneliness and rejection? Do you need to come up with some new coping skills and behaviors? How can you take care of yourself without using or being used by another?

> *Lord, help me to be on the alert for sexual predators. Help me to lean on you and not on my own understanding. Lead me, Lord.*
> *If I do fall down, help me to trust that you'll be there to pick me and put me back on track.   Amen*

WEEK SEVEN: FRIDAY
WHY AM I PROVOKED SO EASILY?

> I said to myself, "I will watch what I do and not sin in what I say. I will curb my tongue when the ungodly are around me." But as I stood there in silence—not even speaking of good things—the turmoil within me grew to the bursting point. My thoughts grew hot within me and began to burn, igniting a fire of words.   Psalm 39:1-3, NLT

"I told you I had plans tonight. You're more than an hour late. Why didn't you call?" a woman demanded of her ex-husband. "This is the fourth time this month you've been late to pick up Sara. And by the way, where's the child support check? My phone bill's past due!"

He looked down his nose at her in disgust. "Good grief, woman. Would you calm down? Hi gorgeous!" He exclaimed as his four-year-old daughter ran into his arms. "Let's get out of here. Mommy's in one of her stinky moods again."

After they left, she called me. "Why do I lash out at him?" she sobbed. "Why does he make me feel as if I'm some kind of out-of-control idiot?"

"Did this happen when you were married?"

She paused. "Well, yeah. He was always telling me I had full-time PMS. He said I should get on hormone replacement therapy, or antidepressants or something. He, of course, considered himself *perfect!* It's like he goads me into losing my temper and then slams me when I do."

" Hmm. Sounds pretty passive-aggressive to me."

"Huh?"

"Well, think about it. He didn't admit that he's done anything wrong. He didn't address being late or the missing child support check either, right? He *is* maneuvering you into losing your temper. It's a control game. By doing something he knows will upset you, and then ignoring it completely, he's really picking a fight with you. He's denying his anger outwardly, but expressing it in covert ways that make you go ballistic. Then, when you grab the bait, he blames it all on you. He didn't lose control by getting upset, so he's OK. He's off the hook. You got upset, so you get to take the fall."

Ever happened to you? Ever done it to someone else? Describe an incident when you provoked someone to anger, or someone did it to you. How do you feel as you write about it now? How would you behave differently if you could replay the scene?

Lord, we play so many games with anger. Please help me to unmask the games I play and to avoid being caught in the traps others set for me. Amen

WEEK SEVEN: SATURDAY
CELEBRATE THE GIFT OF FAITH

> Now faith is being sure of what we hope for and certain of what
> we do not see.   Hebrews 11:1

"Are you *sure* you still believe in God?" she asked me. "After all the crummy stuff that's happened?"

"Of course I do!" I answered. My brain reeled with silent questions: *Why in the world did she ask that, and what could I say to convince her that I really believe, that I'm not some kind of fair-weather believer? Why should I have to measure my faith against hers or anyone else's?*

What is faith? And how do we prove we have it? Do we prove it by devoting our lives to doing good works? Do we prove it by talking Christianese? Is just believing in God enough? No, no, and no. The writer of Hebrews tells us that faith is "being sure of what we hope for." Aside from salvation, what did I hope for back when I first became a Christian? I hoped to know God. I hoped that what he had to say to me would help ease my pain. I hoped he would help me live my life better. I hoped he could give me something solid to hang on to.

The Bible told me this about God: *He says he knows me. He says he loves me. He says he forgives me. He says he honors his promises. He doesn't lie.* I decided to believe him, trust him. Implicitly. Even though I couldn't see him. After all, the other half of this Hebrews 11 verse tells us that even though we don't see God, he's always there. We're absolutely "certain of what we do not see."

I can't prove to anyone that I have the right kind or amount of faith. Like everyone else's (I imagine), mine fluctuates. I have cried and screamed at God. I have turned my back on God. I have also turned to him as comforter, best friend and loving parent. I can only trust that he'll take that tiny mustard seed that is my faith and grow it into a gigantic, fruit-laden tree. Take your journal and Bible to a private place and do an hour-long Bible study on faith. Consider, for example, these passages: Luke 17:6; Romans 10:17; Hebrews 11:7-12. How would you answer the question that woman put to me? Has your faith grown bigger or smaller since your divorce?

Dear Father-Mother God, you do know me, love me, forgive me, and know what's best for me. Help me to trust you, Lord. Speak to me in my heart and show me the way. Amen

WEEK EIGHT

WEEK EIGHT: SUNDAY
TIME OUT TO REOWN MY WORLD

Not in the clamor of the crowded street,
Not in the shouts and plaudits of the throng,
But in ourselves are triumph and defeat.
Henry Wadsworth Longfellow

One of the most empowering things you, as a newly single person, can do is to reown your world. When one's spouse disappears, the ghost of the missing presence hovers around the house for some time. The bed is cold and empty. The nights are long and lonely. There's a pair of invisible, empty slippers next to it, just waiting to be filled. How do we deal with the emptiness? One option is to long for and fantasize about your mate coming to his or her senses and returning. A second is launching an all-out search for a replacement. A third way is to accept your aloneness for now and use this time for healing and growth. This is the most challenging way to go, and it's also the most rewarding. Is it easy? In the short run, no. In the long run, yes!

So can you throw the invisible slippers away? Tonight vow to be a bed hog. Sleep diagonally, on your back. Let your mouth hang open. (Who cares if you snore?) Take some time out and today look around your house. Do a physical and spiritual inventory, then reclaim your house. As your *single home.* How do you do that?

Clean out cupboards. Rearrange furniture. Plan a garage sale. If you're low on furnishings, call up a friend with a wacky knack for decorating and ask for some ideas to make what you have work better for you.

Next phase. Make a list of the places you and your ex used to go to. Not the boring ones, but the ones you really miss. Those Sunday drives or picnics by the lake? An incomparable restaurant? Did you love to go to the movies? Did you have regular tickets for baseball, football, or even opera? Can't you spare a little time to give yourself a treat or two? Can't you go have some fun again with a friend? Yes!

Put a star by those places you used to go that mean the most to you. Now put a second star in front of those that are affordable. Put a third star next to the one thing you want to do most. Get on the phone and make plans with someone to do it with you within the next week. Then go have yourself a good cry.

Father, I know I have to let go of my spouse, but I thank you for reminding me that I don't have to give up everything that brought me joy.   *Amen*

WEEK EIGHT: MONDAY
GETTING EVEN IS EXPENSIVE!

Deceit fills hearts that are plotting evil; joy fills hearts that are planning peace!   Proverbs 12:20, NLT

Working in divorce recovery, I've seen people burn through the equity in their homes and plunge themselves deeply into debt trying to get even. Why? How can revenge be so all-consuming? How can it blind us to the point where we not only turn our present into a nightmare, but also seriously impair our own and our children's future security?

I've seen IRAs cashed in. I've seen college funds dissolved to pay legal bills.

If a judge finds it impossible to see through the muck of a custody battle, he will order a psychological evaluation. The entire family is examined under a microscope. If one or both parent persists in slandering the other, and the maligned parent reacts with fear and anger when unfairly attacked, the issues become even more clouded. It becomes up to the psychologist to discern where the truth is. Psychologists are human beings, and their judgments are no less fallible than yours or mine. They eventually have to make recommendations to the court and this requires that they take sides. They don't always choose correctly.

People fight about *stuff* as bitterly as they do about their children. I recently had lunch with three people, all separated more than two years. None of their divorces were final yet. They were all trying to untangle their property and debts. Their legal bills climbed as their lawyers went back and forth, back and forth. None of them knew how to make it all stop. They all hoped to be finished in three to six months.

If you're feeling lost in the legal maze, see if you can get connected to other people who are struggling with the court system. If there's anything we all need when facing this impersonal but incredibly powerful monolith, it's the support of people who have walked in our moccasins. We can get so caught up in the intense emotional drama of the battle that we lose all perspective.

Have you and your ex had problems splitting up possessions or resolving custody issues? If you haven't, do you know others who are? Spend a few minutes writing down your thoughts and feelings about today's topic, along with today's scripture. Then write a letter to God.

Heavenly Father, I want to plan peace, not evil. Fill me with joy, not deceit. Help me to avoid falling into malicious or greedy behavior.   Amen

WEEK EIGHT: TUESDAY
WHY DOES THIS FEEL LIKE A ROLLER COASTER?

Tonight all the hells of young grief have opened again....For in grief nothing 'stays put.' One keeps on emerging from a phase, but it always recurs.   C.S. Lewis, *A Grief Observed*

When I first began working in divorce recovery, the course material I was given used the concept of the "Slippery Slope" to describe the roller coaster ride that newly single people invariably go through. We move in and out of the phases of grief, often with mercurial rapid-fire motion. One minute we're feeling quite balanced, the next we're in a bellowing rage. Or we go to bed at night feeling okay, and wake up in the morning with a black cloud strangling our hearts.

Have you ever found yourself feeling so grateful, so free because you believe you've finally forgiven (and been forgiven by) your ex? And then, boom! Something happens and the sirens go off again. Every single alert button in your head is activated and flashing at once. Suddenly, you're back at square one, scratching your head and wondering what just happened.

Why is this? Why is this grief process so messy, so unpredictable and so painful? Why does it take so long to get through it? Why—just when we think we've made it—does life pull the rug out from under our feet so that we slip and slide on our rear ends—all the way back down to the bottom again? My opinion is that it's because we humans tend to be impatient. And we Americans live in a quick-fix, microwavable society. We expect ourselves to be over and done with the icky part of divorce ASAP. And often our co-workers, family and friends reinforce that philosophy.

Explain to those people close to you about the Slippery Slope. Ask for their patience and understanding. Invite them to applaud your steps forward, up and out of the pit and ask them to be merciful when you fall back into it. Work towards showing that kind of compassion to others too. Make a list today of those people you trust and make a date to spend some quality time with someone. Share some of the ups and downs of your journey with this person. And then be there for them too.

> *Father, please help me to understand the recovery process and to know you are moving me through it to strengthen, heal and sanctify me.   Amen*

WEEK EIGHT: WEDNESDAY
I LOVE YOU, I HATE YOU!

> This is what God does. He gives His best—the sun to warm and the rain to nourish—to everyone, regardless; the good and bad, the nice and nasty. If all you do is love the lovable, do you expect a bonus? Anybody can do that.   From Matthew 5, The Message

Remember when you fell in love with your former spouse? Oh, sorry.

Come on. Cut me some slack. Take a couple steps back. Women, you did love him once, didn't you? You did think he was strong, virile, handsome, and wonderfully intelligent. Men, you did think she was the most beautiful, sensitive, delightful creature ever created when you married her, didn't you? So how did it get to this place where you hate each other? How did the person you vowed to love until death become your sworn enemy? How did it come to be that a venomous thirst for revenge has wiped out the love in your hearts? What on earth happened?

You know what? It may take you years to figure that out. In some cases, you may *never* figure it out. But God loves you. And He loves your ex too—no matter how badly you've been treated or how much cow dung you've slung at this person you once adored. God wants us to stop hating. He wants us to stop plotting revenge and *love the unlovable*. Often the most difficult challenge of all is to love our ex-spouse. It may take years for you two to achieve a workable, lasting peace. Over and over you may have to say, "Father, forgive her (or him). She (he) doesn't know what she's (he's) doing" as you bite your tongue and will yourself to turn that other cheek.

Remember that saying when we were kids: "Sticks and stones will break my bones, but words will never hurt me?" Not true. Words hurt, especially when flung at you by an ex-spouse who knows you intimately, who knows better than anyone on the planet where the soft, vulnerable, unprotected places are in your soul.

How do we avoid falling into hateful behavior? The only thing that has helped me was to do my own personal Bible study on revenge and loving my enemies. Look in your concordance. Write out as many passages as you need to on this subject. Tape them to your bathroom mirror and memorize them so that when those hateful thoughts catch you by surprise, you can rattle off a centering verse or two.

> *God, th   Thank you, God, for being so majestic that you can love the lovable and the unlovable equally. Protect me from not only the sting of evil words, but from being goaded into returning evil for evil.*   *Amen*

WEEK EIGHT: THURSDAY
STANDING TALL IN THE FACE OF ADVERSITY

David said to [Goliath], "You come against me with sword and spear and javelin, but I come against you in the name of the Lord Almighty.... All those gathered here will know that it is not by sword or spear that the Lord saves; for the battle is the Lord's,

and he will give all of you into our hands."   1   Samuel
17:45, 47

The battle is the Lord's. What a concept! When going to court looms ominously in the background, and stays there looming for months and months, it's easy to believe that God has forgotten us. Like the Israelite army, we're so terrified by this nine-foot giant who comes out every morning to taunt us that we feel like tiny ants, about to be ground into the dirt.

It took a young shepherd boy with a sling and five stones to knock Goliath to the ground. How did David do it? He didn't. He let God do it. His eyes penetrated the giant's gnarly facade and saw him for what he was, a puffed up bully. And he took him out with one shot.

A courageous woman wrote me this note: "I was trying to decide if I should fight for custody of my daughter, since my ex was addicted to meth-amphetamines and had moved his girlfriend in with him. A lady at church whom I barely knew talked to me about the situation. That same week she sent me a card that said, 'Even though your daughter's with you 50 percent of the time, she's with God 100 percent of the time.' That meant a lot to me. I think about it whenever I'm tempted to want to fight him. It keeps me sane."

God is always in control. Always. The things that happen in a divorce are frequently unfair and usually very painful. But the battle is ultimately God's. The most difficult thing that most of us will ever do is to give it up and give it to him. Our instincts as parents and our rage at the injustice being inflicted upon us conspire together to keep us locked into a fight-or-flight mode. Our emotions are running the show, the irrational emotions of fear and anger, not love. The more fear and anger we feel, the less we hear God. The less we feel or express love.

What is your biggest challenge right now regarding this divorce? Are you and your ex still camped out on the battleground? Does Goliath come out every morning just as you're wiping the sleep from your eyes and scare the daylights out of you, messing up your whole day? Read the story of David and Goliath. What is it telling you?

> *God, I need to be reminded that the battle is yours. Help me to let go and trust you, even though everything seems totally unfair and awful right now.   Amen*

WEEK EIGHT: FRIDAY
HOW WAS ANGER HANDLED IN MY CHILDHOOD HOME?

A gentle answer turns away wrath, but harsh words stir up anger.

Proverbs 15:1, NLT

Answer these questions about the way anger was dealt with in your childhood:

1. Who got openly angry in your family? How did they vent their anger? How did everyone else react? How was conflict resolved?
2. Did one of your parents provoke the other to anger and then blame him or her for getting upset? If so, which one? Give an example of how this occurred and how it was resolved.
3. Did your parents dodge anger by being overly busy and avoiding too much close contact? Did their anger ever catch up with them?
4. Did your parents displace their anger, finding a common enemy to join forces against? Did they then direct all their anger at this enemy, avoiding all conflict between themselves? How did you feel when they did this?
5. Were either of your parents chemically addicted? Did one of them get sick a lot, while the other catered to his or her every need? Did the care-taking parent ever rebel? Were you or a sibling expected to be a care taker as well?

6. Did one or both of your parents refrain from getting angry altogether? Was that person always slightly (or deeply) depressed? If you tried to talk to this parent about something that made you angry, how did he or she respond?

7. How did you express your anger growing up? How did your parents respond to you? How do you deal with conflict together now?

8. Did people admit their mistakes and ask for forgiveness in your family? Give an example or two.

    Heavenly Father, help me to be truthful in answering these questions. Please bring to light any areas inside of me that need your healing touch. If I'm ashamed of how I behaved back then, help me to ask for forgiveness. Help me remember I only have the power to change my behavior from here on out.   Amen

WEEK EIGHT: SATURDAY
BEWARE OF THE CROP SNATCHERS!

> You were running a good race. Who cut in on you and kept you
> from obeying the truth?   Galatians 5:7

Achieving a goal is like running a big race. You work out and get yourself in shape so you can go the distance. You psych yourself up. The day of the big race comes, and you're ready! You roar out of the starting gate and tear around the track, lap after lap. But on the last lap, just moments from the finish line, you just can't do it. You're exhausted. Actually, you're beyond exhausted. Suddenly from the sidelines comes a cheer. "You can do it! You can do it!…" You trip and twist your ankle. You pick yourself up and keep running. Your chest is burning. It's hopeless. You'll never make it. But then you notice someone running alongside you. "Come on. Hang in there. Don't give up. You're almost there." You catch sight of the finish line. You stumble across and throw yourself onto the grass, gasping for air. You made it!

The alternate scenario is this: You're back at that last length. Instead of applause, you hear booing. "You can't." Faces jeer at you from the sidelines. Someone runs up to you. "Hey. You are *never* gonna make it. It's just too hard. Quit now before you *really* hurt yourself." You trip and twist your ankle. "Don't get up," the voice says. "I told you to quit. Now look what you did. It's probably broken!" You inch your way off the track and onto the grass, grasping at your leg, tears streaming down your face. You failed! Again!

As a divorced person, and especially as a single parent, you will discover lots of people who will discourage you from daring to dream big. "You'll be lucky just to get by," they'll say. "Play it safe. Keep your dead-end job (they may decide to give you a raise *next year)*, and don't even think about doing something *risky*. Please! Single parents cannot afford to take risks."

A wise pastor told me once to be on the alert for crop snatchers! Met any lately? Who were they and what did they steal from you?

> *O God, thank you that you will never desert me, no matter how arduous the race. Please surround me with encouragers, not crop snatchers.*   *Amen*

WEEK NINE

WEEK NINE: SUNDAY
HOW WE CAN TAKE CARE OF OURSELVES

"The most important [commandment]," answered Jesus, "is this: '...Love the Lord your God with all your heart and with all your soul and with all your mind and with all your strength.' The second is this: 'Love your neighbor as yourself.' There is no commandment greater than these." Mark 12:29-31

"When you're grieving you need to take special care of yourself. Grief is stressful," I counseled my divorce recovery group.

"No kidding!" one woman answered. "I can't tell you the last time I slept through the night. Much less ate a whole meal! My mother thinks I've become anorexic and wants to take me to a specialist!"

One of the guys in the back of the room pitched in. "Yeah. My cooking's worse than awful," he said. "I end up drinking my dinner most nights."

Around the circle the true confessions continued. Our group contained people who were overeating, under eating, dating too soon, working too much, ignoring their jobs, sleeping too much, not sleeping. "I started smoking!" the last woman exclaimed. "I haven't smoked since high school. It's the stress. It's just too much."

Once again, grief is stressful. It can wreak havoc on our bodies, minds, hearts, and souls and turn us inside out if we let it. Each person in my group picked one self-sabotaging behavior to work on that night. We worked on them for a week and then reported back. The smoker didn't quit, but she did cut back. As she told us later, when she talked on the phone at night, she didn't fill her ash tray to overflowing and beyond as she tried to puff away her heartache. The woman who had lost thirty pounds was making an effort to prepare herself a healthy meal every night instead of gobbling a sack of microwave popcorn in front of the TV.

We can take better care of ourselves. We should get regular checkups, take vitamins, eat well, and rest more often right now, especially if we aren't sleeping well. We should get regular exercise, find a friend we can bare our soul to. We should let ourselves cry. Crying loosens up those tight places in our hearts and softens us. It drains out the poisons clogging us and keeping us tied up in knots. For today, make a list of things you can do to love yourself better and help yourself through this time of grief. And commit to doing one thing right away.

Father, the second commandment says that I am to love my neighbor as myself. Right now I need help loving myself. Please help me first of all to love you with all my heart, soul, and might and, second, to care for myself as I would my own children. Amen

WEEK NINE: MONDAY
HOW WAS ANGER HANDLED IN MY MARRIAGE?

"Put your sword back in its place," Jesus said to him, "for all who draw the sword will die by the sword."   Matthew 26:52

Let's answer a few questions about the way anger was handled in your marriage. Often, as marriages disintegrate and communication breaks down, anger becomes the most prevalent emotion in the home.

But here I'd like to ask you to think back to before things got really difficult. Answer these questions about your marriage, not your divorce.

1. Did either you or your spouse get openly angry in your marriage? How did you vent your anger? How did the others in your family react? How was conflict resolved between the two of you?

2. Did one of you provoke the other to anger and then blame him or her for getting upset? How did this occur? How was it resolved?

3. Did one or both of you dodge conflict by keeping yourselves overly busy, avoiding close contact? How did anger ever catch up with you?

4. Did you and your spouse displace your anger, finding a common enemy to join forces against? Did you direct all your energy at fighting this enemy, thus avoiding conflict between you?

5. Were you or your spouse chemically addicted? Did one of you get sick a lot, while the other catered to his or her every need? Did the care-taking spouse ever rebel? Was a child expected to be the caretaker?

6. Did one or both of you refrain from getting angry altogether? Was that person always slightly (or deeply) depressed? How did that person deal with other people's anger?

7. Did you and your spouse ever admit your mistakes and ask for forgiveness? Were you able to ask your children to forgive you when you were wrong?

8. How do you and your ex-spouse handle anger now? What patterns are you beginning to see in your behavior?

Finally, a word about anger and violence and divorce. If you are threatened with physical violence, get a restraining order. If you are a victim of violence, file a police report right away. If you're being stalked, call the cops. It's best to protect yourself.

If you or someone you know feels they're in danger, get help. If a marriage has a history of violence, the violence may well escalate during and after a divorce. Be alert! If you're seriously worried about someone, by all means speak up.

> *Father, if violence is in front of my eyes, let me see it and call it what it is. Give me the courage to speak out and get help. Please reveal the patterns of anger inside my marriage so that they may be healed. Help me to see what I did wrong and to ask for forgiveness where I need to.*   *Amen*

WEEK NINE: TUESDAY
SUFFERING IN SILENCE

> Laugh, and the world laughs with you;
> Weep and you weep alone;
> For the sad old earth must borrow its mirth,
> But has trouble enough of its own.   Ella Wheeler Wilcox

What's the very first thing you do when you're hurt? I mean really, really hurt. When someone says or does something that hurls a spear of agony straight into your heart? Do you cry? Do you lash out in anger? Do you run for the hills? What's been your coping technique in the face of rejection, abandonment, harsh criticism, and betrayal?

Crying wasn't an option for me growing up. Getting angry wasn't either. So I retreated behind a wall of pseudo strength: that thick, tough rhinoceros skin of denial to hide my pain from the world. Eventually I hid it from myself.

Later, when I became an adult and I wasn't held any longer to the confines of the parent-child relationship, the anger surfaced. Did it ever! When wounded, my immediate and involuntary reaction was fury. *How dare that person (or situation) treat me so unfairly? I'll show him! I'll get her!* When the anger didn't work, which of course it didn't, I would go back to plan A. I'd run and hide. I'd suffer in silence. I didn't know how to reach out to another and share my pain. I saw crying as a sign of weakness; when I was able to do it, it was only in isolation.

It took me forty-four years to learn how to cry. Once I started, I cried a reservoir full of tears. Now when I'm hurt, instead of lashing out in anger, my feelings move straight to tears. I cry. I got to the place where I couldn't hide my tears anymore. I had to step over the threshold of shame and fear and *trust other people.*

I have learned that crying with a loved one is a gift that honors the other person; when we cry, we shed our harsh, angry side. Instead of running from this person, we turn ourselves around and walk toward him or her; *we share our truest, most honest and vulnerable self* with the other. It's a gift that brings healing to both people.

How did you express pain in your family of origin? How did you and your former spouse deal with pain in your marriage? How do you deal with your pain now that you're alone? Explore these questions in your journal today. Do you have a safe, accepting friend with whom you can share your painful tears? With whom it's safe to move through your anger and fear into the healing light and loving embrace of God's love?

> *O heavenly Father, I do so desire healing in my life. Touch me in the places that need to be transformed by your love. Let me scream, run, and, finally, cry. Help me to be real, Lord. Help me to understand love as you understand it.   Amen*

WEEK NINE: WEDNESDAY
HOW DO I KNOW IF I'M REALLY DEPRESSED?

> I cry out to God without holding back. Oh, that God would listen to me! When I was in deep trouble, I searched for the Lord. All night long I pray, with hands lifted toward heaven, pleading. There can be no joy for me until he acts.
>
> Psalm 77:1-2, NLT

The loneliness and isolation associated with grief can be overwhelming. We get so low, so depressed that even picking up the telephone to call our closest friend is more than we can handle, yet we feel so desperately empty and lost. Our souls cry out for companionship. Understanding. And compassion. What happens here? How does our grief cross that dotted line and strap us to our beds, as if we were paralyzed with fear, pain, hopelessness, and confusion? Wondering if you're depressed? Well, try answering these questions with a) seldom or never; b) sometimes; c) often or always:

1. I'm incredibly sad and lonely.
2. I'm eating a lot more or a lot less.
3. I'm really irritable.
4. I'm not sleeping well and I'm always tired.
5. I have a hard time getting motivated to do anything.
6. I'm worried that I might get cancer (or some other disease).
7. I beat myself up a lot for my mistakes and failures.
8. I worry about losing my job, my friends, my kids....
9. I feel as if things will never get better.
10. I wish I could die.

Count up your a's, b's, and c's. A's indicate no depression. B's indicate moderate depression. C's indicate severe depression. Most people going through divorce experience many (or all) of these symptoms, either for a short while, intermittently, or long term.

If you feel immobilized by sorrow and unable to find a way out of it, it's time to contact a therapist. If thoughts of suicide plague you, you are in extreme and excruciating pain. Even though you feel hopeless, please know that there is hope for you, and there are people who can help you deal with the pain—before it gets out of control.

Members of my divorce recovery groups say that the months they spent in therapy (and, yes, even on antidepressants) made all the difference in the world. Why? For starters they were able to get out of bed in the morning. The black fog that had enveloped them dissipated; they were able to identify and work on some of the issues pushing them over the edge. Once you've succeeded in improving a single facet of your life, you won't be so inclined to beat yourself up. The face peering back at you from the mirror won't be one you're ashamed to be associated with, much less to own.

Your assignment for today is to call your church and a close friend or two, and ask for the names of good Christian therapists. Even if you don't need the name today, you or a loved one may need it tomorrow, so it's good to have it on hand. And remember, even though you may feel like curling up into a tiny ball and hiding in a corner, don't. Isolation will only make the pain more severe. Call someone. Reach out. Now.

Father, when the walls close in on me and I feel as if I can't go on, please give me the courage to reach out to someone who can help me. Amen

WEEK NINE: THURSDAY
WHAT'S THE PRICE OF DENYING MY ANGER?

Short-tempered people must pay their own penalty. If you rescue them once, you will have to do it again.   Proverbs 19:19, NLT

I know some people who just don't get mad. They live by the "peace at any price" credo and stuff their anger, insisting to the world that everything is delightful. These people hold themselves apart from anger. They avoid conflict whenever they can. When things get hot, they tune out. They keep their mouths shut and wait. As soon as the storm passes, then they block the inflammatory event right out of their minds. The next morning they can calmly ask, "Didn't we have a lovely time?" and mean it.

These folks allow others, who are temperamentally out of control, to run wild. They rescue them and protect them from consequences of their own sinful behavior. As noted in the proverb above, the pattern is easily established and difficult to eliminate.

We all know people whose repressed anger erupts in physical ailments. I've known couples where one partner developed stomach problems, migraines, chronic fatigue, or any number of mysterious ailments. The other partner got so caught up in ministering to the sick spouse that neither ever had to deal with his or her anger. I've known others who start tap dancing the minute a conflict is hinted at. Rushing to meet the needs of the angry person, they'll do anything to diffuse the anger threatening to explode around them. Outside they're cheerful. Inside they're convulsing in agony. As they go about their placating ways, they pile criticism on top of criticism onto themselves. "If only I hadn't left my shoes by the bed....If only I'd remembered to pick up the laundry...."

When was the last time you stuffed your anger? What caused you to do it? What kind of physical problems have you suffered from avoiding confrontation?

> *Dear God, when anger catches me unaware, help me to own up*
> *to my feelings and to examine them in the light of your truth.*
> *Amen*

WEEK NINE: FRIDAY
GAINING CONTROL OVER MY EMOTIONS

Let the godly confess their rebellion to you while there is time, that they may not drown in the flood waters of judgment. For you are my hiding place; you protect me from trouble. You surround me with songs of victory.   Psalm 32:6-7, NLT

"Did you know that we don't have to act on each feeling we have?" the pastor's wife asked our women's group. "We do, however, need to feel it. We do need to be aware of it. We do need to listen to what it's telling us. In fact, we may even want to examine it closely and try to discern its history. Where did it come from? We can give ourselves permission to work through our feelings without judging ourselves harshly because we think feelings are inappropriate, irrational, out of date, or 'stupid.' If we don't work through them, we'll most likely deny them, telling ourselves, *I'm centered. I'm joyful. I'm way beyond this ridiculous emotion.*"

She walked us through Psalm 32 and showed us how David became aware of his feelings. As we read the psalm along with her, we saw how David exalted in the blessedness he felt because his sins had been forgiven. He went on to describe how he felt when he was in denial. His bones wasted away; he groaned all day long; his strength was sapped because of his guilt. Once he admitted his sins, the weight was lifted from his shoulders. He felt peace, forgiveness, and protection. He was surrounded with songs of deliverance.

She gave us five steps to help us gain control over our emotions. They were:

1.   We acknowledge our feelings to God. "This is what happened, Father, and this is where I am."
2.   We admit our helplessness. Only Jesus can calm the raging storms.
3.   We ask for his truth and power to help us. He will counsel us.
4.   We keep on asking, seeking, and knocking. We persevere.
5.   We praise God, as David did, and in faith receive the blessings.

Pull out your Bible and read over Psalm 32. As you compare it to these five suggestions, what comes to mind? How did David find peace? What advice does he give in verses 8-11?

Father, I rejoice in you. You are truly my hiding place, and I trust that you will protect me from trouble if I am truthful and don't cover up my weakness.   Amen

WEEK NINE: SATURDAY
I'M GONNA GET YOU!

Hurt people hurt people. Sandra Wilson, Ph.D.

Sandra Wilson's book, titled *Hurt People Hurt People,* is particularly applicable to people going through divorce. Have you noticed that there's something chillingly similar among those who are the newly separated?

They're in major pain. They're hypersensitive. Their defenses are up. They're fully armed and ready to snap into battle mode at the drop of an insult, even an imagined insult. Like ticking time bombs, they're ready to explode and shower those around them with pain.

I remember the first few months I was single-again. I was always on guard. And I was always getting into scraps with my family, my co-workers, my friends. I was especially dangerous driving to and from work. Someone was stupid enough to cut me off on the freeway? Ah ha! I'd cut right back in front of him, scowling and swearing.

The harder we've always tried to be perfect and lovable, the more susceptible we are to becoming ticking abuse-bombs during divorce. Why? Because we don't have room in our psyches for failure. Failure is unacceptable. It is the opposite of perfection. How have you treated people these past few months? Have you hurt people? Make a list today of people to whom you wish you hadn't done or said things. Next to each name, jot down a yes or a no to indicate if you've yet rectified things. Now call your closest, safest friend and ask him or her to help you work through asking forgiveness of these people.

Father, I know that when I'm hurting, I hurt others. Please help
me to stop, and to ask their forgiveness as I get stronger.
Amen

WEEK TEN

WEEK TEN: SUNDAY
WHEN THE ANIMOSITY GETS OVERWHELMING

> For he will command his angels concerning you to guard you in
> all your ways; they will lift you up in their hands, so that you will
> not strike your foot against a stone.   Psalm 91:11-12

When the storms of life swirl crazily around us, they wipe away
familiar watermarks. It's always "high tide" during a storm. You can't
walk on the beach without being drenched by cold, pounding waves
that threaten to smash you against sharp rocks. At these times we need
to retreat to higher ground. We must find shelter and we wait out the
storm. We stand firm in our faith and conviction that the storm will
pass. The warmth and brightness of the sunshine will return. With the
sunshine will come a carpet of fresh, green grass, and a profusion of
brilliantly colored wildflowers?

The chaos of divorce can unleash monster storms within our lives.
One man had a particularly abusive ex-spouse. She had a nasty habit of
calling him once or twice a week in the latter part of the evening. She'd
claim a legitimate pretense for making the call but within minutes
would launch into a tirade.

"What do I do?" he asked me.

"Hang up. The first minute she gets abusive. You have the right to
draw a line and say, 'Beyond this point I will not go.' When she goes off,

all you need to do is say, 'You may not speak to me this way.' Then hang up."

"That's all?"

Yes. That's all. It's so simple that most people are confounded by it. Just hang up. You don't have to accept abusive treatment. You may have to repeat this process a dozen times. Or two or three dozen. Eventually the person on the other end of the phone line will catch on. The storm will stop.

What storms are you facing right now? Storms are scary. They unleash powerful forces of destructiveness. In the midst of storms, it will be helpful to you to take this journey in your mind. Close your eyes. Imagine yourself climbing up a hill and reaching an overlook where you can see your entire neighborhood spread out below you. How do you see yourself? Your ex? Can you see past your immediate circumstances and feel God's angels lifting you up in their hands so that the sting of the harsh words fades into the wind?

> *Lord, help me to see the big picture more clearly. Give me the gift of perspective. Help me to draw my line and to stand firmly behind it.* Amen

WEEK TEN: MONDAY
REWRITING HISTORY

> Now we see but a poor reflection as in a mirror; then we shall see face to face. Now I know in part; then I shall know fully, even as I am fully known.   1 Corinthians 13:12

We each see things differently. And how we remember an event today won't be exactly the same way we remember it next year or in five years. We all rewrite history to coincide with our current reality.

Look back at your marriage. From the vantage point of a newly separated person, you probably don't have a balanced picture of what it was like. If you're really ticked off at your ex, you probably can't remember much good about being with him or her. In fact, you may wonder how in the world you could have been so *blind,* so *stupid* not to have seen the *real monster* lurking behind that lovey-dovey mask. If you still hunger for your ex, you will most likely remember only the *really good parts* of your marriage. Either way, if we tape recorded your story of the marriage right now and compared it to your ex's story, do you think the two would bear much resemblance?

Do you know people whose accounts of recent history consistently make *them* look good? They're never wrong. The other guy always is! I call that game Villains and Victims. It's so easy to play, especially in a divorce when tempers are hot and people get nasty. In most cases, ex-spouses take turns wearing black hats in the divorce arena. One may lie a lot more and be a lot meaner, but the other one has to be playing too, or the game would not go on. When we're locked into this drama, the best thing we can do is take a time out. Pull out your journal. What did the other guy say happened? What do you say happened? Where was he or she wrong? Where were you wrong? You can't force the other person to speak the truth, but you can be honest with yourself. That's a big step forward.

> *Dear Lord, we humans see things through an unclear lens and we all want to make ourselves look good. Help me to own my stuff and not give in to the temptation to put a black hat on the other guy.   Amen*

WEEK TEN: TUESDAY
HEALTHIER WAYS TO DEAL WITH ANGER

Those who control their anger have great understanding; those with a hasty temper will make mistakes. Proverbs 14:29, NLT

The Bible advises us to resolve our differences and forgive one another. Anger fragments us. It tears relationships apart. Only after we've calmed down and worked through the issues that created the conflict—completely, honestly, and kindly with the other person or people involved—can our relationship be restored to wholeness.

Generally, unhealthy ways of dealing with anger are conditioned responses. They're ways we learned to react early in life. *We aren't acting; we're reacting.* We're not in control of our emotions or our responses. We're on autopilot. We may goad others into rage and then put them down for being out of control. We may be friendly to someone's face but rip her to shreds behind her back. We may stuff our anger and suffer illness and depression. We may try to outrun it by staying overly busy. We may find a common enemy whom we never have to interact with directly and then project all our anger onto him. Reactions!

I remember once complaining to a therapist that I never said the right thing when I was under attack. I gave a knee-jerk reaction and then had twenty-twenty vision in hindsight. The therapist basically said, "If you can think of the right thing to say and do after the fact, then you can train yourself to say and do it at the right time."

"How?!" I asked.

"First of all, stop. Take a deep breath. If you feel as of you're losing control, tell the other you need a time out. Take it! Don't come back until you've sorted through your thoughts and emotions and feel more balanced."

"What if that never happens?"

He laughed. "That's where courage comes in. And practice. It takes practice."

How would you describe your automatic anger style? Ask your most trusted friend if he or she sees your behavior as predictably fitting into one of the categories mentioned above or perceives you as personifying different styles in different situations. When was the last time you got really upset? What did you do?

God, I have so much anger in me right now that it blows me away. Help me to get it out—on paper, by exercising, or with a safe friend—in ways that won't hurt me or other people. Amen

WEEK TEN: WEDNESDAY
HOW CAN I STOP GETTING PUSHED OVER THE EDGE?

Don't copy the behavior and customs of this world, but let God transform you into a new person by changing the way you think. Then you will know what God wants you to do, and you will know how good and pleasing and perfect his will really is.

Romans 12:2, NLT

God heals us. He changes us by the cleansing and transforming of our minds. I wasn't very old the first time I heard that passage quoted. I had absolutely no idea what it meant. What was God going to do, I wondered, have me lean my head over the kitchen sink and turn on the water? Instead of shampooing my hair as my mother did, would he slice my head open and wash my brain? It sounded a lot like getting my mouth washed out with soap, but a lot scarier.

As I grew older, I realized that God isn't going to perform brain surgery on us. (Darn! A quick fix would be so much easier!) But he can and will help us change the way we think. As you've been reading this book, have you started to monitor the things you say silently to yourself? What have you heard yourself saying? Are you unkind to yourself? Do you put yourself down for the way you act, look, and feel? Do you put others down? Are intense feelings, maybe of anger, frustration, betrayal, and fear lurking close to the surface, just waiting for the slightest provocation so they can spew all over anyone who happens to tap lightly on that activate-anger-now button?

How can God help you cleanse and transform your mind so those triggers are deactivated? I see the first step as being ready to hear and record what you say to yourself. Awareness must come first. The last time a major button of yours went off—can you remember what thoughts went through your mind? Write them down. How realistic are they? How kind? How nurturing, forgiving, loving? *They're not?* Now skip a line. Look up Galatians 5:22-23. Write nine new affirming and encouraging sentences about yourself, one for each of the nine fruit of the Spirit.

Heavenly Father, please help me to change the way I think so that my life can be a reflection of the fruit of your Spirit.
Amen

WEEK TEN: THURSDAY
PEACE INSTEAD OF PANIC

You will keep in perfect peace all who trust in you, whose thoughts are fixed on you! Trust in the Lord always, for the Lord God is the eternal Rock. He humbles the proud and brings the arrogant city to the dust. Its walls come crashing down!

Isaiah 26:3-5, NLT

As she poured out her story to me, I could feel the fear in her rolling through the phone lines. She had not lived in this country long—just long enough to establish residency and then have her husband leave her for another woman. The wife was such an emotional wreck that he'd been granted temporary custody of their young daughter. (He wanted full custody.) She was permitted to see the baby only on Wednesday nights and alternating weekends.

I tried to explain the court system to her. I tried to explain the process of a custody evaluation to her. I tried to calm her fears. But she couldn't hear me. Over and over she kept saying, "But he's taken my baby away. He says horrible things about me. They're all lies. I'm all alone here. I have no friends. My family is all back home, and they believe him, not me. He picks up my daughter at day care when it's my day, and I go there and she's gone. I don't even get her when I'm supposed to! The women who run the day care look at me as if I'm a bad person, a bad mother. He's talked to them too. What can I do?! How can I stop him?"

She called me every week or so for about two months. With every call her panic mounted. She became a victim of the system—desperate, hysterical, and incapable of portraying herself as a mature and caring parent. She was a Christian. She knew God, but she couldn't hear God over the howling siren of her own fear. She had no peace. Her husband prevailed, and the temporary custody arrangement was modified further to give him full custody. She was considered so unstable that she was allowed to see her daughter only when a court-appointed supervisor was present.

Did she deserve that? I don't think so. But her fear overwhelmed her and destroyed her ability to portray herself well. She came across as a basket case, and her husband came across as a solid, dependable, and caring parent. Do you know anyone who has been paralyzed by fear? Read today's scripture verse again. What is the lesson here?

Father, thank you for promising that you will keep me in perfect peace if I trust in you and fix my thoughts on you. Hide me in your holiness. Help me to leave the warfare to you.
Amen

WEEK TEN: FRIDAY
TIME OUT FOR CREATING A REFRIGERATOR COLLAGE

All who joy would win must share it,

Happiness was born a twin.   Lord Byron

I shuffled through the two identical stacks of photographs on my kitchen counter. I hadn't been able to bypass a free "second set." But what was I going to do with the extras? I sorted the photos into piles. One pile for the new family album. One pile for my daughter's album. Another pile for my son's. There was a fourth pile. Give-aways to grandparents perhaps? No, the photos I had left would qualify more as out-takes than as grandparent material. They were the ones with the goofy expressions, tongues hanging out of mouths, kids dancing on the coffee table with the dog (theirs) dressed in a tattered old evening gown (mine). You get the idea. They made me chuckle.

Stumped, I went over to the fridge for a swig of milk. Suddenly I got an idea. I took the stack of out-takes and made a photo collage on my counter. Then I stuck tape on the back of each photo and transferred my design to the front of the refrigerator door.

My kids loved it. Together we've kept on our refrigerator a running photo gallery of our adventures. We've made it a point to use our favorite pictures. Whenever we open our refrigerator, we see good times, togetherness. Silliness.

Look back through those stacks of photos that never made it into albums. Pick some of the more hilarious out-takes and make yourself a collage. Promise yourself that you'll update it frequently. Even if you live alone, you'll enjoy the photos, as will everyone who visits you.

Father, thank you for giving me a sense of humor. Help me to remember the joy in silliness and to manifest that joy in my life. Amen

WEEK TEN: SATURDAY
MY EX IS SAYING HORRIBLE THINGS ABOUT ME!

There was given me a thorn in my flesh, a messenger of Satan, to torment me. Three times I pleaded with the Lord to take it away from me. But he said to me, "My grace is sufficient for you, for my power is made perfect in weakness."

2 Corinthians 12:7-9

The Blame Game. It's a way of shifting responsibility over to others. When I'm blaming someone, I'm trying to maintain my power over that person. If I can get him to feel like dog doo, then I feel big and strong.

Anyone who's been caught up in the game will confirm my experience that being blamed for something that isn't your fault is hellish. The game itself is a form of torment that its participants inflict on one another. Back and forth. Back and forth they go. Who can be the meanest, nastiest? Whose words can cut the deepest and draw the most blood? Will one person be able to win by wearing the other one down?

Jim Smoke has a saying I love. "Growth begins where blaming ends." That's a good one to tape onto your bathroom mirror. The AA folks have another saying I appreciate equally. It goes something like this: "When I have one finger pointing at you, there are three pointing back at me." Blaming is a cop out, a growth-stunter, a lose-lose game.

If you want to blame others, rest assured they will turn and lay blame back on you—unless you're perfect. Is anyone perfect here on earth? No. Not since Jesus.

Rather than shining the flashlight on the faults of others, why not turn it on ourselves? Why not look at our own shortcomings, our own weaknesses, and ask Jesus to remove them from us? That's building up instead of tearing down. That's the good stuff of growth. That brings healing.

In what ways have you indulged in the Blame Game with your ex? What have you said to wound him or her? To whom have you said it? What has your former spouse said to defame your character? To whom has he or she said it? It's helpful and necessary to acknowledge our sins before God, to confess them, and to ask for his forgiveness and his guidance in looking for goodness, not fault, in others. Write him a letter today.

> *Father, you know the ugly things I've said and done to hurt this person I used to love so deeply. Please forgive me. Please help me to stop pointing fingers at other people and instead to shine that flashlight into the parts of my own soul that need the light of Christ.   Amen*

WEEK ELEVEN

> Dear friends, be quick to listen, slow to speak, and slow to get
> angry. Your anger can never make things right in God's sight.
> James 1:19, NLT

A year or so into my single-again journey, I decided I wanted to stop
running on autopilot. I was repeating the same patterns, each time
hoping to get better results. It wasn't working. My life wasn't getting
better, and I was frustrated with my own lack of growth. I went to talk
to the pastor of my church after a particularly grueling argument with
someone I was working with in our singles ministry. He gave me some
suggestions on how to deal with all the fury and resentment I felt
towards this woman. "Why don't you start by writing a letter venting all
your angry feelings?" he asked.

"What?!" I cried, visions of poison pen letters flying back and forth
in the mail dancing in front of my eyes.

"No. You write the letter, yes. You mail it, no. Absolutely not! It's a
way for you to work through your anger *without* involving her. You still
have to work with her and it will serve to useful purpose to alienate her
further. Once you've worked off some steam you should be able to get
in touch with what you're feeling—with what's behind the anger. When

you go to confront her, your thinking will be a more clear. I promise you."

"OK," I said, smiling to myself. "This sounds like something I could get into."

"One more idea," he said. "Try redirecting your anger. Whenever someone or something upsets you, try taking long walk on the beach. Or run. Swim. Bike. Go to the gym. It doesn't matter what you do, just as long as it's strenuous."

Try these two approaches. If you're feeling angry today—whether it's at your ex-spouse, a sibling, a parent, your child(ren), your boss or someone else, try writing that person a letter. *Do not mail it!* Then get some vigorous exercise. Finally, come back to your journal and describe your "before" and "after" feelings.

> *Lord, thank you for providing healthy ways to let off steam. Help me to become more aware of my feelings and to act on them in more constructive ways.   Amen*

WEEK ELEVEN: MONDAY
LOOKING IN THE MIRROR

> Why do you look at the speck of sawdust in your brother's eye and pay no attention to the plank in your own eye?...You hypocrite, first take the plank out of your own eye, and then you will see clearly to remove the speck from your brother's eye.
> Matthew 7:3, 5

I was substituting as a divorce recovery group leader. I didn't know any of the five women gathered. All were newly separated except one, I'll call her Sue, who had been *trying* to work through her marital settlement for four years. Her divorce had been postponed repeatedly.

The dynamic in the group had been established prior to my arrival. It was four against one. Sue was an easy target, terrified, timid, totally confused, and used to being ordered around. These four do-gooders banded together and took turns offering her advice. The week before they had talked her into making a to-do list, and now they each chastised her, as they reviewed her list and discovered that she hadn't done *anything* on it. She had, I noticed, perfected the art of faking people out. She promised to do everything on the list the next week, but it was obvious to everyone that she wouldn't. After all, for four years, her therapist, her attorney, her estranged husband, and his attorney had failed to get her to complete the divorce. She groveled and pretended to be submissive, but she was stubbornly immobile.

All the other women in the group had serious challenges of their own to deal with. Their lives had all been turned upside down by their impending divorces. But Sue was a diversion. It was so much easier for them collectively to look at her and focus on *her* problems than it was for them individually to look in the mirror and face *their own* predicaments. It gave them a sense of unity and joint purpose and lifted them above their own misery.

As Jesus so poignantly showed, we humans all get hung up pointing out the specks of sawdust in our brothers' and sisters' eyes. We lose sight of the planks that are blinding us from seeing the truth about ourselves. Have you picked on anyone lately? Or have you been advised or criticized by a blinded do-gooder? What does this verse tell you? What can you do differently to take care of your own problems instead of everyone else's?

> *Lord Jesus, thank you for leaving us with your incredible words*
> *of wisdom and truth. Remove the plank from my eye and help me*
> *to keep from pointing out the sawdust in the eyes of others.*
> *Amen*

WEEK ELEVEN: TUESDAY
GET THE ONCE-A-MONTH LIBRARY HABIT

> A book is a garden, an orchard, a storehouse, a party, a company by the way, a counselor, a multitude of counselors.
>
> Henry Ward Beecher

My kids and I moved to a new city that had a beautiful multilevel library, surrounded by trees, grass, and a pond that played host to migrant birds. To visit there was to step out of Southern California and into another dimension. One of the first things the kids begged for was a trip to the library to get library cards.

We began what has become a once-a-month library habit. Developing a library habit is cost-effective. Books fill up empty hours and nourish our minds and souls in the process. Spending an hour or two in the library is a luxury. So is going to one of those new bookstores around that offer coffee and comfortable couches. It's relaxing and replenishing to take a few hours off to read, especially in a place that's been created as a sanctuary for readers.

Today your assignment is to take yourself to the library. If the one nearest your home isn't aesthetically pleasing to you, do a little research. There's bound to be a good one—or a relaxing, friendly bookstore— not too far away. Get a library card and cultivate this habit.

Dear Lord, thank you for all the ways you provide for me. Open my eyes so that I'll see new ways to expand my world. Give me the courage to step out.   Amen

WEEK ELEVEN: WEDNESDAY
GETTING LOST IN THE BLACK HOLE

[Jesus] plunged into a sinkhole of dreadful agony. He told them, "I feel bad enough right now to die."

From Mark 14, The Message

Right before Jesus was arrested at Gethsemane, he prayed that God would take the cup of crucifixion from him. At that point in his life, he took a major nosedive. He was in the Black Hole. He managed to regain his faith, climb out of the pit, and go on to face his fate with Pilate.

Jesus understands suffering like no one who has ever walked on this earth. He understands with the all-knowing, all powerful, gracious, loving, and forgiving mind and heart of God.

Did you expect that, once you ended your marriage, most of the problems associated with it would disappear? I did. But you may realize, as I soon did, that the ending of the marriage was only the beginning of my journey. Two of my favorite psychologists, Henry Cloud and John Townsend, describe this phenomena in their book *Changes That Heal*. When depression lingers after the divorce is final, they explain, it is often not related to the divorce itself, but rather to older, deeper, developmental character issues. Once the marital conflicts are eliminated, these buried issues surface and we can find ourselves in *a lot of pain*. This in itself can be extremely confusing. We expect ourselves to be getting better, to be healing, but we aren't. We are mired in a sinkhole of agony.

Do you feel isolated and lonely? Hurting? Angry? Depressed? Has it become more intense since you've been on your own? Today, write in your journal about your closest relationships. How do you relate to your mom? Your dad? Your siblings? Your kids? Your friends? Whom do you trust? With whom can you be transparent, honest, completely yourself, to the point of revealing your weaknesses? Are there areas in which you feel blocked or stuck? Write a letter to Jesus, that same Jesus who lost it, and share your brokenness with him.

Lord Jesus, I am so grateful that you know better than anyone about suffering. Now that I am alone, please show me the character issues that need to be healed within me and lead me to people who will help me work through them.   Amen

WEEK ELEVEN: THURSDAY
WHY DO I HAVE THESE MOOD SWINGS?

Zeal without knowledge is not good; a person who moves too quickly may go the wrong way. People ruin their lives by their own foolishness and then are angry at the Lord.

Proverbs 19:2-3, NLT

Mood swings. They're a major complaint I hear from people going through the first year or so of divorce. Mood swings are volatile and embarrassing. Again, divorce is an emotional ride in the last car on a roller coaster. You go up, you go down, you zoom around those corners at break-neck speed. You scream in elation and then recoil in fear as your stomach drops to your feet and then bounces back up into your throat. You yell at the operator to stop and let you off, but he doesn't hear you. You just keep passing the starting gate over and over again as your wild ride continues.

I've seen people rush to the doctor for Prozac to get them off that emotional roller coaster. And some women look into hormone replacement therapy. I'm not a doctor and I'm not anti-medication, but I'm not sure we can or should medicate all the emotions away. With divorce, we should be prepared for some emotional chaos. I've found that if you expect those ups and downs, they aren't nearly so overwhelming or frightening.

What are some of the mood swings you might experience during the first year or so after your divorce? You can expect to jump from love to hate to indifference. You can expect to be consumed with vindictiveness from time to time. You'll wake up some mornings feeling heart sick and weak. Other days you'll wake up and say, "Wow! I'm all better now! I feel great!" But a few days later you'll open your eyes to find yourself in the hopeless grip of depression. You may be hit with a long wave of so-what? apathy.

How have your moods swung this week? Over the past few weeks? Can you describe them? What kind of things did you say to yourself as you rode the roller coaster? How could you change your "self-talk" to be gentler and more patient with yourself? Can you replace your put downs with a loving internal dialogue?

Father, help me to understand that mood swings come with the territory here in divorce country. Teach me to talk to myself as Jesus would talk to me.   Amen

WEEK ELEVEN: FRIDAY
WHEN I'M CONSUMED WITH GUILT

Have mercy on me, O God, because of your unfailing love. Because of your great compassion, blot out the stain of my sins. Wash me clean from my guilt. Purify me from my sin.
                              Psalm 51:1-2, NLT

"If only I had listened to my lawyer and just settled."
"I should've gone back to school when I was still married."
"If only I hadn't shot off my mouth and said all those awful things."

"I should've stood up to him, instead of standing there cowering like a wimp."

Our "shoulds" and "if onlys" are our guilt messages to ourselves. When we hear ourselves parading them out one by one, we can quickly see that we're stuck in the past. The negative messages, repeated and repeated, convince you that you are a first-class failure. Depression sets in.

Answer this question: Can you go back and change the past? No!

Can you revisit the past to learn from it? Yes!

How?

In the above examples, you could: 1) call your lawyer and tell him you've reconsidered and no longer want to continue fighting your ex; is it too late to settle? 2) call the junior colleges nearby and order catalogs for the next semester; 3) call the person to whom you were cruel and apologize; 4) engage in some role playing with a trusted friend to practice standing up for yourself.

Sometimes we've done something wrong. If that's the case, we need to admit it, apologize, ask forgiveness, and move forward. Sometimes we're just picking on ourselves and playing out old tapes from childhood. We're hearing our parents, teachers, and other significant adults scolding us, and we're not even hearing them correctly. Tape this note onto refrigerator: *The next time I say "If only..." or "I should have..." I'm going to catch myself and write it down!* And do it. Then, after the line, write something constructive you can do to solve the problem or avoid the guilt message in the future.

> *Lord, please show me where I'm "guilting" myself out and getting hung up in the past. Help me to ask for forgiveness where I need to.   Amen*

WEEK ELEVEN: SATURDAY
DISCOVERING AND ACCEPTING A NEW IDENTITY

Continue to work out your salvation with fear and trembling, for it is God who works in you to will and to act according to his good purpose.   Philippians 2:12-13

What kind of tapes have been running in your head since the divorce? Do any of these sound familiar? These are the "I can't" or "I'm a failure" tapes:

1.   I thought things would've been better by now. Will it always be this bad? Why won't someone help me?!
2.   I feel so overwhelmed, mistreated, beat up, hemmed in.
3.   I feel stifled, scared, frustrated, powerless.
4.   I don't know what I want out of life. It wouldn't matter even if I did know, because I've screwed up my life and that's that.
5.   I can't afford to quit this job and try something new. No way!

Now read the "I can" or "I'm going to be OK" tapes:

1.   I love God and I know he loves me. I'm created in his image, and I'm unique. I'm learning to treat myself and others better.
2.   I deserve to have a fulfilling life. I don't need to be crippled by fear, guilt, and self-sabotaging thought patterns and behaviors.
3.   I'm learning to solve problems creatively and assertively. I'm beginning to trust my own judgment. I know that God has a plan for me.
4.   I want to be changed. I want to be healed. I want to grow.

Open your journal and jot down any of the messages from either category that you've caught yourself saying internally. Leave a blank line between each one. For each negative message, write an affirming truth from God's Word. For each positive one, write a sentence of praise and gratitude to your Creator.

> *Father, thank you for creating me in your image. Help me to change my operating system from "I'm a failure" to "I'm going to be O.K."*   *Amen*

WEEK TWELVE

WEEK TWELVE: SUNDAY
HOW DO I FACE BITTERNESS AND HOSTILITY?

Therefore, strengthen your feeble arms and weak knees. Make level paths for your feet, so that the lame may not be disabled, but rather healed. Make every effort to live in peace with all men and to be holy; without holiness no one will see the Lord. See to it that no one misses the grace of God and that no bitter root grows up to cause trouble and defile many.

Hebrews 12:12-15

Have you ever popped a pill into your mouth before you had the glass of water ready? Do you remember it dissolving on your tongue and filling your mouth with a disgusting, bitter taste that could be erased only by brushing your teeth? To me, talking to a bitter person is like that. I don't like to be around hostile or vindictive people. The words that come out of their mouths have such a venomous bite that they knock me back against the nearest wall.

I knew a man once who'd been divorced for nearly ten years. Yet his anger toward his ex-wife seemed as fresh and potent as someone newly separated. When he spoke, it was through clenched teeth. He felt life had dealt him a bad hand, and he wanted everyone to know it. He could list his ex-wife's sins, one by one. He was obsessed with the wrongs she'd done him. He complained mightily about how she was raising their children. He complained even more loudly about how much money he was sending her. He was out of control.

It's easy to let the anger that rises up in us during our divorces go to seed within our souls. When that happens, roots of bitterness grow inside us. Soon there is a seedling, then finally a tree. When we allow bitterness to flourish within us, our actions and our words become our fruit. Our words drip with sarcasm. We get a twisted, unhealthy satisfaction from back stabbing, blaming, and name calling. We spend hours devising elaborate plots to get back at the person who hurt us.

Is there anyone you avoid like the plague because of bitter tirades? Have you been put down by someone like that because you wouldn't join in that person's crusade against women, men, the church, the boss, the parents, even God? Have you found yourself tempted by bitterness? In your journal write the above passage from Hebrews. List some of the bitter fruits you've seen growing and being harvested in the lives of bitter people.

> *Lord God, thank you for reminding me that bitterness can start as a tiny seed of unresolved anger in my heart. Strengthen my feeble arms and legs, Father, so I can grow in holiness and not miss out on your grace.   Amen*

WEEK TWELVE: MONDAY
FACING UP TO STARK REALITIES

> Seek the Lord while you can find him. Call on him now while he is near.   Isaiah 55:6, NLT

When we're in pain, setting goals is the last thing we want to do. If we had any goal at all, it would be to stop the pain. "Give me my meds," I heard an expert say more than once, echoing the secret cry of desperately wounded people. For the first few months after a marriage falls apart, most are incapable of getting any further than "stop the pain." Thoughts ricochet back and forth between the past and the present. The future? It looms ahead of us like an oncoming tornado. We just want to run and hide somewhere that's safe. Do we feel confident in our ability to create a new life for ourselves? No! The thought of getting through the day is challenging enough. The idea of planning for the future, of setting goals, is too overwhelming to think about!

Can you relate? I sure can. But what I learned, what we all learn, is that at some point we need to think about setting goals. If we don't, we're guaranteed to flounder along aimlessly, wasting this gift that is life.

God wants you to take this catastrophe that is your divorce and turn it into an opportunity for growth. The most effective way to do that is to start setting goals. But before you can set goals, you need to accept the stark reality that you're in a place you'd never have chosen to be. You're alone. You've gotten custody of yourself, and it's up to you to seek the Lord, to call on him now while he's near. Ask his help and direction.

Where are you today in terms of goal setting? How does the prospect make you feel? Don't rush out and write a dozen goals; for now just meditate on the concept of it all.

> *Lord, help me face up to the fact that I need to take some steps toward getting on with my life. I need you, Father. Draw near to me and hold me. Amen*

WEEK TWELVE: TUESDAY
LET'S TAKE A TRIP TO THE ATTIC

I'm goin' to the attic and I'm gonna go with Jesus,
Yes I'm goin' to the attic and I'm gonna go with Jesus.
Yes we're goin' to the attic and we're gonna get a suitcase
And together we're gonna face the pain.

One day my dog and I were on our daily walk. I found myself singing that familiar oldie "Goin' to the Chapel." This cracked me up. *Here I am, writing a book about divorce, and I'm singing this song about getting married!* Then the words changed, and I sang this new version.

What does it mean? "Goin' to the Attic"? We tend to shove out of our minds any uncomfortable memories. We stash them where they won't bug us. They end up in suitcases, sometimes even wrapped in chains and bolted, up in the attics of our consciousness. The attic is a place we *never* have to go. It's only for discards, rejects, things we were too lazy or too sentimental to throw away. As a child did you ever sneak alone into your grandparents' attic? Pretty dark and scary up there? Full of spiders and dust and all sorts of creepy things? But if you ventured back with a friend and a flashlight, I bet it looked a bit more intriguing. Your fear may have evaporated, if you could see this as adventure!

Set aside some time with your journal. Think about your mother and father and maybe your grandparents. For each person, try to answer the following questions. Can you identify any painful patterns, uncomfortable memories?

1. How would you describe your father or mother? What motivates him or her? What are his or her gifts, talents, and strengths? Weaknesses? What does he or she struggle with as a person? Have dreams been realized?

2. Briefly describe your dad or mom's childhood and adolescence. What kind of relationship did he or she have with your grandparents?

3. How old were your mom and dad when they married? Who ran the show when you were a child? Are your parents still married? How do they get along? How would you describe their marriage?

4. How do you and each of your parents relate? What feelings can you freely express with one another? Are you satisfied with your relationship?

5.   What is your happiest memory of your dad or mom? Your most unhappy one?

6.   How are you like your dad or mom? Unlike?

7.   How did your dad or mom discipline you as a child and as a teenager?

8.   How does your dad or mom treat you these days? Pleased with how your life is turning out? Or have you failed to meet expectations?

After answering for both your parents, take a walk. Sing my silly song if you want! Can you see any patterns within your family that are in need of Jesus' healing touch? Can you describe them?

> *Jesus, come with me to the attic. Help me dig around in the piles of memory for those old suitcases. Help me to see and understand my parents and my relationship to them. Flash your light on any areas that need to be healed. Help me to look inside and face what's there, knowing all the while that you're right there with me, protecting and loving me.   Amen*

WEEK TWELVE: WEDNESDAY
SECRETS—PITTING A CHILD AGAINST A PARENT

Hatred stirs up dissension, but love covers all wrongs.
                              Proverbs 10:12

"Dad," the little girl told her father, "Mom says I can't talk to you about what we do on the weekends...."

"Why not?"

"I can't say. It's a secret."

"We don't have secrets between us, Honey. I'm your dad. You can tell me everything. I promise."

"But you won't get mad at Mommy and quit sending money? Won't we have to go on welfare?"

I've heard different renditions of this story too many times over the years. When the father (or mother) calls me, he or she is always horrified. "She's poisoning our child against me. Just because she doesn't trust me and hates me doesn't mean she has any right to pass those feelings on to our child. Keeping her life a secret from me! How could she do this? What can I do to stop it?!"

Not wanting to hurt the child, I suggest that the parent wait a few days to chill out before calling the ex-spouse and asking for a meeting. To avoid taking unfair emotional advantage, it is best to tell the ex beforehand what the discussion will address. Then I suggest meeting at a neutral, quiet place, such as a diner in midafternoon.

Here are some discussion points. You might explain that you feel you have a right to have a relationship with your child that's healthy and trusting. You might say you feel it's wrong to tell our child things about you that aren't based on fact. Maybe your child is "too young" to understand what's going on between parents, and "digs" and secrets are devastating to a young child. Your child needs love and support from both of you right now. Your child doesn't need to be caught up in the middle of the fight between the two of you. The lies and secrets are hurting your child.

The ex may be grateful for having been forewarned of the topic at hand. It gives the ex a chance to think things through. Sometimes I hear of an ex asking forgiveness, maybe admitting to getting all hung up in wanting to "get back," maybe admitting to being afraid the child would "choose" the other parent. I've seen such conversations help former spouses take giant steps toward forgiveness, especially if both parties genuinely admit their faults, their parental jealousies.

Does this scenario ring true to you? Have you played your child off against the other parent recently? Have you bad-mouthed your ex to your child? Told any sly little lies or big whoppers about your ex to try to look good or steal love?

> *Lord, please bring healing to me and my ex-spouse. Forgive us for defaming each other. Help us to get out of the gutter and find the higher ground.   Amen*

WEEK TWELVE: THURSDAY
PITY PARTIES

> You have put me in the lowest pit, in the darkest depths. Your wrath lies heavily upon me; you have overwhelmed me with all your waves.   Psalm 88:6-7

When I was really hurting after my divorce, I gravitated toward people who were really hurting too. (My church's singles' ministry was full of lonely, aching singles just like me—so sympathetic souls were easy enough to find!) *They* certainly wouldn't try to pull me up by my collar and give me a swift kick in the pants!

There was one person with whom I felt really safe. We let it all hang out when we talked. In fact, we got carried away with ourselves. It became a contest. Every time we talked on the phone, we updated our lists of grievances. She'd tell me her latest life's-not-fair story, and I'd retaliate with my version. Who had it worse? Who had been dealt the lousier hand? Which one of us would win that coveted title, Martyr of the Year? (Can you imagine a TV awards ceremony for *that* one?)

There's something wonderfully comforting in having someone with whom we can share our problems. We understand her pain; she understands ours. We don't judge her; she doesn't judge us. But she and I crossed the line from healthy comforting to unhealthy one-upmanship. We had to *prove* to each other how much we hurt. When I was able to outdo her on the suffering scale, I got a certain weird, momentary satisfaction. But if she one-upped me and proved to me she had it worse, then where was I? I had to come back with something even more spectacularly awful. Ugh. I wasn't taking responsibility for my pain, or doing anything to alleviate it. I was just bragging about it! And there is no reward for being Martyr of the Year. Trust me.

Have you been to any pity parties lately? What were your complaints? When you were a child, was it OK to hurt, or did you have to *prove* that your emotional injuries were *really severe* before your pain was permitted? What do you do now when you hurt? To whom do you turn?

Heavenly Father, help me to stop feeling so sorry for myself. Walk with me through this pit of pain and lift me up so I can stop this wallowing.   Amen

WEEK TWELVE: FRIDAY
PEACE IN THE MIDST OF THE PAIN

The Lord is my shepherd; I shall not be in want. He makes me lie down in green pastures, he leads me beside quiet waters, he restores my soul. He guides me in paths of righteousness for his name's sake.   Psalm 23:1-3

Have you ever seen a cartoon where a character is agonizing over an important decision? She has an angel on one shoulder and a devil on the other, and they take turns giving her contradicting advice?

How many times have these two opposing voices, the black and white, gone to war inside your head? The holy little white voice isn't quite as loud as the black one and can't be heard at all if there is too much chaos in your life. In fact, God speaks so quietly to me that I usually have to go off by myself in order to hear him. He is my Shepherd and he leads me off away from all the craziness. We stop in a beautiful grassy spot right next to a slow-running brook, and he sits me down and lets me reflect on the silence. As I close my mind to everything but his love and the beauty around me, he restores my soul.

You know what? Now that your marriage is over, it's most likely that things are a lot quieter at home. Chances are, the conflicts raging within your marriage wiped out the white voice. You may hear that little devil on your shoulder saying, *It's all his fault! Don't you see that? All of it! Let's get him! After all, he's a lying, cheating, jerk!* That voice can turn against anyone, even you. And it will. *You're a failure!* it told me. *Who would ever want you?*

The next time that nasty voice starts griping at you, urging you to get all fired up for another round of battle, take a time out. Go to your special, personal quiet place, a place of stillness and peace. If you're a single parent, maybe you won't be able to leave the house. That's OK. After the kids are asleep, go into your bedroom and close the door. Read Psalm 23. If you know it by heart, make a promise to recite it to yourself whenever the craziness threatens to overtake you. Then close your eyes and breathe deeply.

> *Dear God, please relax my body, calm my mind, and restore my soul. Lead me along the paths of righteousness, Father. Give me peace.* Amen

WEEK TWELVE: SATURDAY
WHEN I CAN'T STOP WORRYING

> Can all your worries add a single moment to your life? Of course not....Your heavenly Father already knows all your needs, and he will give you all you need from day to day if you live for him and make the Kingdom of God your primary concern.
>
> Matthew 6:27, 32-33, NLT

"What if the judge lowers my child support? How will the kids and I survive?" "What if my ex-wife moves to the other side of the country?"

"What if I never remarry?"

"What if I lose my job (get cancer, get disabled)?"

While guilt traps us in the past, worrying projects us into Tomorrowland. Like science fiction writers, we're trying to predict the future and fix it before it ever happens! If you worry about your ex-wife moving to Florida, will that stop her? Hardly! If you worry about losing your job, will that guarantee you that you'll have it for as long as you want it? No!

Worry is fear-based. Worrying is trying to control things that are beyond our control. It's like trying to play God—but of course we're not God. We're stuck right here in the present, without knowledge of the future. In the Sermon on the Mount, Jesus said a lot about the futility of worrying, and *the antidote for worrying and doubt is faith and trust.*

I try to catch myself in the act of worrying. Then I consciously replace my "what if" with "as if." Instead of doubting whether God is in control, I can choose to believe and act *as if* he is. Instead of worrying about what will happen tomorrow, I can focus on doing my best to solve the problems that I can solve today. I can leave tomorrow to God, because I know he's the big Boss, not I, my ex, the judge, or the bill collectors.

What are some of your worry statements? List them. What is the worst thing you could imagine happening? How often does it flash across the movie screen of your mind? Turn to Matthew 6:25-34. Then read Hebrews 11:1-6. How do these passages speak to your heart?

God, please help me to get out of Tomorrow land and into today.
Help me to replace my "what ifs" with your "as ifs."
Amen

WEEK THIRTEEN

WEEK THIRTEEN: SUNDAY
GOD'S STANDARDS VERSUS VENGEANCE

> You have heard it said, "Eye for eye, and tooth for tooth." But I tell you, do not resist an evil person. If someone strikes you on the right cheek, turn to him the other also.
>
> Matthew 5:38-39

"My husband has just dissolved his corporation and filed for bankruptcy," she told me. "He just got back from a trip to the Caribbean. I'd bet my last nickel that he stashed a huge wad of cash there. Now my house is in foreclosure. I have to move. I'm broke!" And she burst into tears.

Unfortunately this is not an uncommon story. When a savvy and well-informed spouse decides to make off with all the assets, the other can be left high and dry and penniless. Very often there is little the victimized spouse can do. She (usually it's a woman) can file court papers and make accusations, but if the money is hidden well enough, it won't be found.

It can be an ugly world, there's no doubt about it. Accepting this kind of unfair and unethical treatment is difficult, especially from the one person you once trusted above anyone else. I talked to this woman at great length. In her situation it would have been so easy to give into feelings of bitterness and resentment and to spend countless hours dreaming up elaborate and equally vicious plots to take revenge against her cheating ex-husband. By responding to wickedness with wickedness, she would have become hard and ugly herself. She would have been consumed with feelings of hatred, fear, and mistrustfulness toward others. She would have shut out God's voice and heard only the high-pitched whine of the serpent.

But she was a wise woman. When I checked in with her a few weeks later, she was a transformed person. She quoted today's verse to me. "I finally understand what Jesus meant by turning the other cheek. When I turn away from thoughts of revenge, I turn to face him. I am dazzled by his unconditional, overwhelming, divine love. My faith is restored, and I see hope for the future. I see that he will make all things right, in his own time. And I am filled up to the brim with peace."

Whoa. At the same time God instructs us to love our enemies and to turn the other cheek when someone strikes us, he also tells us in Proverbs 24 and again in Romans 12 that revenge is his to take, not ours. Those verses, which reflect God's standards, sustained this woman as she stood firm against the injustice inflicted upon her by her ex-husband. What challenges have you faced where these verses would help you to decide upon the godly course of action? How would you do things today with God's standards firmly planted in your mind?

Lord, I thank you for showing me the way to stand firm against deceitful schemes. Protect me from the temptation to plot and seek revenge. Teach me to leave the vengeance to you.   Amen

WEEK THIRTEEN: MONDAY
WHO'S RUNNING MY LIFE?

The law of the Lord is perfect, reviving the soul. The statutes of the Lord are trustworthy, making wise the simple. The precepts

of the Lord are right, giving joy to the heart. The commands of
the Lord are radiant, giving light to the eyes.   Psalm 19:7-8

Our parents can easily become more parental during a divorce; they
may take us back under their wings, financially or emotionally. I can't
tell you how many people move back in with Mom and Dad. For a
while, anyway. After all, they can't stand to see us hurting. They want to
help. And we need help. When we accept their help, however, we are
instantly, mysteriously transported back to childhood. Mom and Dad
take over, resuming parental decision-making and disciplinary roles.
Only we're not kids; we're grown ups, right? We may even have kids of
our own. So what gives here?

About a year after my divorce, one recently remarried mom told me
something I never forgot: "Watch out for getting too dependent on your
folks. If your adolescence was rocky the first time around, believe me, it
will be even more rocky this time—when you again try to break away
from them! Trust me," she concluded, "I've been there."

Are your parents helping you right now? If so, how is that affecting
your relationship? Have the rules changed? Do you feel like a teenager
again? In your journal, explore these ideas. If you feel moved to write
them a letter thanking them for their help, do so. Then list some steps
you can take to increase your self-sufficiency.

*Jesus, please help me to take responsibility for myself right now
and not lean too heavily on my parents, or anyone else. Help me
to look to you instead so that I can walk in your radiance.
Amen*

WEEK THIRTEEN: TUESDAY
TURN DOWN THE BACKGROUND NOISE!

Surely goodness and love will follow me all the days of my life,
and I will dwell in the house of the Lord forever. Psalm 23:6

"Wow," she said as I sat down on the edge of the pool. "You've lost weight. Looks like you're almost down to your *hunting weight*." Two other women joined in her laughter, as did I—awkwardly. I'd been separated almost two months. I hadn't "hunted" in nearly a decade. Just the idea of making small talk with a man sent shudders up and down my spine.

Yet everywhere I turned, that's what I heard. At work: "So...met anyone interesting yet?" Or, "Come on. Let's go out to Happy Hour this Friday night. I'll come over and help you go through your wardrobe and update it. I guarantee you, when I get finished, you'll look twenty-eight instead of thirty-eight."

I lost weight. I did the wardrobe thing. I went to Happy Hour with the single women from work. I even got chatted up by plenty of men, most of them under thirty who would exit quickly the minute I mentioned my *kids*. "Don't divulge that, silly," my friends said. "You're scaring them all away!" Duh! I lasted a couple of months on the singles' circuit and then I scurried back to the safety of my home. I hadn't liked it at twenty-eight; I liked it far less now.

Have you received a lot of unsolicited social commentary and advice since you lost your mate? Or when you mention to a trusted friend or family member that you're lonely, do you get a lecture on getting out there and meeting people? Try explaining that you're taking some time out to work on yourself, and you get a lecture on the self-absorbed, navel-staring obsessiveness of the Me Generation.

Turning down the volume on the background noise is about figuring out what's best for ourselves. It's about refusing to allow ourselves to be swayed by someone else's opinion. What kind of social pressure and background noise do you have in your life? How have you responded? How would you prefer to respond?

> *Father, please help me to turn down the volume on the background noise so that I can filter out the harmful voices and better hear yours.*   *Amen*

WEEK THIRTEEN: WEDNESDAY
GRACE HAPPENS

> The son said to him, "Father, I have sinned against heaven and
> against you. I am no longer worthy to be called your son." But
> the father said to his servants, "Quick! Bring the best robe and
> put in on him. Put a ring on his finger and sandals on his feet.
> Bring the fattened calf and kill it. Let's have a feast and celebrate.
> For this son of mine was dead and is alive again; he was lost and
> is found."   Luke 15:21-24

I pulled into the church parking lot and noticed the bumper sticker
right away: "Grace Happens." I laughed to myself. Nice! Much better
than the *other* saying. Grace does happen—all the time. What is it? I've
heard it defined as the unmerited favor of God. It's a gift. An unearned,
undeserved gift, like salvation. The story of the Prodigal Son is such a
powerful illustration of God's open-armed, joyous love for us. Even
though this young man had squandered his inheritance, even though
he'd hung out with low lifes and prostitutes, even though he deserved
to be run out of town, he was greeted with hugs, kisses, beautiful new
clothes, and a big party. His depravity was forgotten; his repentant
return a cause for celebration.

That's grace. God performs the ultimate act of grace when he
forgives us. But he keeps on showering us with undeserved, unearned
treasures, those wonderful nuggets of grace all our lives. Yet so much of
the time we don't notice them. We're looking down and out instead of
up. Our eyes aren't on him, so we miss out. How do we become more
sensitive and aware of those nuggets of grace he keeps handing us? It's
sort of like developing a grateful heart. We have to seek his face. And we
have to start looking for grace and expecting it. Every day. There are
gold mines of it out there. Everywhere. What do you think of that? Get

to your quiet place and bask in God's presence. Find an index tab for your journal and write on it "Nuggets of Grace." Any time God gets your attention by giving you a special grace, jot it down in there. By the time you finish this book, you will have a whole collection of nuggets!

Father, please give me eyes to see the evidence and instances of your grace all around me every day. Help me not only to see, but also to praise you and thank you for every unearned, precious gift. Amen

WEEK THIRTEEN: THURSDAY
HOW DO I LEARN TO FIGHT FAIR?

He who answers before listening—that is his folly and his shame.
Proverbs 18:13

I was in my first really serious relationship since the divorce. Both of us had been married before, and neither of us dealt all that well with conflict. We pushed each other's buttons big time. At touch of a trigger, he would flip into a preadolescent fury. I, of course, thought I was far more mature than he, but I wasn't. I just had different buttons. Every time I felt threatened, mine went off. We decided counseling was in order and spent several sessions with a pastor.

We learned that neither of us knew how to fight fair. At least not with a member of the opposite sex. And we weren't really fighting each other anyway. We were really fencing with ghosts, ghosts from the dawn of adolescence. On top of the baggage from our teenage years was heaped piles of unresolved pain and disappointment from the following decades. We struggled for months.

So how can we fight fair? Here are some hints I've learned. It helps considerably if both parties can agree to honoring them before a disagreement begins.

1. Wait to discuss the issues until you are calm.
2. Acknowledge each problem specifically and focus on solving it.
3. Avoid criticizing, blaming, and demeaning the other person.
4. Avoid using extreme words like *always, never, everyone,* and *nothing.*
5. Take one- to ten-minute time-outs, if necessary. During the time-out, each person defines, in writing, the problem as he or she sees it. Areas of disagreement and possible solutions are addressed. After the time-out, the person who has been most upset asks the other to share what he or she wrote.
6. Listen! Take turns talking and avoid interrupting each other. Repeat statements back to each other or ask the other to repeat things if necessary.
7. Don't bring up hurtful things from the past.
8. Be respectful. Successful negotiation requires compromise on both parts.

How do you feel about sharing these suggestions with your ex? If you're not ready, then write them down and post them on your refrigerator. Share them with a trusted friend. Practice them on somebody safe.

> *Jesus, I want to learn to fight fair. I want to stop pushing other people's buttons, and I want to get more control of my own. Please help me. Amen*

WEEK THIRTEEN: FRIDAY
CONSIDERATIONS FOR NONCUSTODIAL PARENTS

Those who bring trouble on their families inherit only the wind. The fool will be a servant to the wise.   Proverbs 11:29, NLT

Here's another one of my lists! I suggest that noncustodial parents post this so you notice it often. It is a gentle but persistent reminder of how much your children still need you in their lives:

1. Make your kids priority one. Call them often. Stay involved in their day-to-day lives. Let them know how much you love them.
2. Hug them often. Touch is vital to their well-being.
3. Spend time with them. You don't need to be a "Disneyland Dad (or Mom)." It's the little, almost inconsequential, things that mean the most.
4. Make sure that their bedrooms at your home are personal, warm, and inviting. Keep clothes, toys, and other familiar, comforting things around for them.
5. Keep your word. Show up when you say you will. Pay your child support, in full and on time.
6. Keep a calendar with their special events on it, so you won't forget birthdays, graduations, school plays, and sporting events.
7. Don't bad mouth your ex-spouse to your kids or use them to carry cryptic messages back and forth.
8. If you're considering a long-distance move in the years after divorce, involve your children in this decision, whether they live with you or not. They want to know that they're important to you and that you value their input. They crave stability.
9. Be aware of their feelings when you begin to date and when you remarry. Go slow and be gentle.
10. Remember that your kids have inherited not only looks from your ex, but also certain personality traits. Don't hold it against them!

    Father, you know how difficult it is for me now that I'm no longer living with my kids. Help me to be the best noncustodial parent I can be. Amen

WEEK THIRTEEN: SATURDAY
A FEELINGS CHECK

The Lord is close to the brokenhearted; he rescues those who are crushed in spirit.   Psalm 34:18, NLT

"Mom, can I hang out with you today?"

"Why sure, honey. I'm just going to the grocery store and the bank and the...."

"I don't care where we're going. I'm lonely for you."

We hugged. We spent that Saturday together, running errands. Midway through, we stopped at Burger King and picked up a couple hamburgers and sodas. Even though it was chilly, we took our food down to the beach and huddled together on a ratty old blanket.

Gayle was feeling lonely. Her best friend had moved away, and she hadn't connected with a new buddy yet. She felt alienated from the other kids at school and uncomfortable with me being gone all the time now that I had a full-time job. She missed me. So did her brother.

"Honey, when I worked at home, you got used to having me around every afternoon. It was nice. It was much easier for the three of us, but I can't do that right now. I need this job to get money for food, health insurance, clothes, rent."

We talked through her feelings. I shared some of my feelings about being away for so many hours. I'm grateful she took the initiative to pull me aside for a day, so we could do a feelings check. I'd been so caught up in my job and family chores, that I'd lost sight of her needs. Thank God, Gayle caught me and got me back onto the main track before our relationship derailed.

Feelings checks are critical, especially when time together is at a minimum. What kinds of feelings will kids express during and after a divorce? At first you can expect them to have a lot of fear. They'll feel rejected by the parent who left. They'll also express anger, loneliness, guilt, confusion, and powerlessness. When we parents witness painful emotional outpourings from our children, we often feel compelled to rush in and fix things for them. Much of the time we can't. But we can listen, try to understand, and offer love and support. Try it. Don't wait till your kid begs for your attention. Take a time out and do a feelings check today.

God, I praise you for giving me the gift of my children. Help me to take the time to check in with them and listen to them. Amen

WEEK FOURTEEN

WEEK FOURTEEN: SUNDAY
ALIGNING THOUGHTS AND WORDS

> Friend deceives friend, and no one speaks the truth. They have
> taught their tongues to lie; they weary themselves with sinning.
> Jeremiah 9:5

One night a couple of years into my divorce I was sitting on my
couch with a man I'd been dating for a while. I liked him a lot and I
wanted him to like me, perhaps even love me, so I was on my best
behavior. I don't remember our exact conversation. But I do remember
an alarm going off in my head about halfway through the evening.
Brrrring! Brrrring! *Hey, Ann,* an inner voice said. *Hello?! Do you know
that the words coming out of your mouth bear no resemblance whatsoever
to what you're thinking?* On the outside I was agreeable, pleasant, even
charming. On the inside I was screaming, *Stop! You can't mean that!
That's wrong! No—o—o—o!-o!*

As I grew up I received no training in speaking tricky, troublesome
truths. Pleasant, happy ones, yes. We loved those! But we preferred to
pretend that the other kind didn't exist. I'd learned that speaking my
mind might be too messy or make me look silly, weak, needy, or, to
borrow a phrase from my daughter, dorky. It's obvious from this verse
that, even in Jeremiah's time, people were wearing themselves out
deceiving each other trying to get their needs met.

But actually, I'm a lousy phony. I'm incapable of being sweet and pleasing enough consistently enough to get my way without anyone knowing I'm conning him!

Now I had to quit conning myself. If I had to lie about myself to get someone to like me, I wasn't going to be very happy spending time with him, was I?

Think back to a time when your brain and your mouth were out of sync. Describe it. If you could replay the scene, what would you say this time? What feelings does speaking the truth bring up? Explore those too.

> *God, thank you for your alarm bells. Teach me, Father, to stand up for truth as Jesus did, with love and compassion, not hatred or cruelty.   Amen*

WEEK FOURTEEN: MONDAY
FEARS, LET'S NAME 'EM AND TAME 'EM

> For God hath not given us the spirit of fear; but of power, and of love, and of a sound mind.   2 Timothy 1:7, KJV

One night I jokingly compared my nine-year-old son's facial expression to that of someone he didn't like. He burst into tears. "Mom, how would you like it if I said something like that to you? How would you like it if I called you ——— ? How could you do this to me? How could you hurt my feelings like that?" His tears lasted awhile. I was wrong; I told him that. I asked his forgiveness. But he couldndn't forgive me right then. His feelings were too raw. Later that night I went into his room. We talked and hugged, and he was able to forgive me.

A few weeks later his feelings were hurt again—but by someone other than me. This time he sat there, tongue-tied and stone-faced, his body clenched like a tight fist. It was obvious to me that he was hurting but equally obvious that he didn't intend to show it. Later in the conversation, the person who had insulted Derek asked him to express his feelings. Derek started to giggle, uncontrollably until he was asked to leave the room.

Later I asked him, "Why is that you feel safe getting angry at me, but with other people you clam up or get the giggles?"

"It's my fears, Mom."

"What are you afraid of? Being hit? Being laughed at? Being punished? What's the very worst thing that could have happened if you'd spoken the truth today?"

"Well, he could have hit me. Or yelled at me. Made fun of me."

"Would he hit you?"

He hesitated. "No. I guess not."

"How would you feel if he made fun of you or yelled at you?"

"I guess I wouldn't die, would I? I'd feel better than I do now. Now I feel stupid. I really did have a lot to say. I don't know why I got so scared and acted so babyish."

That day we invented a game called Name 'Em and Tame 'Em. This is how you play. When those tendrils of fear start choking the breath out of you, stop yourself. Grab a piece of paper and a pen. Make two columns. Label the first "what am I afraid of?" Name your fear. Label the second column "what might happen?" In this column write the numerals 1 through 5. Then list: (1) the very worst thing that could happen; (2) the second worst; (3) something that would have a neutral effect on you; (4) the second best thing that could happen; (5) the very best outcome possible.

What's worrying you right now? Name your fears and play the game. Give yourself a time-out and come back to your list of consequences. Describe your feelings now.

Father, I know that I shouldn't worry as much as I do. Please help me to name and tame my fears so that I won't be paralyzed by them. Amen

WEEK FOURTEEN: TUESDAY
CHALLENGING THAT NASTY LITTLE VOICE

Elijah: "I alone am left, and now they are trying to kill me, too."

God: "Yet I will preserve seven thousand others in Israel who have never bowed to Baal or kissed him!"

1 Kings 19:14 and 18, NLT

Have you ever noticed that our nasty little voice tends to exaggerate? In 1 Kings 19, Elijah has just won a big victory for God. Under his leadership the people rebuilt the altar of God. They destroyed the false prophets of Baal. You'd think Elijah would have been elated by this. But no. He got a message from Jezebel saying she was going to get him; she said he'd be dead by morning. Instead of resting in his faith in God, Elijah freaked out. He took off. He felt abandoned, alone and useless. He wished he could die.

Like Elijah, we all tend to get irrational when our panic buttons have been pushed. In this story, God puts on a great show for Elijah. He sends a windstorm to the mountain. Then an earthquake, and then a fire. But the Bible tells us that God didn't come to Elijah in these natural disasters. God's voice came as a gentle whisper. He didn't beat Elijah up for losing his faith and running away. God quieted Elijah's fears. God let him know that actually he *wasn't* alone in his resistance to Baal; seven thousand others in Israel had never bowed to Baal.

God challenged Elijah's fears. His fears were irrational, and so was his depression. The voice in his head that convinced him to run away because life wasn't worth living was the voice of those irrational fears. Think back to the most recent time you panicked and spun out in fear. What set you off your panic buttons? What kinds of things did your nasty voice tell you? Respond to this voice as God did to Elijah. Rationally. Gently. What's the real truth here? Write in your journal.

Dear Lord, when panic wants to tell me otherwise, please help me to remember who you are. Calm my spirit, Lord, with your gentle whisper. Amen

WEEK FOURTEEN: WEDNESDAY
THOSE CLEANSING TEARS

To weep is to make less the depth of grief.
                          William Shakespeare

"The American culture is relationally deprived," the divorce recovery speaker said in his lecture. "And the American male is friendless."

Later in my group I suggested we discuss these two topics. "What do you think he meant?"

One man said, "We guys talk business, sports, and the news. Try bringing up anything deeper and we get real uncomfortable."

A woman spoke up. "They're islands, independent and aloof. They don't have any need for intimacy. Unless it's sex, of course." Nervous laughter.

"That's not true," the man countered. "It's just that we're always supposed to be strong. We're not supposed to show weakness. Heck, we can't even cry."

"I couldn't cry either," a second woman said. "Big girls don't cry. Babies cry."

In divorce recovery meetings we always have plenty of tissues on hand. It's a necessity. We never know when the flood gates are going to open. This was one of those nights. Around the room the tears overflowed. We discovered that most of us cried in the dark, in our rooms, late at night after everyone else had gone to bed. We were all embarrassed to show up at work with red, swollen eyes.

I used to be like that. My tears were locked up tight and had been for most of my life. I didn't cry easily. I'd want to, I'd try to, but most of the time I couldn't. Until my first serious post-divorce relationship ended. I think I cried a lifetime's worth of tears that summer. I went to sleep crying. I woke up in the middle of the night crying and again at dawn, crying. Once that dam broke, I cried until that reservoir of tears was dry. But, subsequently, tears became my tender friends, not my enemy.

What is your history with tears? Trace it back from your childhood, through your adolescence, and all the way to the end of your marriage. If you're a man, do you feel stuck in the sports, news, and business rut? How do you communicate with your same-sex friends? Your opposite-sex friends? Is there a difference?

> *Dear Lord, help the flood gates of my heart to open, so that I may be cleansed by my tears. Please help me to seek out friends with whom I can get past the superficial niceties.*   *Amen*

WEEK FOURTEEN: THURSDAY
SPINNING OFF INTO ORBIT

> The wounds of the past continue festering. The warping effects ...keep us from seeing reality clearly; we make the same errors, the same mistakes over and over, all the while believing what we think we see and not what is.... Deep grieving purges.
> Robert Hemfelt, Frank Minirth, and Paul Meier, *Love Is a Choice*

"Have you ever had emotional vertigo?" the pastor asked the group. *What's that?* I wondered.

He continued with an example. "Do you know how a scuba diver tells which direction is up? He follows his bubbles. If he had no air bubbles to tell him where the surface was, he'd have no way of knowing how to reach it. He'd panic, which would deplete his oxygen supply in a hurry."

Suddenly I understood. It was like Hansel and Gretel after the birds ate all their bread crumbs. They lost their compass. They couldn't see where they'd come from and so had no idea of how to get back home. Kathy and I call it spinning. Not exactly a grounded, secure, or comfortable feeling. "What causes emotional vertigo?" I asked.

He smiled. "I was waiting for that question. If you were brought up being told that things were good when they weren't, or if you weren't allowed to be angry, then you won't trust your feelings. You'll repress them. You'll deny them and then hate yourself when they come out in spite of your best efforts to contain them. If you were mistreated and told you were being well-treated and that you should be grateful for it, you'll be even more confused. You won't trust your perceptions. You'll be easily deceived, because you've taught yourself to ignore red flags. Basically," he concluded, "you won't know which end is up."

Read today's quote again. Write it in your journal. *It is profound.* Have you accepted lies in place of the truth? Are they clouding your vision and causing you to lose your way, spinning through the same mistakes again and again? Explore emotional vertigo and its relation to your wounds.

Dearest Father, sometimes I get to spinning so badly I can't tell which end is up. Please show me the truth and ground me in your love.   Amen

WEEK FOURTEEN: FRIDAY
REACHING OUT—TO GIVE AND TO GET HELP

Yet I am poor and needy; come quickly to me, O God. You are my help and my deliverer; O Lord, do not delay. Psalm 70:5

When I heard that a neighbor, a single mom, had lost her job, a friend and I invited her to dinner. After she poured out her story to us, we gently reminded her that God was in control and that he'd provide for her. Somehow. Some way. And that he'd work all this painful stuff together for good. Somehow and some way.

She was quiet for a few minutes as the conversation drifted to other things. When she spoke again, her words surprised me. "When you guys called and invited me over, I was blown away. I'd never felt so rejected and alone in all my life. I was so grateful that you called. You know, I've never reached out to people who are hurting before. I always let them come to me. I'd be there if they asked, but I'd never make the first move. I don't want to be that way anymore. I want to be proactive from now on. Thank you for showing me that."

So many of us are reluctant to approach a hurting person. Likewise, we retreat from friends and family when we need them the most. We need to reach out to others as much as we need people to reach out to us. When we give people the gift of our time, love, and compassion, it blesses them. It blesses us too.

Today read Matthew 7. Then read James 1. What is God saying to you? To whom have you reached out lately? With what do you need help? Who can help you?

> *Lord, thank you for the wondrous promises you've made to me.*
> *Help me to remember to ask when I need help and to reach out*
> *to help others too.   Amen*

WEEK FOURTEEN: SATURDAY
HEY! NOW I'M THE LITTLE ENGINE THAT COULD....

> *"Whatever I have, wherever I am, I can make it through anything*
> *in the One who makes me who I am. I don't mean your help didn't*
> *mean a lot to me — it did. It was a beautiful thing that you came*
> *alongside me in my troubles.""   Philippians 4*
> The Message

Do you remember the story of the little, bitty steam engine? She had a long train of cars to pull. No big deal. Everything went along quite swimmingly until she came to steep hill. No matter how hard she tried, no matter how much she huffed and puffed, the train just wouldn't go up that hill.

Finally, she gave up. She left the train and went to look for someone to help her. She found one, strong big steam engine standing on a side track. "Will you help me over the hill with my train of cars?" she asked. He wouldn't. He'd finished his day's work and gotten all spiffed up for tomorrow. He wasn't about to mess himself up. "Nope. Sorry, I can't help you," he told her. She found a second big steam engine. No go there either.

Finally, she found another little, bitty steam engine just like herself. "Will you help me?" she asked. "Hey! No problem!" he told her and off they went to the waiting train of cars. One engine went to the head of the train, the other to the end. Puff! Puff! Choo! Choo! Off they went. Slowly the cars began to move. Very, very slowly they began to creep up that steep hill. As they climbed, the little, bitty engines began to sing in elation: "I think I can, I think I can, I think I can. I know I can, I know I can I know I can."

Well, you can too. You can do all things through Him who strengthens you and if you search, you'll be able to find loving, helpful people who'll rally beside you in your times of trouble. Can you think of a time in the not-too-distant past when you chose to persevere (and succeeded) instead of giving up (and failing)? What did you pray for? Who helped you? Now flip to the Thank You Note section of your journal and thank God for giving you the strength to pull through.

Heavenly Father, thank you for your perfect love that strengthens me. Thank you for teaching me perseverance and enabling me to make it through the really tough times. *Amen*

WEEK FIFTEEN

WEEK FIFTEEN: SUNDAY
TIME OUT TO DEVELOP THE ENDORPHIN HABIT

He is the rich man, and enjoys the fruits of riches, who summer
and winter forever can find delight in his own thoughts.
Henry David Thoreau

There are two things in life that raise my endorphin levels high
enough to deposit me on a big, wide plateau of peace and well-being.
They are exercise and chiles. Of the two, I'd have to admit that exercise
is the more universal choice.

How long has it been since you took a good, long walk that lasted at
least an hour? Or a bike ride? When was the last time you went roller
blading? Or swimming? Or cross-country skiing? The kind of exercise
I'm talking about here isn't an aerobics class or a workout on the
machines at the gym. That generates endorphins for sure. But it's the
outdoor stuff—exerting myself physically in God's world *by myself*—
that really raises my spirits.

I'm a walker. A swimmer. An occasional bike rider. A kayaker. Our
dog walks, swims (in the ocean), and even rides in my kayak with me! I
like his company; it's devoted companionship and solitude all rolled up
into one. I didn't used to like the solitude. In fact, I remember the first
few times the dog and I walked along the beach. I marched through the
tiny waves at the high tide line, and my eyes took in the surfers sliding

gracefully down the faces of the waves. I saw brown pelicans coasting over the water, swooping high up into the air, and splashing down to scoop up fish.

Why didn't I have anyone to share this with? In my heart I ached for someone to talk to. I was so lonely! I walked for two hours that day. About halfway through, my attitude changed. Dramatically. I'm sure it was partially the endorphins kicking in from the exertion. But more than that, I suddenly realized I had someone to talk to! There was someone with me that day, and he exercises with me always now. We have some pretty incredible talks. Guess who?

Exercise really does nourish the heart and soul even more than it tones up the body. Even if you are a gym goer, try spending some time alone moving through God's world. With him. (Dogs optional. Chiles afterward optional!) That's your assignment for today.

Father, thank you for creating such a magnificently beautiful world. Let's go outside today, Lord, and generate some endorphins together. Amen

WEEK FIFTEEN: MONDAY
ACCEPTING GOD'S NO'S

Let there be tears for the wrong things you have done. Let there be sorrow and deep grief. Let there be sadness instead of laughter, and gloom instead of joy. When you bow down before the Lord and admit your dependence on him, he will lift you up and give you honor.   James 4:9-10, NLT

I remember when my first serious post-divorce relationship ended. We hadn't been getting along *at all* and I knew both of us had a lot of humbling growth to go through before our relationship got to a healthy place. I was actually quite *relieved* at first to have him out of my life. But, a few weeks later, when the initial shock wore off, I realized that *I missed him. Something fierce.* It was so fierce it scared me even more than being lonely

did. *How could I have missed seeing all his good qualities when we were together?* I wondered. *How could I have been such a, well, shrew? Where was my submissive, gentle spirit? Why did I have to go head-to-head with him on every issue? What was wrong with me?* I began to pray and pray for reconciliation.

Did we reconcile? No. In fact, he found himself a new girlfriend before the first month was out. As I prayed and as I cried, it began to occur to me that maybe I wasn't praying the right prayer. God was definitely giving me a big no on the getting back together thing. At least for the moment. It hurts when we pray so desperately for something, especially reconciliation of a relationship, or healing of a loved one from a deadly disease, and God doesn't come through for us. But what is he trying to tell us in these circumstances? Why does he say no or not now?

I think he's telling us that we're not praying the right prayer. I think he's also reminding us that we don't know what's best for us, that we aren't always going to get our own way on this planet. He wants us to trust him, to lean on him, to believe in him even when it's hard, even when it hurts like crazy to do so. He wants us to believe that his grace is indeed sufficient for us. He wants us to believe that all things come together for good for those of us who love him. He wants to grow our faith. And saying no to our urgent, desperate pleas makes us grow.

So what should we pray for? Instead of praying for this man to love me and forgive me, to ask my forgiveness for letting me down, should I have prayed instead that God show me the areas in my character that needed work and asked him to help me do the work? Should I have prayed for the grace to become the woman he intended me to be? Should I have prayed for peace of mind, strength, and courage? Should I have prayed for the hand of God to touch this man's heart ever-so-gently and nudge him, too, back into a desire to get right with his Creator? That's what I finally prayed, and the dark cloud of no lifted from me.

What are you praying for? What *no's* and *not nows* are you getting? What could you pray for instead?

Awesome Father, you always know what's best for me. Help me to lean on you, trust you, believe in you even when it hurts like crazy. Please give me peace of mind, strength, and courage. Holy Spirit, teach me to pray. Amen

WEEK FIFTEEN: TUESDAY
CELEBRATE THE EVENING MEAL

Always remember to forget the troubles that passed away, but never forget to remember the blessings that come each day.

Anonymous

Is your house anything like mine? For too many years after the divorce, I'd fix some quick and easy kid food for dinner. Chicken nuggets, macaroni, hot dogs, canned ravioli, canned beans, and the like. Frozen or canned food cooked quick in the microwave and delivered to my children at the kitchen counter. I didn't sit down. I ate on the run. I wandered around my kitchen snacking, tidying up, doing dishes, talking on the phone. Dinnertime at our house wasn't a time for togetherness. At Kathy's house next door it was pretty much the same, only her kids ate on paper plates in front of the TV while she raced around in the kitchen.

I didn't like what I saw at her house; she didn't like what she saw at mine. So we put our heads together and joined forces. Just because we felt like fractured families didn't mean we had to act fractured. We started having dinner together once or twice a week, all seven of us. It became a tradition. I decided to change a few things at my own house.

So did she. I modified my menus to blend kid food with what I call "real people food." I bought fresh flowers for the table. I taught my kids to set the table. We used place mats and occasionally even cloth napkins!

We sat down together. We took turns saying grace. We made dinnertime into what it used to be for us—a time of family togetherness and sharing. And afterward, sometimes, for a treat, we'd crank up the stereo and dance!

Do you live alone? If you do, there isn't any law that says you have to eat standing up in the kitchen. Honest! You can put flowers on the table, set it nicely, and feed yourself balanced, well-prepared meals. Once or twice a week, invite someone over. Pretty soon they may be inviting you back, and you'll have the beginnings of a social life!

Father, help me to see how you bless me. Help me to treat myself better, Lord, and to share my blessings with others.
Amen

WEEK FIFTEEN: WEDNESDAY
THE NUTS AND BOLTS OF FORGIVENESS

If you forgive those who sin against you, your heavenly Father will forgive you. But if you refuse to forgive others, your Father will not forgive your sins.   Matthew 6:14-15, NLT

Let me tell you a few things about forgiveness. First off, it's hard work. It isn't something that happens magically, even to Christians. You can't expect that to wake up one morning, say six months or a year after your divorce is final, and jump out of bed with these words on your lips: "I've done it, Lord! Today's the day I've forgiven my ex! Hallelujah!"

Forgiving someone is making a conscious choice to love, more specifically to love someone who's not easy to love. It's based on a decision to be obedient to God. It's *not* a feeling, and it doesn't happen all by itself. Forgiving someone shows that person mercy even if the injury she did to us was deliberate. If you're anything like me, it takes you a whole lot of struggling to get to the place where you can look past the offenses. Yet doing that allows us to accept the other person as he (or she) truly is. Once we quit trying to punish or fix him, we're able to move aside and give God the room to work in his life.

Forgiving someone is the only way we can be fair to ourselves, because when we clutch to our hearts all the injustices we've suffered, all the sins that have been committed against us, our souls just percolate with hatred and bitterness. The poison running through our veins doesn't hurt the person who did us wrong; it hurts us!

Forgiving allows God's loving, gracious touch to penetrate our hearts and heal *us*. It frees us from the past and provides us with a clean slate, a new beginning. In Matthew 18, when Peter asked Jesus how many times one should forgive someone, Jesus answered, "seventy times seven." He meant we shouldn't even attempt to keep track of the times we forgive others, because, being human, they will mess up again and again. We all do! That's why we all need a Savior!

When we've wronged someone, it's also necessary for us to ask that person's forgiveness, and you know what? Asking forgiveness is risky business. It requires vulnerability and courage, because we may be scorned. But it's as necessary as confessing our sins to God and asking for his forgiveness. Write down five things in your journal about forgiveness. Write as many reasons as you can for forgiving someone. Then make a list of people you need to forgive and what their offenses were. Now make a list of the people you've wronged and what you did. Then pray...

> *Father, I want to be obedient to you. Please help me see where I've hurt other people and give me the courage to ask for forgiveness. Help me also to show mercy to those who've wounded me, so I'll feel your mercy. Amen*

WEEK FIFTEEN: THURSDAY
SO THIS IS MY SEASON OF GRIEF?!

> There is a time for everything, and a season for every activity
> under heaven: a time to be born and a time to die, a time to
> plant and a time to uproot, a time to kill and a time to heal, a
> time to tear down and a time to build, a time to weep and a time
> to laugh, a time to mourn and a time to dance.
>
> Ecclesiastes 3:1-4

I think grief has two faces, like the two Chinese symbols that spell the word *crisis*. The first face of grief corresponds to the Chinese symbol for *catastrophe*. When a marriage ends, it is a *death*. The death of a sacred relationship. We are *uprooted* from our homes. Our identities as halves of a greater whole are destroyed. This is a *killing*. We are *torn down* and our children are ripped away from us. They may live with us five days a week, or every other week, or every other weekend. When they're with us, we're on overload. When they're gone, we're desolate. We *weep*. We *mourn*.

Ecclesiastes 3:1-8 describe the grief process pretty accurately, if you ask me. And it can get so bleak and dark and miserable and lonely that we're sure it will last forever. Yet the writer of Ecclesiastes assures us of God's promise. We will pass through this season of grief.

The second Chinese symbol in the word *crisis* is *opportunity*. It is *birth, planting, healing, building, laughing, dancing*. Finally, it is *peace*.

Write the Ecclesiastes 3 passage down in your journal in colored ink, so it will stand out. Whenever your spirit is heavy and hurting with the burdens of letting go, read it and remember that there will be other seasons following this one. As a last thought for today, think back to another time in your life when everything seemed to be coming apart. What happened? How did it all turn out?

Father, thank you for these incredible, encouraging words. Thank you for assuring me that there will be other, joyful seasons in my life. Amen

WEEK FIFTEEN: FRIDAY
CHILDREN OF DIVORCE—BILL OF RIGHTS

But the Lord said to me, "Do not say, 'I am only a child.' You must go to everyone I send you to and say whatever I command you. Do not be afraid of them, for I am with you and will rescue you."   Jeremiah 1:7-8

Jim Smoke distributes this Bill of Rights as a handout at each of his divorce recovery workshops. I urge you to copy this and share it with your ex-spouse. If signing your names to it will help you both to abide by this bill of rights, then by all means sign! Remember, the kids are priority one. From now on they (not revenge) are the focus of your relationship with your former mate!

CHILDREN OF DIVORCE—BILL OF RIGHTS

1. *THE RIGHT to know that I am loved unconditionally.*
2. *THE RIGHT to know I didn't cause my parents' divorce.*
3. *THE RIGHT to know what caused the divorce.*
4. *THE RIGHT to the security of knowing where I will live and who I will live with.*
5. *THE RIGHT to be aware of how stress affects my life so I can adapt to it in a healthy way.*
6. *THE RIGHT to be a kid and not be afraid of being myself.*
7. *THE RIGHT to know that my physical and emotional needs will be met.*

8.   THE RIGHT *not to be a victim of the divorce and be used as a pawn by my parents.*

9.   THE RIGHT *to have my own space for privacy to ensure respect of my person.*

10. THE RIGHT *to have a normal household routine and discipline so I can feel secure.*

11. THE RIGHT *to have positive images of my parents so I can love them equally.*

12· THE RIGHT *to have access and time with each parent equally.*

Father_____Mother_____ Date_____
   Lord, I know that one of the biggest challenges facing me as a divorced parent is leaving behind the animosity between me and my ex. Help me, Father. This is something I can't even begin to do without your help.   Amen

WEEK FIFTEEN: SATURDAY
TIME OUT TO MAKE A BLESSINGS COLLAGE

> Enjoy the blessings of this day, if God sends them; and the evils of it bear patiently and sweetly; for this day only is ours; we are dead to yesterday, and we are not yet born to the morrow.
>
> Jeremy Taylor

Do you have a box somewhere, stored in your garage or basement or attic, with old art projects from your school days? Or an old, embarrassing notebook full of poems you wrote to your first adolescent love? No. Well, neither do I. Some parents save *everything!* I don't know what you'd call my dad, but he's the opposite of a pack rat. He gets tremendous joy from cleaning out the garage. He threw away everything I was trying to save for my own children, even my Barbie collection!

I can't find much tangible proof of the blessings I had growing up. But I went on a scavenger hunt recently in my own house. I wanted to make a blessings collage, so I would have something concrete and uplifting to look at when life threatened to toss me back into the toilet bowl.

I got a big, strong piece of cardboard and some powerful glue. I gathered together some special photos of my kids, family, and friends, postcards from favorite vacation spots over the years, some sea shells, a sand dollar, a pressed flower. With colored markers I made a list of ten things I had to be grateful for. I added little pieces of poetry I had written. I found a few memorable cards from friends and a copy of the first article I had published. Then I arranged everything on the cardboard and glued it down. I hung that blessings collage on the back of my closet door, where I could see it every morning when I got dressed. Can you try this one?

God, you bless me in so many ways that I overlook. Help me to refocus my eyes so I can see all the great things you do for me every day.   Amen

WEEK SIXTEEN

WEEK SIXTEEN: SUNDAY
FORGIVENESS AND GETTING RIGHT WITH GOD

> Blessed is he whose transgressions are forgiven, whose sins are covered. Blessed is the man whose sin the Lord does not count against him and in whose spirit is no deceit.
>
> Psalm 32:1-2

Children do it often if they're feeling needy and insecure: To attract Mom's or Dad's attention, they misbehave. The pattern seems to repeat throughout life. I'm not sure why that is, I just know it's true.

When I've needed love the most is often when I've acted the most unlovable. With significant men in my life. With my sister. My parents. Apparently acting up was easier than admitting my weakness and vulnerability. Most of the time I couldn't admit it even to myself.

What did I really need back then? What do we all need when we behave in this way? What I needed, what I longed so desperately to experience, was love, God's love. But before I could fully experience God's love, I needed to get right with him. I needed to clean up my act. What does that mean? Read Psalm 32:1-5. That about says it all, doesn't it? Bottom line is, when we aren't right with God, we're like Adam and Eve in Eden, hiding something shameful. It clogs up the receptors in our hearts and minds that let us experience God's love!

Recently I was struggling with some extremely painful issues. I had been thrashing about, looking for someone else to pin the blame on. I was short-tempered with my kids; I didn't return phone calls from friends; I felt abandoned and alone. I groaned all day long and my strength was sapped. I prayed, I prayed, and I prayed. Nothing happened and nothing helped. Then it occurred to me as I was vacuuming (!) that I was praying for healing in a relationship *without getting right with God first*. I fell to my knees and sobbed my heart out. As God revealed them to me, I listed all the things I had done wrong and vowed to correct the things I could correct and ask forgiveness for the things I couldn't. The list was longer than I would have expected. But I did correct all I could. And I felt the assurance of his forgiveness. I was able to receive, experience, his love. Try it. You'll be blown away.

> *Father, my bones are wasting away from my groaning. I want to get right with you. Please show me the places in my life that need to be cleaned up. I want my soul to be without deceit. I want my heart to be receptive to you.*   Amen

WEEK SIXTEEN: MONDAY
HELP! LET'S GET UNSTUCK!

> For he will command his angels concerning you to guard you in all your ways; they will lift you up with their hands, so that you will not strike your foot against a stone. You will tread upon the lion and the cobra; you will trample the great lion and the serpent.   Psalm 91:11-13

Neither Kathy nor I was very good at taking risks, though for different reasons, with different styles. I was good at faking it. Afraid to stop and analyze the situation, I'd get spinning so fast I was going nowhere, running in circles. She was good at avoiding it for fear something would go wrong.

So we did some research on how to break the deadlock of fear. We came up with some ideas on how to move ourselves off ground zero. Here's a synthesis:

1. Identify the ineffective things we do to get approval, reassurance, comfort.
2. Identify the ways we try to get others to take care of us.
3. Identify the ways we conform to the expectations of others.
4. Identify what makes us dependent, insecure, and needy.
5. Make a list of the things we love to do best.
6. Describe how we'd act if we were the best person we could be.
7. Make a list of things we could do that would make a difference.
8. List the things we *really* want to do that people might criticize us for.

Do you have a close friend who's pretty much at the same place you are? Make a date for dinner with this person and bring this book and your journal along. Brainstorm together, not only on ways you two can better yourselves, but also on ways you can get yourselves off ground zero. Be there for one another. Be accountable to one another. The two of you will be far more successful than one of you alone. And as you find yourselves making healthier choices, you will discover that your self-esteem will rise. And you can celebrate this together!

> *Father, help me to let go of my outdated, useless, toxic, and paralyzing choices. Help me to become the person you intend me to be.*   *Amen*

WEEK SIXTEEN: TUESDAY
OPTING FOR TRUTH AND KINDNESS

Your own soul is nourished when you are kind, but you destroy yourself when you are cruel.

Proverbs 11:17, NLT

Choosing mercy and kindness over bitterness and revenge seeking can be the toughest thing you've ever had to do. It may require more courage, commitment, and self-control than you've ever had to exert before, along with a monumental dose of perseverance. It's about going that extra mile, again and again, and developing those muscles of mercy and forgiveness.

Before we can be merciful and forgiving of others, we have to be honest, with ourselves and with God. We have to own up to our sins and ask for his forgiveness. We have to make a solemn promise to do our very best to do the godly thing the next time. We may not always succeed at showing mercy and forgiveness to those who have hurt and continue to hurt us. In fact, at first we may fail much more often than we succeed. But if we hang in there, eventually God's way will triumph more frequently than the world's way within our lives.

One of the best ways to stay on track with our new, loving behavior is to ask a trusted friend to share the journey with us. Is there someone you know who would help you maintain accountability, without criticizing or judging you harshly when you slip up? Ask that person to be your mercy and forgiveness partner. Share with that person the things you have done to hurt others and to hurt yourself. Get your fears and resentments out of the attic. Expose them to God so that he may heal them with the light of his truth. Expose them to your friend also. If you feel compelled to ask someone's forgiveness, do so. If you aren't ready to do it yet, pray that God will keep working in you until you're ready.

Owning up to things, offering mercy and forgiveness, and asking for forgiveness in return are important stepping-stones to a healthier, more God-centered life. It's how we let go of the pain of the past. It's how we're set free.

Sometime today take this book, your Bible, a concordance, and your journal and find yourself a quiet place. Look up references to *mercy* in the Bible and write your own definition of it. Do the same for *kindness* and *forgiveness*. Now close your eyes and pray.

> *Father, I want to own my stuff and to receive the blessings of your forgiveness and mercy. Bring to the surface my buried fear and resentment. Show me where I've been wrong and help me to choose a safe, loving partner with whom to share this journey of healing. Amen*

WEEK SIXTEEN: WEDNESDAY
LISTEN, LEARN, LOVE

> Listen, my child, to what your father teaches you. Don't neglect your mother's teaching. What you learn from them will crown you with grace and clothe you with honor.
>
> Proverbs 1:8-9, NLT

"Thanks, Mom. I loved how you put that note in my lunch."

I smiled. I knew Derek missed my being home after school. I'd recently taken a job after years of working out of my house. I missed him too. He was in my thoughts when I was at work, and I wanted him to know it. "In your office did you hang that picture I made you?" he added, practically reading my mind.

"Of course I did. Everyone who came by commented on what a good dragon-drawer you are. They especially liked all the wild colors." I took his hand and led him toward the couch. We snuggled in together. "So tell me about your day. I want to hear everything. Did you guys dissect that owl pellet?"

We didn't have this conversation by accident. The note was a conscious effort on my part to let him know I was thinking about him during the day. Taking some time alone with him to ask questions and really listen was another way I'd decided I would express my love to him.

After I'd been at my new job for a month, I'd seen that I needed to come up with a plan, to keep my life from running away from me. My neighbor Kathy and I set aside a Saturday (when our kids were gone) to do some brainstorming and goal setting. We made a list of the things we wished we had time to do with our kids. We made another list of the values we wanted to impart to them. Then we made a list of the things we could do to ensure that our kids felt our loving presence, when we were home with them and when we were at work.

Finally, we made a list of the household chores, and we split them up among our kids, so it wouldn't always be Mom cooking dinner, doing laundry, making lunches, and cleaning up after everyone else. We made those chores age-appropriate, but we also assigned a monetary value to each one. If our kids wanted their allowance, or if they wanted to go to a movie, their chores had to be done.

We each held a family meeting where we laid out the new "plan" and asked for feedback from our kids. Mine made a few ridiculous suggestions and so did hers, but overall, they caught the spirit of love that was motivating us. Freeing up our time enabled us to have more quality time with our kids. Having a plan and sharing our burdens has enabled us to be better listeners and teachers.

I suggest you get together with another single parent and have a brainstorming session. Make a plan and help each other stick to it!

> *God, I want to be a good teacher, a better listener, and a more loving parent. Help me to come up with a plan to make this happen. Amen*

WEEK SIXTEEN: THURSDAY
BUILDING MY HOUSE ON A ROCK

But anyone who listens and doesn't obey is like a person who builds a house without a foundation. When the floods sweep

down against that house, it will crumble into a heap of ruins.
Luke 6:49, NLT

Remember those three little pigs? They set off on their own and each of them built a house to live in. The first pig was in a hurry to get the work done so he could play. He built his house out of the first material he came across, which was straw. When the big bad wolf showed up, he had no trouble leveling that straw house. Pig number one ran to his brother's house. But his brother had been too lazy or too busy with other things to spend much time house building. He had quickly thrown a bunch of sticks together and called it home. A couple of good huffs and puffs, and the wolf blew down his house.

What about brother number three? By the time the other pigs showed up, he was just putting the finishing touches on his brick house. He'd taken the time necessary to build a solid home with a strong foundation. There was no way that nasty old wolf could blow his house down. His wisdom, patience, and maturity saved the family.

As single parents, we usually have more stuff on our plates than we can handle. So we may neglect building a strong, rock-solid biblical foundation for our families. We know that temptations will come. We know that our enemy is lurking outside waiting to devour our children. So how do we integrate basic scriptural principles into our lives so he can't blow our houses down and run off with our kids?

It's easier said than done. We can identify some principles, explain them to our children, and try to live them. Here's another list for your refrigerator. If you pay attention to them, they will help you all become more Christlike. Biblical principles for my family:

1. Accept each other as you are. Too many people grow up feeling that they aren't good enough, because they haven't been accepted in their own family.

2. Memorize the fruit of the Spirit: love, joy, peace, patience, kindness, goodness, faithfulness, gentleness, and self-control (Galatians 5:22-23). Work to incorporate them into your life.

3. Help each other out. Become a team with the mission statement— to bear one another's burdens. This exemplifies love in action.

4. Be forgiving. God commands it and it keeps the love flowing.

5. Develop servants' hearts. Anticipate one another's needs and "do" for one another, rather than focusing primarily on getting your own needs met.

Jesus, I want to become more like you, and I want my children to do so also. Help us to integrate these biblical principles into our daily lives.   *Amen*

WEEK SIXTEEN: FRIDAY
MAKING A STRESS-BUSTER LIST

What do we live for; if not to make life less difficult for each other?   George Eliot

At the single-parents' meetings at church, I noticed people, primarily women, sitting in a circle, complaining. What did we gripe about? The universal single-parent problems: money (or lack thereof), the difficulties of coparenting, the kids, the lack of understanding for single parents at work, nonexistent social lives, dwindling friendships, and, of course, lack of free time. Basically we were all stressed out, doing too much for everyone else, and overcome with guilt if we did *anything* to nurture ourselves.

I got an idea. I wheeled the modern equivalent of a chalkboard into a hole in the circle. "Let's make a list of stress busters," I said. Hands went up. Within ten minutes we had twenty-five great ideas:

- Enjoy beauty.
- Be thankful.
- Listen to your kids.
- Play with your kids.
- Tell your kids all the reasons you love them.
- Take time-outs when you're about to yell.
- Take time to talk through a problem with a kid.
- Do things just for you.
- Say you're sorry when you're wrong.
- Get regular exercise.
- Eat well.
- Set, evaluate, and update goals.
- Laugh.
- Say no, *without feeling guilty.*
- Stop trying to do it all and perfectly.
- Compliment someone.
- Dance.
- Take a drive and sing at the top of your lungs.
- Do a good deed.
- Call a friend or family member whom you've neglected.
- Be kind to your ex the next time you see him or her.
- Talk to or write a letter to God.
- Go to a movie by yourself.
- Sign up for that class you've been putting off.
- Go to the library or a museum.

Someone copied these down and typed them up for distribution. The stress busters worked. Our group became endowed with a pioneer (we can overcome anything!) spirit. It was quite a change from a bunch of sad-faced complainers.

Copy this list and put it where you will see it often. Delete any that don't apply. Make it a point to read it over at least once a day. It will transform you!

Father, please anoint me with a pilgrim's can-do spirit. Teach me that I can take care of myself while I'm taking care of everyone else. Amen

WEEK SIXTEEN: SATURDAY
SUPPORT GROUPS, SUPPORT SYSTEMS

Who alone suffers, suffers most in the mind, leaving free things and happy shows behind. But then the mind much sufferance doth o'erskip when grief hath mates, and bearing fellowship.

William Shakespeare

"Why should I join a support group?" she asked me. "I'm doing just fine on my own. I don't want to hang out with a bunch of whiners."

I was having coffee with this newly single mom. I took her hand and looked into her eyes. "We're not whiners. Not me, not the people in my divorce recovery group, and not you. We're just scared and lonely travelers down the dusty back roads of divorce country. We've lost our mates. We've lost our support systems. We need to rebuild."

This woman had a stigma about "support groups." She thought that by participating in a "recovery program," she was labeling herself as something akin to an alcoholic or drug addict. She couldn't see that she needed to find a new community of loving, supportive friends who would walk with her, run with her, cry with her, and hold her hand when she needed it. She chose instead to stand tall, straighten her shoulders, pull in her stomach, and march on alone. Stoic. Lost, lonely, and too filled with fear to admit her neediness.

We need strong support systems so we can heal the wounds of past relationships. Our wounds come from our marriages, our relationships with our parents, from people we've dated, and hurts over the years that have never been forgiven. We also need help in identifying and changing the patterns (perhaps intergenerational) that have led us into trouble before—or they will keep causing us to fall flat on our faces.

Basically, we need help with everything, from car maintenance to baby sitting. We need to create new "family systems" that work for us and our children. God never intended for us to be lone rangers. He created us to be relational, and when our marriages die, we lose our mates, our partners, our back-ups. We need to fill this void with friends—a network of people who will support us.

I have seen people begin divorce recovery workshops alone and terrified. Several weeks later they walk with lighter steps and with smiles. Where there was silence, there is laughter. They've made new friends. Have you joined a support group? If you feel resistance in your heart toward doing so, examine those feelings. How have you filled the void left by your former spouse? What else can you do?

> *Lord, I come to you on my knees. I need help. I need a new community. I'm overwhelmed, lonely, and scared. Lead me toward people who will share my burdens and lighten my heart. Help me to lighten theirs too.   Amen*

WEEK SEVENTEEN

> In the same way, the Spirit helps us in our weakness. We do not know what we ought to pray for, but the Spirit himself intercedes for us with groans that words cannot express.
>
> Romans 8:26

The first time someone recited this verse to me, I was stunned. I had known that God could read my mind. I understood that he could see what was in my heart a lot more clearly than I could. Yet knowing those things hadn't comforted me a whole lot; in fact, I wasn't sure I liked the idea of someone knowing more about me than I did! It made me feel, well, naked.

Then I read this passage. I began to comprehend the immensity of God's love for me. *He loved me in spite of all those dark little secrets I had stored away in the attic of my mind. He loved me even though I didn't begin to have a handle on any of this forgiveness stuff. He loved me even though I was a long, long way from being sinless. And he promised to stand in for me and pray for me when I felt too beaten down and ashamed to pray myself.* Wow!

Today let's take time out to look at our prayer lives. (Every so often I like to do this. It's like spiritual spring cleaning.) If you can, write the Lord's Prayer from memory. If you don't know it, turn to Matthew 6:9-

13. Copy it down in the prayer section of your journal. Then go to Psalm 23 and copy it down. If you don't know these passages, try memorizing them. They're incredible to have at hand when we don't have any words to pray with.

When was the last time your prayer life dried up? Have you ever just thrown up your hands in resignation and asked the Holy Spirit to *please, just take it from here?*

> *O holy God, thank you for giving me the gift of your Holy Spirit to comfort me and intercede for me when I'm without the means to pray. Remind me to ask for your help, Father. Remind me to just ask. Amen*

WEEK SEVENTEEN: MONDAY
MODELING HONEST BEHAVIOR

An honest answer is like a kiss on the lips.   Proverbs 24:26

Even though they aren't much in fashion anymore, I learned a lot from old-time tales and fables. There are a lot of truths tucked away in these stories. Whenever my sister or I misbehaved or were confronted with ethical problems, my dad sat us down and read one of these stories to us. One of his favorites was *The Boy Who Cried Wolf*, which Dad laid on us every time one of us was caught telling a lie.

Do you remember it? A young shepherd boy got bored tending his sheep and decided to have a little fun with the people in his village. So he ran toward them crying at the top of his lungs, "Wolf! Wolf! Help me! The wolves are eating my sheep!" The villagers rushed to help him. But when they arrived, the boy laughed at them. He did this a second time and once again the villagers rushed to his rescue. Again there were no wolves, and he mocked them. But then one day the wolves came, and when the shepherd boy cried, "Wolf!" no one believed him. He lost all his sheep.

The moral of this fable is this: When people lie, after awhile no one believes them, even when they're telling the truth. Today's Bible verse is the flip side of this message. "An honest answer is like a kiss on the lips." Telling the truth isn't just something we need to lecture our kids about. Telling the truth is a biblical mandate that we need to teach by example. If children catch us lying (and believe me, they will if we do!), then we become like the boy who cried wolf. Our own kids won't believe us.

What kind of values are you modeling to your children? Are you walking your talk? What areas of your behavior could you change?

Lord, I know that we all sin and fall short of the mark. I have failed to walk my talk in the following areas: (confess). Please help me and my children to draw closer to you.
Amen

WEEK SEVENTEEN: TUESDAY
GETTING OVER IT BY GOING THROUGH IT

I waited patiently for the Lord; he turned to me and heard my cry. He lifted me out of the slimy pit, out of the mud and mire; he set my feet on a rock and gave me a firm place to stand.

Psalm 40:1-2

Remember? It takes a *minimum* of two or three years to work our way through the grieving process. And that doesn't count detours. *Detours?* you ask. *What's a detour?* Well, a detour is a supposed shortcut that ends up taking us the long way around. Like opting for the romantic solution—falling in love with someone who's as mixed up, hurting, not-ready, and not-healthy as we are. And then having to deal with the grief when that ends, plus the leftover grief from this divorce. That's a detour. A common one.

Modern America prefers quick fixes and bright, happy smiles to long, drawn-out, messy, icky, sad, teary stuff. Who wouldn't? I mean, wouldn't you rather be off and running in a successful new life than sitting in a divorce recovery meeting with red, running eyes, crying your heart out? Of course you would! But the truth is, if you don't do the hard, dirty work now, it's going to come back at you, and you're going to have to do it later. With yet another pile of pain heaped on top of the pain you feel now.

"Express your feelings. Take ownership of them. Repress them and they will own you." I heard that in church. You know, your pain doesn't *really* want a quick fix. It doesn't want an easy, pat answer. It wants to be known, felt, and validated. It needs to be acknowledged before it will go away.

Several years ago I put this little sentence on my bulletin board: "The shortest distance between two points is a detour." (It takes a minute for the meaning to sink in.) At least that's how my shortcuts always turned out. I finally got sick of lengthening my journey by compounding my pain. I made a commitment to do my best to avoid those "quick" solutions. Have you taken any shortcuts that turned into detours? Describe them.

> *Father, thank you for the promise that you will lift me up out of the slimy pit, if I can find courage to trust you. Please give me that courage.   Amen*

WEEK SEVENTEEN: WEDNESDAY
CAN WE SET SOME LIMITS ON THIS SUFFERING?

Then [Elijah] went alone into the desert, traveling all day. He sat down under a solitary broom tree and prayed that he might die.

"I have had enough, Lord," he said. "Take my life, for I am no better than my ancestors." Then he lay down and slept under the broom tree. But as he was sleeping, an angel touched him and told him, "Get up and eat!"   1 Kings 19:4-5, NLT

Read again the verses above. Let any feelings of depression you have today rise to the surface of your awareness. Feel them. Write them down. When you're finished, get up and go outside. Find the most beautiful flower or plant in your backyard or patio and walk over to it. Touch it. Smell it. Look at it from as many different angles as possible. Get up close to it and try to commit to memory every single detail of its structure, form, color, and fragrance. Now go back inside and answer this question: How do you feel now? Better?

Most people do feel a tremendous lightening of their spirits when they take the spotlight off of their depressing feelings and shine it on something else. Psychologists tell us that while it's important for us to acknowledge and feel our pain, we'll be better off if we don't wallow endlessly in self-pity.

How can we avoid getting stuck in the quicksand of our depression? By setting time limits. Feel like crying? Allow yourself five minutes to cry, right before you go to bed. If you find yourself obsessing about your ex and all the injustices associated with your divorce, set aside a few minutes before you go to bed to sit down and write out those feelings. Commit to doing it, once a day, at a scheduled time. Don't allow yourself to be swallowed up by those feelings whenever they pop up to the surface. Instead, gently remind yourself that the nightly pity party is scheduled for ten o'clock and make a mental note to save your hurt, anger, sadness, and overall misery for then. Try it. It works!

Lord, thank you for reminding me, as the angel reminded Elijah, that I can't live on my depression alone. Feed my mind with nourishing, healing thoughts, and help me to limit my suffering to a set time every day.   Amen

WEEK SEVENTEEN: THURSDAY
LEST WE FORGET—GOD IS JUST

He is the Rock, his works are perfect, and all his ways are just.
Deuteronomy 32:4

Have you ever read the story of Lazarus the Beggar in Luke 16? This Lazarus was a beggar covered with sores who hung out at the gate of a very rich man's house begging for scraps. He was so pathetic that dogs came and licked his sores. Both Lazarus and the rich man died about the same time, only Lazarus was carried to Abraham's side by angels and the rich man went to hell.

He caught a glimpse of Lazarus and Abraham across the chasm that separated them and begged for a drink of water. Abraham refused him the drink and reminded him that in his lifetime he'd received an abundance of good things, while Lazarus had suffered mightily. He further explained that the chasm separating heaven and hell was unbreachable. The rich man begged Abraham to send Lazarus back to his father's house to convince his five brothers to mend their ways. Abraham again refused, saying that "If they do not listen to Moses and the Prophets, they will not be convinced even if someone rises from the dead."

I heard this story twice on the radio within the same week, and I wondered what God was trying to tell me by it. I had been really upset by the lack of justice in the world, particularly as it related to me as a single mom. God is just. Those folks who do bad things will, eventually, see the error of their ways. Whether it's in this life or when they're leaning across the chasm begging for relief from the scorching heat— one day they will see. If they have closed their minds to Scripture, then the eye-opening moment won't be a pleasant one. But, it proves irrevocably that the verse from Deuteronomy 32:35 is true: "It is mine to avenge; I will repay." He will. Life may not always be fair, but in the final analysis—God is.

Once again, pull out your journal and your Bible and go to a special, quiet place. Read about Lazarus the Beggar. In his place, put someone who has hurt you deeply without remorse.

> *Dear Lord, I am so grateful that your ways are just and your works perfect. Please help me to turn my tormentors over to you. Help me also to forgive them because — to use Jesuss' words— they don't know what they're doing.*   *Amen*

WEEK SEVENTEEN: FRIDAY
HELPING EACH OTHER SOAR

To love someone means to see him as God intended him.

Fyodor Dostoyevsky

Recently I was looking out to sea and noticed a flock of seven pelicans swooping by, surfing up and down the air currents in a V formation. They banked around the bay and took off to the northwest. I wondered why they chose to fly in a V. What benefit did they derive from it?

A little research revealed that birds are less vulnerable to attack from predators when traveling in a group. By flying in that V formation, the flock can fly 71 percent farther than if each bird blew on its own. Why? Because the uplift created by the flapping of the preceding bird's wings eases the next bird along—all the way down the line. Amazing, huh? And I also discovered that the birds take turns flying in the lead position. It's a matter of who's the strongest and best prepared to take the lead at any given time. The lead bird flies until it gets tired and rotates back. Then another bird comes forward to take its place.

As I thought this over, it occurred to me that pelicans, geese, and other birds that fly in V formations are supporting one another. They take advantage of each other's strength. They lift others up and give of themselves when needed.

How, I wondered, can friends do that for each other? We are all members of the same flock, God's flock. How can we help each other to soar?

Think of your three closest friends. How do they delight you? What special activities do you most enjoy doing together? What has each of them done to lift you up and help you soar? How have you encouraged and supported them? A friend of mine keeps a stash of cards. Whenever he feels compelled to let someone know he cares, he sends a card. Another friend always seems to know when I need to hear her voice. She calls. Another e-mails me daily. No matter how lonely I feel, there's always a sweet note awaiting me from her. Still another brings me fresh flowers from her garden when we get together.

When was the last time you did something really nice for a friend? Go to prayer for a few minutes and pray this prayer:

> *Father, thank you for these friends of mine. Thank you that they've loved me through the tough times and that they've been there with a smile and a laugh in the better times. I want to help them soar, Lord. Help me.*   Amen

WEEK SEVENTEEN: SATURDAY
IS IT TOO SOON TO DATE?

Do not hold against us the sins of the fathers; may your mercy come quickly to meet us, for we are in desperate need.

Psalm 79:8

A husband cheated on his wife repeatedly in their marriage. When it came time to break up, he tormented her with dates, times, and places of his liaisons. Horrified, she listened. For a year afterward, she had a hard time leaving the house. She couldn't even contemplate making friends with a man, much less dating. She attended a divorce recovery program and was encouraged to join a singles' group. She went once but felt awkward walking around by herself with a red name tag on (which let everyone know this was her first time there) and trying to make small talk with strangers.

Even though it was a Christian group, she never went back. "How do I know when I'm ready to date?" she asked me. "My mom and dad are on my case. My married friends are on my case. They want me to be part of a couple again, so I can be included in the social functions. Every time I get set up on a blind date, I freak out. It feels too weird. I don't know how to act. Why can't I go to a party by myself? Why am I excluded unless I'm with a man?"

"Beats me. It's just a fact of life, I'm afraid. The only people I've found who are comfortable hanging out with me and my kids are other single parents, a few single men without kids, and childless couples." Precious few two-parent families have included me and my children. I'm never invited to couples' functions unless I have a man on my arm. I have friendships with married women, but we see each other without the husbands around.

Lots of people begin dating before they're comfortable because of this left-out feeling. We all long to belong, and single-again adults, particularly single parents, too often feel like square pegs trying to fit in round holes. No go.

"Don't push yourself," I told this woman. "Focus on building friendships with people who make you feel safe, accepted, and understood. Give yourself time. Remember that baby-step thing. Don't be pushed into dating before you're ready. Trust your own heart."

Have you dated yet? Conventional wisdom says to wait, to deal with your pain and your baggage, so you don't dump it into some new person's lap. When you look at members of the opposite sex as possible dating partners, what feelings come up in you? Men, how many women *friends* do you have? Women, how about you? How are those relationships valuable to you?

> *Father, help me to know when it's time to venture out into the world of dating again. Show me how to take baby steps. Let me first focus on building friendships. Help me to take it slow and easy.*   Amen

WEEK EIGHTEEN

Then he got into the boat and his disciples followed him. Without warning, a furious storm came up on the lake, so that the waves swept up over the boat. But Jesus was sleeping. The disciples went and woke him, saying, "Lord, save us! We're going to drown!" He replied, "You of little faith, why are you so afraid?" Then he got up and rebuked the winds and the waves, and it was completely calm.

Matthew 8:23-26

I love the ocean, and I check my tide chart daily. At low tide a strip of beach appears between the cliffs and the waves. The dog and I love to walk on the sand. Off goes the leash. Off go the shoes. His pace matches mine, and our feet making tiny splashes in the gentle, lapping waves.

One morning recently I checked the chart. Yes, there would be lots of beach, or so I thought. I set off with a smile. The first big storm of winter was on its way, however, and the ocean was wild, angry, churning, and foreign. Waves pounded the cliffs with exploding walls of water. My tide chart with its neat little predictions had been rendered temporarily meaningless.

The storms of life are like that. They take us by surprise; they churn up the sea around us and threaten to beat us to death if we don't retreat to higher ground. We can become so caught up their intensity that we forget they end. Like Jesus' disciples, we're sure we're going to drown.

When the familiar and expected is obliterated by a storm, Jesus can calm us. He can bring us peace, if we let him. Paul says it best in Philippians 4:6-7. Read the verses in your Bible. Open your journal. Write these two verses in it and write a letter to God sharing with him your fears of being overcome by the storms of life.

Dearest Jesus, calm my internal storms. Help me to turn them over to you. Give me the peace that transcends understanding, Lord.   Amen

WEEK EIGHTEEN: MONDAY
YOU MEAN I GET MORE THAN ONE CHANCE?

> Then the Lord spoke to Jonah a second time: "Get up and go to the great city of Nineveh, and deliver the message of judgment I have given you."   Jonah 3:1, NLT

Our God is the God of second chances. He wants us to build on our hopes, not become paralyzed by our hurts. He wants us to move forward into the future, not remain stuck in the past. And finally, he wants us to move forward in a spirit of faith, not get stuck in the quicksand of "I'm a failure."

Yet we're all going to fail. Remember when you first tried to drive a car? (Make that a stick shift!) How did you do? Did you hop in, turn the key, fire up the engine on the first try, shift smoothly into reverse, back right on out of the garage, and cruise off down the street, doing everything with ease, right down to perfect parallel parking?

I don't think so! Failure is a part of life. It just is! We all want to excel, succeed, and look good. We hate to admit defeat. We hate to admit that we can't master this one new thing as quickly as we'd like. But God is patient, a lot more patient than you or I. *And he doesn't want us to get all hung up on thinking we're no good as people just because we failed at something. Even a marriage.*

What have you failed at recently? Or what have you had more difficulty mastering than you'd anticipated? How did you react? After reading today's verse, do you think God will give you another chance? (Stop and read the whole biblical book of Jonah—two pages long.) Do you think he still loves you as much as he did before your failure?

> *God, thank you for allowing me the freedom to fail. Help me to pick myself up, dust myself off, and get back on track. Don't let me wallow too long, Lord.* Amen

WEEK EIGHTEEN: TUESDAY
NEW TRADITIONS FOR OLD HOLIDAYS

> Hold on to the pattern of right teaching you learned from me. And remember to live in the faith and love that you have in Christ Jesus. With the help of the Holy Spirit who lives within us, carefully guard what has been entrusted to you.
> 2 Timothy 1:13-14, NLT

Because I became single-again in November, the holiday season was upon me almost immediately. Thanksgiving, Christmas, and New Year's hit me in rapid-fire succession. I pretty much sleep-walked through the holidays that first year. At parties I surrounded myself with family and friends, people who wouldn't ask me a whole lot of uncomfortable questions. I was not up to discussing the changes in my over hors d'oeuvres, thank you very much. When some well-intentioned acquaintance or relative caught me without my body guards and pelted me with a barrage of intrusive questions, I found myself mumbling incoherently and making the quickest exit possible.

I made it through—barely. In January I sleep-walked through my daughter's sixth birthday (it was a slumber party; need I say more?), and before I knew it, I was flipping my calendar over to February.

Valentine's Day. The holiday that means a dozen red roses and a mushy card. A candle-light dinner with my honey, complete with gently entwined fingers and tender, loving looks passing back and forth. That's the fantasy, right?

Or how about this cynical view? Valentine's Day, that ridiculous, commercial holiday created by the media specifically to separate people from their money and to make the singles feel miserable, totally alone, and like bonafide, certified failures at love. I didn't want to buy into either of these mind sets, so I put on my thinking cap.

I called Kathy. We made a pact then and there to have dinner together on Valentine's Day. We hired a sitter to watch all five of our kids. We dressed up and took ourselves out to a delicious dinner at a trendy beach-side eatery. We did this three years in a row. Finally the fourth year, she had a date with a man. Rather than sit home and pout, I took my kids out for a spaghetti feast. We toasted our love for each other with sparkling cider. We had a blast!

It's important to be creative and come up with some new, upbeat traditions for the holidays. Otherwise, we're guaranteed to find ourselves facing an emotional and spiritual crisis that is likely to end up with us crying sad, lonely tears into our pillows. Is your family nearby? If not, do you have close friends who will include you at Thanksgiving and Christmas dinner? Several years ago, the singles' group at my church had potluck dinners for people alone at the holidays. They had a Mother's Day brunch where the single dads and kids cooked up a feast for the single moms. On Father's Day the moms and kids cooked for the dads. It was great fun. Get together with some of your single friends and do some planning. It will help keep those holiday blues at bay!

Father, help me to begin building some new traditions for the holidays. Help me to focus on your Spirit of power, love, and self-discipline so that I don't get stuck feeling sorry for myself. Amen

WEEK EIGHTEEN: WEDNESDAY
TIME OUT TO PLANT A GARDEN

Some people are always grumbling because roses have thorns. I am thankful that thorns have roses.   Alphonse Karr

As you begin today's reading, please understand that I have no idea what time of year it is. It could be December; it could be August. It doesn't matter. You can begin planning and planting a garden today. I'm talking fun plants—not just grass and ground cover and bushes. I'm talking flowers, herbs, vegetables, and fruit.

First of all, a trip to the library is in order to check out some books on gardening in your area. What grows well in your climate? When are the best planting times? Now you need to evaluate your backyard or patio. How much space do you have for a garden? How much sunlight do you get at different times of the year? Look at the pictures and let yourself imagine the plants flourishing outside your home. Imagine backyard barbecues in the summer with a profusion of flowers blooming and watermelon or zucchini to pluck from their vines. Can it be done? Yes! Jot down some ideas from the gardening books.

Next, take a serious inventory of the lighting inside your house or apartment. Do you have a window with great northern light in the winter? Do you have a west-facing window that gets filtered sunlight all year 'round? If you have houseplants, check them out. Which ones are doing the best, and in what kind of light?

After you've done your preliminary research, take a trip to the nursery. Try to go when it won't be busy, so you can ask for advice. Take notes. Go back again if you need to. You can start seedlings in the house and transplant them later. It's the cheapest way. You can involve your children. And when your garden blooms, *your hearts will overflow with gratitude.*

> *Father, thank you for creating so many things of such exquisite beauty in this world. Please help me to bring some of your world into my home and to let my garden remind me always of your majesty.*   *Amen*

WEEK EIGHTEEN: THURSDAY
CAN I REALLY CONTROL MY ANGER?

> A fool is quick-tempered, but a wise person stays calm when insulted.   Proverbs 12:16, NLT

The details are immaterial, suffice it to say that an estranged husband and wife were standing in the kitchen of the home they had shared for years. Later she told me what happened. She felt provoked, and, she said, "I lost it. I must've spewed for ten minutes. Then he started in on me. I couldn't believe it. The words that came out of that man's mouth! Our son was sitting at the kitchen table patiently waiting for his food and here's his father, swearing at the top of his lungs. The things he called me! It was the worst ever, by far. I've never been called those names in my life! He scared our son right out of the room." Then she laughed.

"What's so funny?" I asked.

"I was drinking this glass of milk. All I can see when I replay the scene in my mind is his beat-red face all twisted up with rage. I looked from him to the glass in my hand. In my mind I saw my arm go back and then let go with a snap of the wrist, showering him in milk. I wanted to do it so bad! But something stopped me. The grace of God, no doubt. I didn't do it. I just took a deep breath and let him vent. Then he stormed off."

Later he apologized. She continued, "I am so glad I didn't throw that glass of milk in his face."

How does this story speak to you? Does it strike any familiar cords? Have you ever found yourself in the middle of a hideous argument with your ex, ready to really let him or her have it, when suddenly, and out of nowhere, you felt an invisible tap on your shoulder? At times like that, it's as though God is saying, *Hello! Time out! Disengage!* Have you heard him?

> *God, please help me to hear your gentle nudging voice, to keep a*
> *bridle on my mouth and to stay calm when insulted.*
> *Amen*

WEEK EIGHTEEN: FRIDAY
REAPING POISONOUS WEEDS

> They spout empty words and make promises they don't intend
> to keep. So perverted justice springs up among them like
> poisonous weeds in a farmer's field.
> Hosea 10:4, NLT

I've often wondered why so many fathers have such a hard time paying their child support, so I asked several men what they thought. I also read what Judith Wallerstein says on the subject in her book *Second Chances*. Here's what I gleaned: The man writes a check each month to his ex-wife. If there is unresolved anger between them, this check serves as a nagging reminder, not only of the fact that his children are no longer there to greet him at night when he comes home from a hard day of work, but also that his ex-wife can spend *his* money however she pleases.

"She could manage without my money," one man told me. "I feel like I'm just supplementing her lifestyle. I'm sure she spends my money on getting her nails done. Perms. Clothes. I bet only a little of it goes to the boys. I resent it. I feel cheated. And I dock her check whenever I can."

He sounded like a parent docking a naughty child's allowance. "But isn't this about your kids?" I asked him. "What makes you think your money isn't going for their food, clothing, and shelter?"

"Please! There's no way she could spend all that money on my sons. If she gave me a monthly breakdown with receipts, well then maybe I'd believe her. But as it is, she doesn't have to be accountable in any way."

"Would you mind terribly if I asked you how much you pay?"

"Seven fifty a month."

"For each child?!"

"No. For all three boys. Total. That's more than she needs."

I was stunned. This guy had a new car, a nice house. He had a decent job. His ex-wife and kids lived in a run-down apartment. She worked full-time and left her children to fend for themselves after school. She was always exhausted and broke and complained bitterly about her ex-husband's extravagant lifestyle.

The money that passes from hand to hand every month can be a source of serious, ongoing strife. But it's for the children, right? What would you tell this man? What would you tell his ex-wife? How could they manage the situation more effectively?

Father, help me keep my promises so I'm honorable in my dealings with my ex. I want to get past the blaming, and grow in goodness, kindness, and love.   Amen

WEEK EIGHTEEN: SATURDAY
MON (DAD) NEEDS TO GET A LIFE!

> Are you tired? Worn out? Burned out on religion? Come to Me. Get away with Me and you'll recover your life. I'll show you how to take a real rest. Walk with Me and work with Me—watch how I do it. Learn the unforced rhythms of grace. I won't lay anything heavy or ill-fitting on you. Keep company with Me and you'll learn to live freely and lightly.
>
> From Matthew 11, The Message

It's easy to get in a rut. Especially during the long winter months, single parents can find themselves home alone with their kids night after night after night. Weekends can be filled to the brim with soccer, baseball and basketball—activities that revolve around the kids. On weekends when the kids are at their dad's, Mom is catching up on laundry, cleaning, and bill paying. She doesn't have a life. She feels as if she's been sealed off in a tomb of isolation.

This happened to Kathy when I moved away for a year. She called me one Saturday morning. She was crying. "I don't have a life," she said. "Since you've gone, I'm all alone. Alone. Alone. Alone. It's just me and my kids, day in and day out. Night in and night out. How do I get a life?"

Not being a highly social person, this was more of a challenge for her than it would have been for me. "How long since you've gone out with a grown up?" I asked.

She laughed in spite of herself. "Are you kidding? Once. Since you left."

"Have you been to church?"

"No. I can't seem to get up the energy. When my kids are here, they complain and say they don't want to go. I get so tired of fighting with them over it, I've just given up even trying. When they're gone, I can't seem to get myself out of bed weekend mornings."

"Well, dear. You aren't going to get anywhere unless you get yourself off ground zero. You are stuck and you are also the only person who can change that! So let's come up with some ideas to get you unstuck."

We put our heads together and came up with a list of four friends she could call and make plans with. She agreed that she needed to go to church—the next day—and try going to her church's large, active singles' group on Sunday night. Within a few months, she'd reconnected with one old friend, made a couple of new friends, and was feeling as if she had a life again. Are you feeling stuck? Burned out? What can you do to change that? Read again the passage from Matthew 11, above. Then brainstorm. Make a list. Do it! You deserve to have a life.

God, sometimes I feel so lost and so alone. I want to keep company with you and learn how to live freely and lightly. Amen

WEEK NINETEEN

WEEK NINETEEN: SUNDAY
911—RESCUE ME!

> Yet I am poor and needy; come quickly to me, O God. You are
> my help and my deliverer; O Lord, do not delay. Psalm 70:5

Being lonely is hard. It's so easy to run out to a bar, to answer a
classified ad, to go online to a singles' chat room, to join a singles' group
with a looking-for-love attitude, or to accept that blind date your friend
has been urging you to go on. Hoping. Hoping. Hoping to be rescued.
It's not just women who want to be rescued. Both women and men miss
having a mate. Both long for the completion that marriage brings. I
think it's harder to live without it when we've already had it, when we
know what we're missing.

Where do you turn when the loneliness gets overwhelming? Look
again at today's Bible verse. When we are poor and needy, desperate and
overcome with longing, the place we can turn is to God, the true lover
of our souls. Have you done that? Have you ever read Song of Songs
with the idea in mind that it's God's love we crave most, that satisfies
most deeply? Try doing that today.

> *God, I come to you poor and needy. I need you to come quickly*
> *to me. I need you to fill me up with your Spirit of love and*
> *comfort. Amen*

WEEK NINETEEN: MONDAY
REDISCOVER THE KID STUFF IN LIFE

I know that this world is a world of imagination and vision.
William Blake

What kind of stuff do kids like to do? Well, they like to stomp in puddles when it's raining. They like picnics, even when there are ants. They like trips to the beach where they can collect shells and sand crabs, go boogie boarding, and build sand castles. They like bike rides, walks in the woods, camping trips, swinging in hammocks, flying kites. They love scavenger hunts and treasure hunts of all kinds, whether they're searching for leaves, colored pebbles, bugs, tadpoles and frogs, birds' nests, crawdads, or tennis balls. They love to point flashlights at the stars and name the constellations. They love to play tag, Marco Polo, and Red Rover. They love to sing around a campfire, to laugh at silly jokes, and to create their own plays and dance productions.

Kids are amazing. But about the time we all hit junior high, we become either too self-conscious or too *cool* to do much kid stuff. We sort of forget about it in bits and pieces as the years progress. Once we get divorced, we believe we've forfeited our right to play. Life is too difficult, too painful, too much of a struggle.

Right now, take another index tab and write on it "Adventure Journal." Make a list of all the kid stuff that sounds good to you. Then take a day off this weekend and do kid stuff—whether you're with kids or kidless. It's your assignment! Don't forget your camera. These adventures belong on your refrigerator door.

Father, thank you for creating kids with an innate playfulness.
Help me to rediscover mine and use it to bring joyfulness to me
and those around me.   Amen

WEEK NINETEEN: TUESDAY
PRACTICING NEW COMMUNICATION STYLES

A friend may well be reckoned the masterpiece of nature.
Ralph Waldo Emerson

After we get divorced, our friends become far more important to us. We don't have a built-in, live-in best friend anymore, so we have to look outside of our homes for companionship. I was blessed to have Kathy as a neighbor for so many years. I never had to go more than a few steps to have someone to talk to.

Early on in our friendship, she and I decided we didn't have good communication skills. We had spent our married years either blaming, covering up for, or ignoring our husbands. Neither of us knew how to face conflict head-on and negotiate our way through it to a successful, loving conclusion. We were more the "Well-if-that's-what-you-think-then-fine-I-don't-even-want-to-discuss-it" mentality, better known as "my way or the highway." Not a real effective way to communicate.

So we made a pact to practice healthy communication styles on each other. We challenged ourselves to learn to speak the truth in love. To each other's faces—not behind the other's back. We shared our deepest, scariest secrets with each other and found, for the first time in our lives, acceptance. Affirmation. She's a songwriter, and I listened to her sing her songs. She read what I wrote. We lifted each other up when we were in the pits of despair. We encouraged when encouragement was called for, and we did a knock, knock, knock on the head to the other when she was off track.

Have we fought? Oh sure. We're human! I remember one morning we stood on opposite sides of my driveway yelling at each other. We'd been trying to start up a business together, and I felt I was doing more than my share. I was ticked off. She was ticked off at me for being such a martyr. We yelled. We cried. It was really tense. I was sure this was "it." We were done, finished, over as friends. I wanted to run inside and slam my door. But I didn't. Neither did Kathy. Somehow, by the grace of God, we finished venting our hurt feelings without trashing each other completely. Within fifteen minutes we were both hugging, laughing, and apologizing.

It wasn't easy. I haven't always been successful in working through conflicts with my friends, but I am incredibly grateful for all the lessons I've learned through and with Kathy. Her friendship is one of the greatest gifts God has ever bestowed on me. So today I ask you: Who is your closest friend? How do you communicate? Are you truly open, honest, and transparent with each other? What new, healthier styles of communication could you practice with each other? Call up your friend and read this passage aloud. Let your journal know the response.

Father, thank you for my friends. They are such an awesome gift. Help us to work together for our healing and your glory, Lord. Amen

WEEK NINETEEN: WEDNESDAY
"NO ONE PAYS ATTENTION TO ME ANYMORE"

Jesus loves me this I know, for the Bible tells me so.
Little ones to him belong. They are weak but he is strong.
Yes, Jesus loves me! Yes, Jesus loves me!
Yes, Jesus loves me! The Bible tells me so.

Anna S. Warner

My friend remarried a few years ago. She has two daughters, one from the new marriage; her new husband has two sons, both teenagers. This couple did their best to prepare for becoming a "blended family." They went to premarital counseling at their church. They read. They prayed. They still do. Only now they've seen firsthand that no one adequately prepared them for the realities of daily life in a blended family.

Her husband has 50 percent custody, so his sons spend every other week with him. My friend has her older daughter 70 percent of the time. The new daughter lives with them 100 percent of the time. Obviously, their kids are *always* on different schedules. When the boys are there, the household revolves around their activities. The toddler, being a toddler, consumes her mother's time and energy. There is precious little left over for her older sister, who's eight and introverted. She spends a lot of time in her room alone. She doesn't like her step-brothers, because they run the show when they're there. And they pick on her. My friend hasn't figured out a way to manage her new family's chaotic schedules. She tells me that "being in a blended family's a lot like being in a blender."

I've known other children who've faced problems when one of their parents remarried. After weekend visits with her father, his new wife, and their baby, one girl would come home to her mother crying. The girl felt like an afterthought. Or an instant baby-sitter. She didn't like it.

The girl's mother has a good rapport with her ex-husband. When she told him their daughter had problems, the two of them sat down together and brain stormed. They came up with some ideas for how they could help their daughter be more comfortable with the blended family at Dad's house. The situation improved drastically.

Is your ex-spouse remarried or living with someone? Are you considering remarriage? Are there other children in either new family? Are the needs of each child being addressed or does someone (or everyone) feel invisible, left out, and lonely? If this scenario fits you, is there someone you can talk to about it? If not, ask around. ASAP.

Jesus, help me to let my children know that you love them—way more even than I do—and that you'll be with them wherever they are. Help me to face any problems with new and blended families

with courage and grace—for the children's sake. For mine. For
yours.   Amen

WEEK NINETEEN: THURSDAY
SETTING PERSONAL GOALS

Friends, don't get me wrong: By no means do I count myself an
expert in all of this, but I've got my eye on the goal, where God
is beckoning us onward—to Jesus. I'm off and running, and I'm
not turning back.   From Philippians 3, The Message

About six months into single-again life, I was regaling a friend with
stories of my first foray into the dating world. I'd just been to a singles'
party, where I'd stood alone, glass in hand, sipping nervously and
holding in my stomach as I watched the seasoned veterans work the
crowd. No one talked to me. No one. I felt awkward, out-of-place, old,
and *really* dumb. It was like being in junior high again. A bona fide
wallflower, I wanted to fade into the background. Actually, I told my
friend, I wanted to be invisible. Inevitably it dawned on me that what I
really wanted was to be out of there! So I bailed.

She laughed. Then she said, "You know, Ann, you should write a
book!"

I looked at her as if she were nuts.

"No. Really. You should."

I went home and thought about it. I went to the beach, and I prayed
about it, talking with God at length as I walked along the shore. Finally,
a couple of weeks later, I found myself drawn to my computer. I was
writing with a fervor I'd never experienced before. Powered by the
emotions surging within me, I made a goal to write a novel. I did it.
Then I wrote another one. I committed to learn about and practice the
craft of writing so I would be taken seriously. It took seven years before

my work was published. I may not have had control over who would publish me or when, but I did have control over my own actions.

To do. To be. To have. To help. What would you do if you knew you couldn't fail? What would personally enrich you? If you don't name it, set a goal, and work for it, it's unlikely you'll ever get it.

Single parents, in particular, tend to focus the majority of their energy on their kids. Between the children, working, and running a household single-handedly, it's too easy to end up emotionally and spiritually bankrupt. Don't let your hectic life keep you stuck. Sit down today and make some personal goals—goals for *you* (not for your children). What would you love to do? (A goal should reflect your gifts, passions, abilities, style, and life experiences—not someone else's idea of who you ought to be.) What skills and personal qualities do you need to develop to reach a goal that will stretch you but one that is reasonable and attainable?

> *Father, I want to do what it is you created me to do. I want to be the person you created me to be. Show me the way, Lord. Amen*

WEEK NINETEEN: FRIDAY
THE MIRACLE OF ACCEPTING RESPONSIBILITY

> Ironically enough, true growth happens when you accept responsibility for things you're *not* responsible for.
>
> Jim Dyke

Pastor Jim Dyke consistently inspires me. As a guest speaker at our divorce recovery session, he gave the statement above. Twice so we'd all be sure to write it down. I sat up straight in my chair, pen poised, eyes wide open, mouth wide open, mind wide open. My entire being was in a receiving posture. Was he saying that no matter who's dumped on me—no matter how badly—I have to take responsibility for it? Then whom would I blame? Myself?

As I listened, a gigantic light bulb went off in my head. I remembered Jim Smoke's saying: "Growth begins where blaming ends." Wow! I got it! *I was going to have to take a giant step beyond the things other people had done to hurt me. I'd have to say, Yeah, some pretty raunchy things have happened to me. Now what? Do I whine for the rest of my life? Or do I move forward?*

We humans may have been created in the image of God, but that image has been shattered by the reality of sin in our lives. When I look at myself, the image staring back at me is distorted, as if I were looking at myself in a fun-house mirror. The same is true when I stare at others. We are all capable of great kindness; we are all capable of great cruelty. We perpetuate a cycle of cruelty if we get stuck in the mire of keeping track of the sins of others and craving retribution. I decided to make a choice for growth.

What painful things have happened to you that you weren't responsible for? List as many as you can. Have they become part of you? Can you take responsibility for moving beyond them? Explore this miracle-making concept in your journal.

> *Dear Lord, thank you for the wise people you bring into our lives. Please give me ears to hear their words, eyes to see the truth, and the courage to grow.   Amen*

WEEK NINETEEN: SATURDAY
BECOMING A RESOURCEFUL PROBLEM SOLVER

> The man who had received the five talents brought the other five. "Master," he said, "you entrusted me with five talents. See, I have gained five more."

His master replied, "Well done, good and faithful servant! You
have been faithful with a few things; I will put you in charge of
many things."   Matthew 25:20-21

Kathy called me from work one day. Her three boys were begging to
sign up for spring baseball, but she didn't know how she was going to
come up with the cash. We brain stormed for a few minutes, and she
hung up. Two hours later she called back. "Guess what?" she said. "I got
scholarships for the boys! All three of them!"

"How did you do it?"

"Well, I had to work my way up the ladder. It took me seven or eight
phone calls. Finally I was able to reach the guy who's in charge of the
whole program. When I got to him, I explained that I'm a single mom
with three boys who doesn't receive child support. I told him my boys
were dying to play baseball, and there was just no way I could afford the
fees or the uniforms. He said he wasn't sure if he could help, but he'd
make a few calls himself."

This man called her back within the hour. He'd located some
scholarship money, and her boys were able to play baseball.

Over the years I've marveled at Kathy's ability to pull things like this
off. She's incredibly resourceful. By that I mean that she's a creative,
tenacious problem solver.

When faced with a challenge, she brainstorms about it with someone
she trusts. When she's come up with a few different courses of action,
she diligently pursues each one until she has the problem solved. She
has an I-can-do-this attitude, and she has faith in her ability to pull
things off.

From Kathy I've learned that creative problem solving takes self-
confidence, determination, and self-discipline. It also requires courage
and boldness. Calling someone she didn't know and speaking in a timid
voice wouldn't yield the desired results. Neither would giving up easily.
It took seven or eight phone calls to find someone willing and able to

help her boys. She faces her problems directly and doesn't let fear paralyze her.

Whom do you know whose problem-solving style you particularly admire? If you know how he or she responds to a potential crisis, describe it. If not, call and ask her to tell you. Then describe it in your journal. What kind of problem solver are you? How could you become more like Kathy or the people whose style you admire?

Lord, I know that you want me to become a resourceful person.
Please lead me to people who are creative problem solvers so that
I can learn from them.   Amen

WEEK TWENTY

WEEK TWENTY: MONDAY
TIME OUT TO SEEK MY HEART'S LOVE

> All night long on my bed I looked for the one my heart loves; I looked for him but did not find him. I will get up now and go about the city, through its streets and squares; I will search for the one my heart loves. So I looked for him but did not find him. The watchmen found me as they made their rounds in the city. "Have you seen the one my heart loves?" Scarcely had I passed them when I found the one my heart loves. I held him and would not let him go till I had brought him to my mother's house. Song of Songs 3:1-4

Can you remember a time when you were wildly, crazily in love, but separated from your loved one? The longing. The aching. The agonizing. The wanting, needing, missing.

Do you love Jesus that way? Can you imagine running through the streets in the middle of the night crying out for him—asking everyone you come across if he's been seen? Can you imagine your fear; what if he's lost to you forever? How will you survive? Can you imagine that incredible rush of relief you get when you finally, actually find him and hold him again? Can you see yourself taking him to the safest place you know?

Jesus wants us to love him and want him and seek him with an all-encompassing passion. Most times, it is when we are single—alone and without a mate—that we can turn our passion toward him. It's easier to put him first because there's no other lover competing for our passion. (Even as a man, you can make the Spirit of Christ the love of your life, because you know that, as God, he transcends sexuality.) As Paul says in 1 Corinthians 7:32-33: "An unmarried man is concerned about the Lord's affairs—how he can please the Lord. But a married man is concerned about the affairs of this world—how he can please his wife—and his interests are divided."

Today, take your Bible and your journal and retreat to your sacred place. Write a love letter to Jesus.

> *Jesus, help me to fall completely, utterly, totally in love with you. Show me how I can please you, Lord, so that you will be first in my life from here on out. Amen*

WEEK TWENTY: TUESDAY
SETTING GOALS FOR MY FAMILY OF ORIGIN

> Just see what this godly sorrow produced in you! Such earnestness, such concern to clear yourselves, such indignation, such alarm, such longing to see me, such zeal, and such a readiness to punish the wrongdoer. You showed that you have done everything you could to make things right.
>
> 2 Corinthians 7:11, NLT

Making things right. What a concept! Our sense of self-worth is directly affected by the amount of emotional baggage we carry around, and that most of that baggage comes from our family of origin. Now, I'm not saying that "blame your parents" is the answer to anything.

Blaming anyone keeps us stuck. Remember, "Growth begins where blaming ends." Blaming Mom and Dad isn't the answer.

The rather rigid, controlling extended family of one divorcing woman rallied around her and helped her financially. At first she was incredibly grateful, but then the criticism set in. They wanted to dictate where she worked, whom she hung out with, what sports her children played, and even how she dressed and wore her hair. She tried and tried to assert herself, but the family dynamic was firmly entrenched. There were several of them and only one of her, and their perceptions of her kept forcing her back into the mold they'd created. After a great deal of frustration, she broke away from them altogether. They didn't speak for over a year. Walking away hurt her deeply, but she found great reserves of strength within herself. And she learned, she grew, she changed.

The last time I spoke with her, she'd been reconciled with her family for a while. "Things are so much better now," she said. "My parents and brothers haven't changed. They still try to run my life, but I can say no now. At first it was hard, and they raised a ruckus, but they're adapting. Each time I stand up to them, it gets a little easier. And I *know* I'm a much better role model for my kids now too."

A little later she said something that blew me away. "I probably love my family more than ever. I now see that they're doing the best they can, and I don't keep getting upset because *they're* not who I want them to be. I've come to accept them. I want the time we have left to be as good as it can be, and I know that God wants that for us too."

How are things in your family of origin? Are you able to accept and forgive others, which can keep clear your relationship with God? Or are you stuck in the blame game? Set some goals for yourself in this area. Seek supportive friends who have worked through some of their first family issues, and let them come alongside you.

Dear God, I want to learn to be accepting, forgiving, honest, and kind. Help me to forgive my parents for not being perfect.
Amen

WEEK TWENTY: WEDNESDAY
JUST ENOUGH GRACE FOR TODAY

I am the Lord, I am the Lord, the merciful and gracious God. I
am slow to anger and rich in unfailing love and faithfulness.
                                           Exodus 34:6, NLT

Here's an interesting theological point to ponder today: God's
holiness demands that sin be punished, yet his mercy compels him to
love that same person who committed the sin. So here's deserved
punishment on one hand, and mercy on the other. Which do we get?
Well, because Jesus died for us, he paid the penalty for us. That ultimate
punishment: death.

With that unbelievable act of grace, Jesus made it safe for us to be
honest with God. Now we're allowed, even encouraged, to step into his
presence and pour out our hearts to him. We don't have to hide behind
our secrets, hoping somehow that he won't find them out and punish
us for them. No. He already knows, and he wants us to own our sins,
take a deep breath, and ask for forgiveness.

Grace is undeserved favor and mercy. God bestows it on us daily, in
all sorts of ways. It may be a phone call out of the blue from a friend
who's moved away. It may be that check that came in the mail just in
time to pay the utility bill. It may be the delight you feel as you see a
flock of geese fly in a perfect V formation. It may be the awe that
overwhelms you when you hold a newborn in your arms for the first
time. It may be the unexpected joy that accompanies the reconciliation
and restoration of a broken relationship, even a marriage. It may be as
simple as basking in the beauty of a rose. Or as complex as the breaking
of a pattern of intergenerational sin.

Remember that tab I asked you to put in your journal: "Nuggets of
Grace"? Have you been noticing any of those nuggets of grace in your

life over the past weeks? How about committing today to start looking again. Remember, our healing is helped along as we look out and up instead of down and in.

Think back on the last week. What grace has God bestowed on you? Document it. From now on, every day when you write in your journal, ask yourself if there isn't an instance or two of undeserved mercy and favor that deserves to be written down. It will change the way you look at the world, I promise!

> *God, give me the ability to see the nuggets of grace you place in front of me every day. Thank you for loving me more than I can comprehend!   Amen*

WEEK TWENTY: THURSDAY
"BUT I WANT TO GO LIVE WITH DAD!"

> Discipline your children while there is hope. If you don't, you will ruin their lives.   Proverbs 19:18, NLT

He'd lived with his mom and siblings since he was five. His mom was gone from eight in the morning until six at night, five days a week. When she got home at night, she rushed around making dinner, doing laundry and other chores. She had a short fuse and yelled a lot when the kids goofed off or fought. She didn't have a lot of time or energy for him. She never seemed to have enough money.

She annoyed him to no end. While he sat alone in the house, afternoon after afternoon, playing video games or making a stab at doing his homework, he played different versions of the same fantasy over and over in his head. It always began the same way. He started by packing his bags. Methodically, he emptied out every drawer into a huge suitcase. Nothing was to be left. He took the bag to the living room and parked it by the front door. Then he took his computer apart and lugged each component out by the suitcase. Next he dismantled his TV and Nintendo set. Last he foraged through the kitchen and filled a grocery bag with snack food. He opened the fridge and took out a soda, sipping at it as he wrote a cryptic note to his mom: "I've gone to live with my dad." He didn't sign it.

The doorbell rang. Jubilant, he ran to open it. There stood his dad on the doorstep with open arms and a huge smile. The boy catapulted into his father's embrace. They hadn't seen each other for three months. Together they loaded up the car and drove off into the fading daylight.

When kids live with an overworked, stressed-out single parent, they often fantasize about going to live with the other parent. Sometimes, especially when they're older, a change of residence can be beneficial. But often they're just angry at Mom. And they're idealizing Dad. They imagine a perfect life with him and convince themselves that if they could just get away from the "old witch," everything would be better. Way better.

Is something like this going on in your family? If so, can you go off somewhere private with your child and do a feelings check? Can you allow the child's anger to spill out without reacting to it? Can you put together a plan with your son or daughter so that you're more available? Can you work together to find some constructive creative outlets for your child? Get together with a trusted friend or your single parents' group and brainstorm. Talk to God about it. Facing the problem of a resentful child is difficult. But facing it is the first (giant) step.

> Dear Lord, help me to face and deal with the challenges of being a single parent..   Amen

WEEK TWENTY: FRIDAY
FLIRTING AT FORTY?!

> "The Lord bless you, my daughter," [Boaz] replied. "This kindness is greater than that which you showed earlier: You have not run after the younger men, whether rich or poor. And now, my daughter, don't be afraid. I will do for you all you ask. All my fellow townsmen know that you are a woman of noble character."   Ruth 3:10-11

In our teens my girlfriends and I worked to perfect the art of "flirting." To entice the opposite sex, we rehearsed witty lines and charming facial expressions in front of the mirror. We wanted the boys we had our eyes on to really like us. Maybe even fall in love with us.

Been on a blind date lately?

Did you find yourself sitting across the table from a virtual stranger, choking down a cup of coffee while fielding questions such as, "How long have you been divorced? What went wrong with your marriage? How do you get along with your ex? How old are your kids? How much time do they spend with you? Are you in therapy? What kind of books have you read lately?" And finally: "What are you looking for in a dating relationship?"

In case you haven't caught on—this is *not* a casual conversation! It's an interview for the position of Significant Other. I've been on more than one such date, and, if you ask me, it amounts to nothing less than an interrogation. Get all that dirty laundry out there up front, and if the guy isn't scared away, well then, hey, maybe there's hope. (Unless of course he's Mr. Fix-It on the lookout for a new project.) If you botch the interview, you can expect the great hook to appear from stage left, grab you by the neck, and whisk you away. Off stage. Out of sight. Out of the running. Next! Not!

Our society shoves its notion of romantic love down our throats. The media saturates us with it. But, having gone through a painful ending of our most significant relationship, we approach love at midlife with caution. We know better than to trust that overpowering rush of emotions—the urge to merge with another. But how do we avoid swinging to the opposite extreme, allowing caution to turn to paranoia?

I was kayaking with a friend a couple of years ago. I was sharing my loneliness with her and wondering aloud how I could meet a compatible man. "Just do what you love to do," she said. "Pursue your interests, like kayaking. Be yourself and live your life well. He'll show up."

I thought about that a lot. Maybe this formal, awkward, juvenile thing called dating wasn't the answer at my age. Maybe friendship was. What do you think? What adventures have you had in reaching out to the opposite sex?

God, thank you for reminding me to live my life well first of all.
I trust that you will bring new opposite-sex friends into my life.
Help me to appreciate them and to get to know them slowly.
Amen

WEEK TWENTY: SATURDAY
POURING MY HEART OUT TO GOD

O Lord, you are so good, so ready to forgive, so full of unfailing love for all who ask your aid.   Psalm 86:5, NLT

I'm about to refresh your memory and again lay out that paradoxical quote: "True growth begins when I take responsibility for things that were not my fault." Memorize it. I did. I needed to have it in my memory bank to draw upon whenever necessary. It reminds me that even when someone hurts me deeply and unfairly, it's *my* responsibility to get past it. Not his. Mine. But how do I do it? How do I forgive the one(s) who hurt me so badly? Especially if I can't communicate with him in a healthy way? Consider what Oswald Chambers said about being beaten down and broken: "The call of God has nothing to do with our own elevation, but with the lowering of self. To be made broken bread and poured out wine."

Close your eyes and think on that for a moment. When we go through trials, God uses this time to humble us and teach us, so we can fulfill the purpose he has for us. Although it hurts like crazy to be stomped on and torn up, there's a lesson for us hidden behind every adversity, if only we can hang in there and make it through the painful part.

Pastor Don Seltzer once remarked that it wouldn't be so bad if God used his own fingers to break us and his own feet to crush us. But he doesn't. On the contrary, he uses someone we dislike. Or someone we still love who doesn't love us. Or he uses a set of circumstances to which we've sworn we'd *never* submit. When he uses painful situations and nasty people to crush us, we don't like it! Not at all!

But broken bread and poured out wine are the symbols of the body and blood of Christ. If we're ever going to become like him, we have to be broken. We have to submit to the process, knowing that we will be changed in the process, for the better; knowing that God is using this suffering to grow us up, deepen our compassion and ready us to be used in ways that will help his other children. For this process not to make us bitter, we have to learn to forgive. It's paramount. Crucial. Mandatory.

What unfair things have happened to you since your divorce? What people have wronged you? What did they do or say? Pour your heart out to God today in your journal. Give him all your pain, anger, and frustration.

> *Jesus, I give you all the hurt I can find within me. I carry it to you, to the foot of the cross, and I leave it with you there. I want to be as broken bread and poured out wine. Help me to see the lessons. Help me to forgive.* Amen

WEEK TWENTY-ONE

WEEK TWENTY-ONE: SUNDAY
IDENTIFYING SAFE PEOPLE

> When you knock on a door, be courteous in your greeting. If they welcome you, be gentle in your conversation. If they don't welcome you, quietly withdraw. Don't make a scene. Shrug your shoulders and be on your way.
>
> From Matthew 10, The Message

Who are safe people? Henry Cloud and John Townsend have written a great book titled *Safe People*. They provide several personal traits they list by which you can identify people who will be good for you:

Safe people admit their weaknesses. Safe people are spiritual. They're open to feedback. They're humble. They apologize and change their behavior. Safe people deal with their problems. Safe people admit their faults and earn trust. They take responsibility for their problems. Safe people are truthful, growing, and changing.

How do safe people connect with us? Safe people connect intimately. They're concerned about others. Safe people encourage the freedom of others. Safe people confront us with the truth, but they're also forgiving. They relate to us as equals. Safe people are considerate over time, and they're a positive influence on our lives.

What about the other guys? The unsafe, toxic folks? What do Cloud and Townsend have to say about them? How can we spot them? Here are the traits unsafe people exhibit:

Unsafe people appear to have it all together. They're religious (rather than spiritual). They're defensive. They're self-righteous. They do not apologize. Unsafe people don't work on their problems, because they claim to be perfect and thus "don't have any." They demand that we trust them. Unsafe people blame others for their problems. They lie and they deceive. They're stagnant.

How do these toxic people relate with us? They avoid closeness. They're concerned only with themselves. They're controlling. Unsafe people will flatter us, but they'll also condemn and criticize us cruelly. They relate to us as a parent to a child, making us feel small, weak, and stupid. Unsafe people are unstable over time, exerting a negative influence over our lives.

Phew! Make a list of eight to twelve of the most influential people in your life. This list can include parents, siblings, other relatives, friends, former friends, and even your ex-spouse. Which of the safe and unsafe traits does each exhibit? Which of the safe and unsafe ways of connecting does each exhibit in relationship with you? We become like the people we associate with. *Commit to God right now to move toward safe people and away from unsafe ones.*

> *Father, I want to be a safe person. I want to glorify you, through who I am, how I behave, and whom I associate with. Move me toward safe relationships. Open my eyes so that I can see the unsafe ones and move away from them. Thank you, Lord for loving me so.   Amen*

WEEK TWENTY-ONE: MONDAY
HIT THAT NOTE!

The passion which resides in an individual is new in nature, and none but he knows what this is which he can do, nor does he know until he has tried.   Ralph Waldo Emerson

A year or two ago I was watching the Golden Globe Awards on TV. Dustin Hoffman received a special honor for his lifetime achievements in motion pictures. His acceptance speech revolved around a theme central to all artists: hitting that note. What did he mean? He explained that musicians always strive to find that perfect note, the note that captures and embodies what they hear in their hearts. An actor's note could be the moment he merges with his character and brings to life the essence of that person's struggles and triumphs. Painters and photographers hit their notes when the images captured on paper move people powerfully. For a writer it's finding the words that ignite people's hearts and minds.

Whether we are musicians, actors, artists, writers, or...we all long to hit our notes. We all long to do something meaningful that will touch others deeply. You may be saying right now, *Well, I am no artist, thank you very much. My life is boring, boring, boring. And so am I.*

That's not true. God created you as a one-of-a-kind being. He gave you your personality; he gave you your body; he gave you your intelligence, your sense of humor, your emotions, and your talents. He also gifted you spiritually. The passion in you is "new in nature," unique. Your spiritual gifts make you soar. They minister to the hearts, minds, and souls of others. I remember a pastor saying that our gifts are usually noticed and called out by others; we tend to overlook them in ourselves.

Have you ever considered taking a class on spiritual gifts? I did once and I loved it. If your church doesn't offer one, ask your pastor if he or she would be interested in starting a Bible study on gifts. Do it and you will hit that note. You will!

Father, please lead me to your people who will help me to uncover and nurture my spiritual gifts and my special talents. Thank you for creating me in your image, Lord, and let me not forget how much you adore me.   *Amen*

WEEK TWENTY-ONE: TUESDAY
HOW DO I COMMUNICATE EFFECTIVELY WITH MY EX?

If you have legal disputes about such matters, why do you go to outside judges who are not respected by the church? I am saying this to shame you. Isn't there anyone in all the church who is wise enough to decide these arguments?

1 Corinthians 6:4-5, NLT

At a single parents' group a few years ago, we put together a list of tips for maintaining ongoing communication with one's ex-spouse. You may want to copy them down and keep them handy.

- When dealing with your ex, put your children's needs first. Always.
- When you have a difference of opinion with your ex regarding the children, communicate it in a respectful, polite, and honest manner.
- Listen to the other party so you can understand his or her position.
- Think creatively as you problem solve together.
- Be flexible and don't keep score, but be willing to say no if you need to.

- If things get heated, make every effort to maintain your self-control. Take a time-out if you're on the verge of losing it. Try not to take things too personally.
- Make sure you keep your word. This is a critical part of building and maintaining trust, which is the foundation of any healthy relationship.
- If you're facing a volatile, acrimonious ex-spouse in front of a third party, pray with a close friend or pastor beforehand. Commit the relationship and the situation to Christ and let your heart not be troubled.
- Hold fast to hope. God is with you. He also moves mountains.

Lord God, I want to develop effective, loving communication with my ex. I want to be an example for others to follow. Help me to keep you before me, always.   Amen

WEEK TWENTY-ONE: WEDNESDAY
GOD WILL MEET MY NEEDS

I've told you all this so that trusting me, you will be unshakable and assured, deeply at peace. In this godless world you will continue to experience difficulties. But take heart! I've conquered the world.   From John 16, The Message

The story of God coming to the rescue of a desperate single mom is told in 2 Kings 4:1-7. One day the widow of one of Elisha's fellow prophets came to Elisha in tears, because a creditor was demanding that she sell her two sons into slavery to repay her debt. This penniless woman had nothing left in her house except a flask of olive oil. The prophet instructed her to borrow as many empty jars as she could from her friends and neighbors. Then she was to go into the house with her sons, close the door, and pour olive oil from her flask into the empty jars.

She did as he instructed. Soon every jar in the house was filled to the brim. When she was finished, she ran to tell Elisha what had happened. He told her to sell the olive oil, to pay her debts and then to support her family.

Are you at the end of your rope? Do you feel as if you have nowhere to turn and nothing to give? God has given you a flask of oil, just as he did the widow. Just open your eyes and you'll see evidence of his gifts around you. They're there. Something as insignificant as a flask of olive oil could very well be the answer to your prayer; it could be just the thing that will save you! God expects you to use what you have. After all, he promises us that if we use our gifts well, if we are good and faithful servants, he will multiply what we have.

Your assignment today is to read Matthew 25:14-30 and 2 Kings 4:1-7. Then take a good, hard look around you. Ask God to help you discover your flask of olive oil. Ask him to show you how to use it—to help yourself and your children and to help others around you who are in need.

> *Lord, I want to be a good and faithful servant. I want to discover what it is that you've already given me and use it as you desire so that it will multiply, gifting not only me and my children, but others as well. Amen*

WEEK TWENTY-ONE: THURSDAY
CALLING IT QUITS

To have such lawsuits at all is a real defeat for you. Why not just accept the injustice and leave it at that? Why not let yourselves be cheated? But instead, you yourselves are the ones who do wrong and cheat even your own Christian brothers and sisters.

1 Corinthians 6:7-8, NLT

A man went through an ugly, expensive custody battle and lost, only to have his ex turn their son over to him a year later. He put it this way: "I'd wake up at three or four in the morning, head pounding and pulse racing. All I could see was her face. I wanted to smash it in with a shovel. Then I'd take a gun and shoot out both of her knee caps. Hers and her lawyer's. Next I'd tear their fingers off, one at a time. I'd inject them both with arsenic so they'd die slow, agonizing deaths."

He continued, "For too many years we treated our son like a piece of property. She wanted him. I wanted him. We hated each other, so there was no way we could even conceive of sharing him!" Because I could sense that he'd overcome his anger, I asked him how he'd managed to get past it. "I just burned out. It took too much energy to keep on hating her like that. And I finally came to understand that we were hurting our son most of all. We needed to treat each other decently, for his sake."

His relationship with his ex will always be challenging, but he found a way to douse the fires of hate, and since then things have been far more peaceful. When I heard his story, I wondered: How does one put out a wildfire? How does someone replace bitterness, blaming, and hatred with kindness, forgiveness, and love? Does someone wait until the fires burn themselves out, or does one grab a fire extinguisher and start dousing the flames?

Do you fight crazily with your ex? If not, do you know people who do? As a Christian, how would you describe the way we're supposed to respond to vicious, slanderous, unfair attacks? What does today's scripture say to your heart? If you followed it, how would your actions and words change?

Heavenly Father, I need a change of heart. Too often I find myself getting caught up in the battle, flinging fire bombs and stink bombs at my ex. Help me to stop this, Lord. Show me how I should behave.   Amen

WEEK TWENTY-ONE: FRIDAY
SELF-CONTROL, WHO NEEDS IT?

> Remember how the Lord your God led you all the way in the
> desert these forty years, to humble you and to test you in order
> to know what was in your heart, whether or not you would keep
> his commands.   Deuteronomy 8:2

I keep a card taped to my computer that lists nine qualities from
Galatians 5:22-23 that I want to cultivate. The fruit of the Spirit: "love,
joy, peace, patience, kindness, goodness, faithfulness, gentleness and self
control." When I get to the last one, I can't help but remember my good
friend, Kim's comment that once stopped me dead in my tracks: "The
only real control is self-control."

Think about it. Who else's behavior can we control except our own?
And how successful are we at that?

What is self-control? We think it's about conquering our bad habits.
If we give up cigarettes, alcohol, sex (if we're single), swearing, or
whatever plagues us, we get to feeling smug and self-righteous. Like the
ex-smoker who is loudly intolerant of second-hand smoke, we look
down our noses at people who appear to have less self-control than we.
There must be more to self-control than triumphing over sinful habits,
because self-righteousness is not one of the fruit of the Spirit!

Ditching our bad habits is a start, but it is not enough. Learning self-
control is about being tested on every level and flunking a whole bunch
of times. It's about humiliation—that ugly, helpless feeling that comes
when we finally accept that we can't do this. *We can't do it on our own.
We have to rely on God and obey him.* We would really rather not obey.
We would really rather be in charge and do things *our* own way!

God doesn't teach us self-control in the easy times. He teaches us
self-control when we're lost in the wilderness, when we're down, dirty,
hungry, broken, and humiliated. It's only then, when we're beyond the

end of our ropes, that we turn to him and trust him. Completely. *It's only when we realize how much it hurts—how destructive it is to us to be disobedient—that we resolve to obey. And mean it.*

The biblical epistle of James has a lot to say on self-control. So does Proverbs. Check them out today when you retreat to your private place with Bible and journal in hand. In what areas could you use more self-control?

> *Father, I need self-control in every facet of my life. Please help me to keep my eyes on you, so I may experience the joy that comes from submitting to you. Amen*

WEEK TWENTY-ONE: SATURDAY
WHAT IS EMOTIONAL MATURITY ANYWAY?

> Love is patient, love is kind. It does not envy. It does not boast; it is not proud. It is not rude, it is not self-seeking, it is not easily angered, it keeps no record of wrongs. Love does not delight in evil but rejoices with the truth. It always protects, always trusts, always hopes, always perseveres. Love never fails.
> 1 Corinthians 13:4-8a

I doubt I will ever become fully mature evolved while I am here on planet Earth. I doubt that any of us will. We'll be in process until the day we die and leave this Earth. That's what God wants from us, I think. He wants us to keep on keeping on—growing and seeking Him the entire time we're here. So while I don't think I'll ever be able to puff out my chest and say, "I have reached the pinnacle. I'm emotionally mature now, thank you very much!" I do want to move in that direction.

So how do we know if we're growing in emotional maturity anyway? Well, I believe that our first clue would be that we're becoming aware of our feelings. We're learning to listen to the messages we give ourselves.

We've listened to those crusty old tapes running through our heads a few times and actively challenged what they told us. Feelings that were once hidden from us, and ran our lives by remote control, are now increasingly becoming visible. Our buttons from childhood are being exposed, one by one and gently deactivated. We are learning to be gentle and accepting of ourselves and others. We see better, we hear better and we do truth better now.

We're also learning to admit our mistakes and ask for forgiveness. We're working at developing our empathy for others. As we replace our sour, critical old tapes with new ones that love, nurture and encourage us, we are increasingly able to act kindly and generously towards other people as well. Our awareness is coupled with self-control as we do less and less of the things that would hurt us and impede our growth, and learn to treat ourselves as beings worthy of dignity and respect. We're learning to set goals and work towards them. We're finally outgrowing our Disneyland mind set because we're not living in Fantasyland, Frontierland or Tomorrowland anymore. And we know that if we miss the raft and get stuck on Tom Sawyer's Island—we'll make it through the night!

Look in two or three different sources and come up with your own personal definition of emotional maturity. How have you grown in the past months? Which areas would you like to concentrate on for the next few months?

> *Father-Mother God, help me to stay in touch with my feelings.*
> *Help me to see and hear more clearly. Help me be gentle with*
> *myself and others, and help me to grow in self-control.*
> *Amen*

WEEK TWENTY-TWO

WEEK TWENTY-TWO: SUNDAY
STANDARDS, BAGGAGE, AND BOUNDARIES

> Our sexual behavior is determined by our standards, our
> boundaries and our baggage.   Jim Dyke

One of the best talks I ever heard on the subject of sex and
dating was given by Pastor Jim Dyke. He gave his discussion the
appropriate and humorous title of "Sex without the Theology."
Rather than laying a bunch of legalistic "thou shalts" and "thou
shalt nots" on the group, he told us he was determined to take a
kinder, gentler, less antagonistic approach. Read the quote for
today again. *Standards, boundaries* and *baggage*. That's what
defines us sexually.

Being a realistic man, Jim knew that people who make the
commitment to remain celibate *only* because they're *supposed to*
don't have much success remaining celibate. I've seen statistics
where single-again Christians admit to having sex by the third
date, on the average. My experience with singles' groups parallels
that. Sex and dating are synonymous in modern America.

Jim said, "If you don't know what your *standards* are, then ask
yourself : *What is best for me?* Consider your own boundaries. He
went on to explain that our *boundaries* are built by what we say yes
and no to. Our boundaries come from our sense and awareness of
our own personal value. People with poor boundaries often say

yes and wish they'd said no. Why? Sometimes we're incapable of placing a value on ourselves. We externalize. We judge ourselves by others' standards and feel diminished when they don't appreciate us as we'd hoped they would.

That brings our *baggage* into play. Baggage is our old, unfinished business from the past. We may fear being rejected. We may fear making another mistake. We may believe we're "tarnished goods," forever doomed to living without love and sexual fulfillment. The only way to dump our baggage is to open those suitcases and slay the dragons hiding inside. The only way to discover our true worth is to go to the right source. Once we do, we'll come to see that we are people of infinite worth to God. And that will allow us to say yes when we mean yes and no when we don't. It will help us to protect ourselves from making poor choices sexually—choices that demean rather than celebrate our personhood.

What are your *standards, boundaries* and *baggage* with regards to sex and dating? In an honest, vulnerable way, write a letter to God and express your thoughts and feelings to him.

> *Father, dating and sex confound me. Please help me to see that I am a person of infinite worth to you and to avoid giving myself away cheaply.*   *Amen*

WEEK TWENTY-TWO: MONDAY
GETTING A HANDLE ON FINANCES

> Trust in the Lord and do good. Then you will live safely in the land and prosper. Take delight in the Lord and He will give you your heart's desires.   Psalm 37:3-4, NLT

If you're like many newly single people, just surviving from month to month is almost more than you can handle. Chances are, your standard of living isn't quite what it used to be and money never seems to stretch far enough. So you're probably sitting there saying to yourself, *Come on. Don't even ask me to set financial goals! I can't see any way out of this hand-to-mouth existence. Save money?! Please!*

But you know what? Paul went from living in luxury to being thrown in prison, to being shipwrecked, to living under house arrest in Rome. And he learned the big secret: He learned how to be joyful and grateful no matter where God sent him. He was joyful because he knew he was doing God's work. He was grateful because Christ gave always provided him with the strength he needed to get the job done.

When you've just gone through a divorce and your finances have been torn asunder like everything else in your life, it's critical that you not hide your head in the sand. It's necessary to face your financial situation with your eyes open. It's important to take charge of it and to do research, ask a lot of questions; learn as much as you can so you can plan for your financial future.

Banks, churches and community colleges all offer courses in financial planning. You may be screaming silently, *No! I hate that stuff! Please don't ask me do it!* But you know what? Learning how to plan for the future financially may be a pain; it may be a bore, but if you don't do it, you'll wish you had someday.

Your assignment for today is to sit yourself down and review your finances.

The first step is to find out where you are right now. The next is to decide where you

want to be and to formulate a plan for getting there. If you don't know the first thing

about money management and you're feeling completely overwhelmed, make some calls. Find a friend who can help you, or sign up for a class. Remember, most of us struggle financially for *years* after our divorces are final. Understanding your financial situation is half the battle. Figure that out and you'll be half way to getting where you want to be!

Father, help me to learn the secret of being joyful and grateful, no matter how much money I have. Help me also to set some financial goals so that I can move forward responsibly and hopefully. Amen

WEEK TWENTY-TWO: TUESDAY
SURVIVE OR THRIVE?

[God said,] Who has the wisdom to count the clouds? Who can tip over the water jars of the heavens when the dust becomes hard and the clods of earth stick together?

Job 38:37-38

What's a survivor? Isn't it someone who can *endure*, who can hang in there during the stressful times, and who doesn't cave into despair when facing great personal trials? That sounds pretty good, I wonder if it's good enough. Is it enough for you to merely hang in there when things are incredibly difficulty, hoping somehow that your circumstances will right themselves and things will turn around, eventually?

That sounds honorable, but unfortunately it doesn't lead to spiritual growth! Have you ever read the book of Job? I remember an instance several years ago when a man I thought loved me very much dumped me for his former girlfriend. It was a messy ordeal that took place smack in the middle of our church's singles' ministry. Ugh. It left me and my children wondering what in the world we'd ever done to deserve *this!* I didn't understand how God could let this happen to me. I was trying to hang in there (by my fingernails), when someone suggested that I read the book of Job.

Craving understanding, desperate to find some relief from my pain and humiliation, I retreated to my sacred place and read the entire book.

I delve into Job now whenever I'm facing a personal trial (also James 1). It helps to remind me that Job lost virtually everything—his children, his worldly possessions, his health. As he struggled to *endure* and to comprehend why all this was happening to him, his friends sat around and picked on him. They were discouraging. They were critical. They were pious. Yet just at the point when Job could have given in to despair, something happened. Step by little step, his attitude improved as he turned away from his preoccupation with guilt and punishment and began to focus instead on the mystery, holiness and divinity of God. And what do you know? God spoke to Job. He pointed out to him of all the wonders of creation. God's creation. And Job saw. He understood and he was humbled. His life was restored. He didn't merely survive his trial. He triumphed over it and he thrived.

What does it mean when we say someone has the "patience of Job?" I don't think it means that she has tenacious endurance. I think it means that she has the courage not only to wait on God, but to struggle like Job for understanding. To search for God's lesson in the adversity and to focus her eyes on His majesty, perfection and holiness. What do you think?

> *God, You are an awesome God, there's no doubt about it. Help me to do more than just endure trials. Help me to keep my eyes focused on you.   Amen*

WEEK TWENTY-TWO: WEDNESDAY
MAKING PEACE

The humble will see their God at work and be glad. Let all who seek God's help live in joy. For the Lord hears the cries of his needy ones; he does not despise his people who are oppressed."
Psalm 69:32-33, NLT

She was a legend in the singles' group. Who was she? She was someone who'd actually made peace with her ex-husband. I heard rumors about her. Apparently the first few years after their divorce were pretty brutal. How had it all turned around? I wondered. I sought her out. After I heard her story, I asked her to come speak to my divorce recovery group. "They need to hear this," I told her. "Hey. We all do. Again and again."

Her husband left her for another woman. They got married as soon as the divorce was final, moved an hour away and had a child of their own within the next year. Every weekend this woman's daughter was shuttled out to a new town in the backcountry where she knew no one and had to fend for herself much of the time. She became sullen and withdrawn. Her schoolwork began to suffer.

The mother had gone back to work full time and wasn't on top of the situation. The ex-husband blamed his ex-wife for their daughter's problems and sued for custody. Their battle raged on for two years, depleting the mother's savings and nearly destroying her career. "I was so miserable," she said. "So angry and scared. There wasn't anyone on Earth any angrier than I was. And the one I was most angry at was God."

But she prayed persistently for a miracle. She took her anger to God and she turned the other cheek with her ex and didn't allow herself to play his games. She was steadfast. She remained focused on her daughter's needs and it kept her from going off the deep end when everything else in her life seemed to be out of focus.

Three years later, her ex-husband and his wife became Christians. What was once a strained, difficult relationship gradually transformed. "You wouldn't believe it," she said. "God has moved a mountain here. Make that an entire mountain range! We talk now. We laugh. We sit together at soccer games. My daughter spent last summer with them. She learned to ride a horse. She helped with her stepsister. They go to church together now. I'm almost embarrassed to say this, but *I like my ex-husband. I like his wife.* Isn't that a miracle?!"

Is there someone within your circle of friends or family who has persevered through a difficult trial and come out on the other side? Seek that person out. Have this person speak to a group of newly single-again people. Or take him or her out to lunch.

God, I am so grateful for the shining stars you put in our midst.
Let me see someone who has struggled with courage and faith so
I may be encouraged by that person's example.   Amen

WEEK TWENTY-TWO: THURSDAY
FOR IT IS IN GIVING THAT WE RECEIVE

Brothers and sisters, we urge you to warn those who are lazy. Encourage those who are timid. Take tender care of those who are weak. Be patient with everyone. See that no one pays back evil for evil, but always try to do good to each other and to everyone else.   1 Thessalonians 5:14-15, NLT

I read an article recently in *Single-Parent Family Magazine* about Hope House in Mechanic Falls, Maine. Run by Jan and Bruce Wilson, this center offers a free "thrift store" where single moms can trade in their kids' outgrown but wearable clothes for ones that fit. It offers various classes and support groups, counseling, child care, a library, and a coffee shop. The Wilsons operate it out of an old parsonage. And get this! At least sixty single moms visit there every day. These moms befriend, encourage, support and affirm one other. They donate their time, energy and whatever else they can to help the center operate.

The verses quoted above urge us to warn those who are lazy. Single parents operate on overload most of the time, and this mind set of not having enough time, energy, support and resources can easily make us negative and spiritually stagnant. Why? Because all that focus on what is missing from our lives makes us want to repay evil for evil. We're too busy trying to make ends meet and we're so consumed with feeling sorry for ourselves that the idea of helping someone else seems ludicrous.

It takes too much effort to be encouraging, patient, good and loving. Or does it? What does scripture tell us? *It tells us over and over again to love one another.* Whatever we give will be multiplied and returned to us. But we have to take that first tentative and terrifying step. We have to give of ourselves when we feel like we have nothing whatsoever to give. And we have to give with the humble hearts of servants—who give because we genuinely care, not because we want to manipulate people into meeting our needs.

When was the last time you did something really unexpected and maybe a little bit wonderful for someone else? What was their reaction? How did you feel? What blessings came your way afterward? Open your eyes. Be creative. How can you help those in need around you? If the successful story of Hope House touched your heart, borrow it. I'm sure the Wilsons won't mind.

> *Father, I don't want to be self-pitying and lazy. I want to be loving, encouraging, patient and tender. Give me the humble heart of a servant, Lord. Amen*

WEEK TWENTY-TWO: FRIDAY
THE INCREDIBLE GIFT OF AN APOLOGY

Yet I hold this against you: you have forsaken your first love. Remember the height from which you have fallen! Repent and do the things you did at first! If you do not repent, I will come and remove your lamp stand from its place.

Revelations 2:4-5, NLT

Several months ago I was listening to the radio in my car. The subject under discussion was forgiveness, specifically teaching or children about forgiveness. At a stop light, I pulled a pen out of my purse and jotted the following three things onto a scrap of paper:

· I was wrong.
· I'm sorry.
· Please forgive me.

Three simple steps that start with the admission of wrong-doing, move toward the offering of an apology, to the final step of asking for forgiveness from the person we have wounded. As the speaker cautioned in the broadcast, receiving the forgiveness requested in the third step may take time. If we have hurt someone deeply, time must pass before the words can penetrate that person's heart. Healing usually doesn't happen like a flash of lightening. Sometimes it does, but most often it takes longer. A person we have wronged must know that we are sincere. That person needs to feel safe in trusting us again. They have the right to say, "yes," "no," or "not now."

Did you learn these three basic steps for healing your relationships when you were growing up? I sure didn't. Back then It wasn't OK for parents to admit wrong-doing. It somehow diminished their status as parents. They held themselves aloft, on pedestals high above us and dictated our behavior from afar. For a parent to admit wrong-doing to a child, to apologize, to ask for forgiveness (which cannot be demanded from another but must be given freely) is to give our children an incredible gift. It affirms the child's value as a human being. It requires that we as parents be humble. That we pull ourselves down off our pedestals and fall to our knees in front of God, like any other sinners.

How much better our marriages would have been if we'd learned to ask for, accept and give forgiveness! If only we'd these three steps tattooed into our hearts back then! What better role models we can be for our children if we learn them and practice them now.

Think of someone you've wronged recently. Call that person. Go through these three steps with them. Describe the incident in your journal. Describe your feelings before, during and after.

Father, help me to admit it when I do wrong to others. Give me the courage to admit wrong doing, to apologize and to ask for forgiveness. And finally, provide me with the patience that will allow you time to work in the other person's heart so that he or she can truly forgive me. Amen

WEEK TWENTY-TWO: SATURDAY
ACCEPTING MYSELF AS I AM TODAY....

So I pray that God, who gives you hope, will keep you happy and full of peace as you believe in Him. May you overflow with hope through the power of the Holy Spirit.
Romans 15:13 NLT

Do you believe that you are exactly where God intends for you to be today? Try saying it out loud: "I am exactly where God intends for me to be today." What?! Doesn't it follow then, that you should be thanking God for the circumstances, feelings and thoughts that are you today? Can you do that? Or does it seem like expressing gratitude to God for a life that feels like it's in the toilet bowl is way too much of a stretch?!

You know what? The paradox, the miracle of acceptance is that *it works!* First we have to accept our feelings. Own them. Only when we've worked through all our feelings of sadness, outrage, terror, shame and self-pity will we be able to get to the gratitude. Only then will we be able to accept our circumstances. Only then will we be able to accept ourselves and begin to grasp how great is God's love for us. Only then will we be able to see that *we are right where God wants us to be.* Then, and only then will we find the where-with-all to stop fighting and trying to control things.

Remember the Serenity Prayer from Alcoholics Anonymous? It's so helpful to me when I'm struggling to get to acceptance when dealing with any challenging aspect of my life. Here it is:

Lord, give me the serenity to accept the things I cannot change,
the courage to change the things I can,
and the wisdom to know the difference.

It starts with acceptance. Acceptance brings with it that peaceful inner sigh of serenity when we come to the realization that we are powerless over this situation and we're able to *let go of it.* Acceptance opens the door for courageous action when we've come to see that *we can change something here—most often our own behavior.* And wisdom comes from prayer. From surrendering our confusion to God. He provides us with the discernment so that we can know whether to play, hold or fold the cards we hold in our hands.

So, explore the questions I asked in the first paragraph in your journal today. Explore the concept of acceptance. If you've been focusing on the negatives in your circumstances and in yourself, try focusing on the positive. What is beautiful and good about you? Your life? Feel the gratitude?!

Thank You, Father for the miracle of acceptance. I ask You for
the serenity to accept what I can't change, the courage to change
what I can—and the wisdom to know the difference.
Amen

WEEK TWENTY-THREE

WEEK TWENTY-THREE: SUNDAY
CAPTURING THOSE MAGIC MOMENTS!

Young man, it's wonderful to be young! Enjoy every minute of it. Do everything you want to do; take it all in. But remember that you must give an account to God for everything you do. So...remember that youth, with a whole life before it, still faces the threat of meaninglessness."   Ecclesiastes 11:9-10, NLT

"Lighten up, Mom! You are taking things way too seriously!"

I sat down. Abruptly. I wasn't used to being lectured by an eight-year-old. "What?!" I exclaimed after I'd caught my breath.

He sat down beside me and patted my hand. "You worry too much. Everything's gonna be OK. Gayle and I can help you. It won't be so bad."

I don't even remember what triggered those remarks from my son, Derek, so many years ago. What I do remember was the shock I felt as an alarm bell went off in my head. *Brrring! Hello? Anyone home here?* The not-so-subtle sound of a wake-up call.

I woke up that day and faced myself in the mirror. The woman I saw there had narrow, suspicious eyes. Her lips were drawn together tightly. Her teeth were clenched and her jaw was rigid. She was not a happy camper. I asked myself why, and the woman in the mirror responded that she felt overwhelmed, overburdened, over stressed, under loved, under supported, and under funded. Whew! What a load! Derek was right. I did need to lighten up. Big time.

I sat down with my kids that evening and did a feeling check. How was everyone doing? What complaints did we have? How could we pull together to make things better? I got a lot of good information from them. They wanted us to laugh more. When I asked them how we could do that, they took turns regaling me with funny stories from school. Pretty soon we were all roaring with laughter. We made a pact to do our best to remember the hilarious, or even moderately amusing things that happened during our days and recount them to one another at dinner.

They asked me to take them to the park and swing with them after dinner. To play basketball and hide and seek. They asked me to rent *Christmas Vacation,* which has to be the silliest movie ever made. Then I came up with a few ideas of my own. "How about if we limit your TV watching so we'll have more time to spend together? How about if we put on some dancing music and rock out every so often? How about if we award a prize to the person who can go a whole week without griping once?"

They liked most of my ideas and I liked most of theirs. Bottom line was, the atmosphere in our home "lightened up" and we were all a lot happier. Take a look at yourself in the mirror. Do you need to lighten up? Call a family meeting tonight and come up with a plan!

Father, thank you that you created me with a sense of humor and a great capacity for joy. Help me rediscover mine and share it with my children and friends.   Amen

WEEK TWENTY-THREE: MONDAY
WHO DID GOD CREATE ME TO BE?

I praise you because I am fearfully and wonderfully made; your works are wonderful, I know that full well. My frame was not hidden from you when I was made in the secret place. When I was woven together in the depths of the earth, your eyes saw my unformed body. All the days ordained for me were written in your book before one of them came to be.

Psalm 139:14-16

If you were raised in a family, or if you were in a marriage, where your gifts were suppressed, your entire being may have ended up being squashed and forced into a mold that didn't fit you at all.

If someone raged at you or mocked you when you expressed your personhood, whether it was a parent or your spouse (or both), you were no doubt overcome with fear. For much of my life, I hid my vulnerable, creative, gifted self away where it couldn't be "touched." Did you do this?

Now, here you are in the middle of a divorce. If your spouse belittled you, well, he or she's not there anymore. There's no excuse to hide your light under a barrel. Who does God intend you to be? What gifts has he given you? What light to share with the world? At this juncture you can choose: Are you going to live out the script has written for you, or are you going to let someone write your script?

Here are some more questions. Who's in charge of your life? You? Your ex? Your mom or dad? When you take a step out on your own, are there still people on the sidelines of your life who keep demanding that you *justify* your behavior to them? Such so-called authority figures assume the right to determine what's right or wrong for you. How do you feel when these folks get on your case? What steps can you take to protect yourself from these belittlers and surround yourself with people who will encourage you to see and explore the gifts God has given you?

Next assignment: Think of your favorite elderly person. Describe him or her. Think of the most bitter, crabby oldster you know, and describe that person too. Now picture yourself at that age. How would you describe *you?* What would you like to be remembered for? What kind of changes would you have to make in your life to become this person?

> *Father, You knew me before I was born and even then you knew everything that would happen in this life of mine. That idea boggles my mind, Lord, but I agree with David that I am fearfully and wonderfully made. Thank you for reminding me that you have a plan for my life. Help me to put the past behind me and move ahead on the path you've ordained for me.*
> *Amen*

WEEK TWENTY-THREE: TUESDAY
WHAT HAS GOD PUT IN MY HEART?

> God said to Solomon, "Since this is your heart's desire and you have not asked for wealth, riches or honor, nor for the death of your enemies, and since you have not asked for a long life but for wisdom and knowledge to govern my people over whom I have made you king, therefore wisdom and knowledge will be given to you."   2 Chronicles 1:11-12

If you absolutely couldn't fail, what would you do with you life? If you aren't sure, is there a restless growing conviction inside of you that's urging you to become involved is something? If there is, acknowledge it. Explore it and learn as much as you can about it. If you feel like you aren't qualified to pursue it, relax! You can be assured that God will reveal a gift within you that's necessary for your involvement. It may not happen overnight, and you may have to put in some hard work, but as God shows us in this conversation with Solomon, he's put certain desires in our hearts and he blesses us when we choose to follow them.

My friend Nancy has recently developed a heart for missions work in Mexico. She, who used to cringe at the thought of going camping (and refused to go) is now traveling into Mexico, sleeping on bare mattresses and taking cold (or no) showers. And she's learning to speak Spanish too. She's definitely stretching in new directions and occasionally it's a bit disconcerting to her. But she'd be the first to tell you that the discomforts she's experienced have proven to be inconsequential compared with the joy and satisfaction she gets from helping these illiterate, impoverished Indians. She knows God has led her to do this, and she's following him with a grateful heart.

So how do we discover our heart's desires? How do we find out what God wants us to do, ministry-wise, career-wise, relationship-wise? When I was taking a spiritual gifts class several years ago, one of the things the leader said really stuck in my mind. It's this: *"Much of what God wants of you is written directly into your heart. All you have to do is look within."* Wow. What it took for me was to begin taking those long walks on the beach, alone with God. He was (and is) always right there in my head and heart, ready to listen, and ready to answer me.

Looking back over my class notes from back then, I saw that I had responded to the question "What is my heart's desire?" with these words: *I want to write a book about surviving and thriving after divorce.* Need I say more?!

Answer the questions posed here today. Go for a walk alone with God.

> *Father, when I'm alone with you today, please show me what you've written directly into my heart. Show me what you have planned for me. Amen*

WEEK TWENTY-THREE: WEDNESDAY
GETTING THAT LOG OUT OF MY EYE

> I will give you a new heart and put a new spirit in you; I will remove from you your heart of stone and give you a heart of flesh.   Ezekiel 36:26

To comprehend the concept of forgiveness, we have to work at extricating a large log out of our eyes. Why? Because, as Jesus so poignantly reminded us in Luke 6:41, we're nearly blind to our own shortcomings while we're so aware of those of others. How is this connected to forgiveness?

Consider the man whose wife left him for a guy at the office. He's living alone, without his kids 85% of the time in a barely furnished apartment. A good chunk of his check goes to her for spousal support and to the kids for child support. He hasn't been able to focus since the divorce. His job as a sales rep has suffered and his income has diminished in direct proportion to his misery. He sits through a divorce recovery session on forgiveness and seethes.

Forgiving his ex-wife is impossible, he says. She hurt him and she deserves to get what's coming to her! He's the one who's sitting there alone, night after night nursing a broken heart. He's the one with all the financial problems right now. It just isn't fair! Who in the world can expect him to forgive her when *she ruined his life?!*

Forgiving, while it seems unfair, is really the only way to be fair to himself. Getting even is a game for losers. It only compounds the frustration and prolongs the agony. As he plays the hurts over and over in his brain, he gets hooked into feeling sorry for himself, into hurting and feeling victimized. Every time he plays that tape, he reinflicts the wounds on himself. Like a coyote who chews at his ankle to free himself from a trap, he may end up chewing off his entire foot before he escapes the steel jaws of his prison.

This guy, like all of us, needs to see his own part in the death of his marriage. The pain won't go away until he stops blaming his wife and lets go of his need for revenge. He needs to acknowledge his own sin. He needs to get right with God on that—to ask for and accept God's forgiveness, to forgive himself—then to release another sinner, his ex-wife, from her sin. Love the sinner, hate the sin. And we all sin.

Remember the woman caught in adultery? Jesus didn't condemn her because her accusers were sinners just as she was!

What blame have you heaped on your ex? Are there any other people (girlfriends, boyfriends) that you blame also for your divorce? How are you chewing at your foot over this? How much do you want to be free of the churning anger and pain that's eating you up inside?

> *Oh God, I do so want to get past all this craziness. I need a heart of flesh and a new spirit, Father. Please help me to soften, to lighten up, to begin owning my stuff and not hanging onto my ex's for dear life. Thank you.   Amen*

WEEK TWENTY-THREE: THURSDAY
TIME OUT TO FIND A LITTLE LUXURY

He is a wise man who does not grieve for the things which he has not, but rejoices for those which he has.   Epictetus

When was the last time you took a walk in the rain? When was the last time you sat out a stormy day with a good book, or a stack of movies, several bags of microwave popcorn and a roaring fire? When was the last time you took a long walk in the country? When was the last time you went fishing? Or rode a horse? Or basked in the sun? Ladies, when was the last time you had a manicure and pedicure? Have any of you had a massage since you got divorced?!

For touch-deprived single people, a massage can be a gift to the soul. Too expensive you say? A friend told me recently that she went to a massage school and was able to get a very cheap rubdown. Similarly, other people I know go to beauty colleges to get manicures, pedicures and facials, for next-to-nothing.

Get out your journal right now and turn to the Adventures tab. Make a list of things you consider luxuries. Put a check by the ones you can do alone, and a star by the ones you prefer to do with someone. Now put exclamation points next to the ones that are affordable. Every single one I listed above can be experienced for relatively little money.

These days we think we're being frivolous if we take time out to pamper ourselves. I learned, the hard way (of course), that if I don't take time to treat myself to little luxuries, I get really crabby. Then I get a martyr's attitude and resentment oozes out from my pores. I get sarcastic, mean, nasty. Pretty soon I'm upside down! When I can no longer stand to be in the same room with myself (or even worse, the same house, or the same town) it dawns on me that it's time to quit being superwoman before I end up babbling incoherently in a corner, waiting for them to come and take me away to the funny farm!

Promise yourself that this coming weekend, you will pick one item from your luxury list and do it—whether you do it alone, with your kids, or with a friend.

Dear Lord, I know you created the Sabbath for rest and restoration. Help me to make and take time for myself so that I don't burn out. Amen

WEEK TWENTY-THREE: FRIDAY
BECOMING A RISK TAKER

For it is by grace you have been saved, through faith—and this is not from yourselves, it is the gift of God—not by works, so that no one can boast. For we are God's workmanship, created in Christ Jesus to do good works, which God prepared in advance for us to do.   Ephesians 2:8-10

Should I or shouldn't I? We face that question every time we take a tentative step or an enthusiastic leap into the unknown. We have to consider all the risks and weigh the possible benefits we stand to reap at a future time against the negative consequences we may face. Do we take the *road less traveled,* or do we instead stay on the secure and familiar path we're on now?

Becoming a risk taker means daring to deviate from the known and take those first, terrifying steps into the unknown. When it's a career change or a move to a new city or even mustering up the guts to take another chance at love, it can catapult us into crisis mode. Taking a new path means stepping away from our safety nets. If you take a job doing something you *love* instead of something that will merely pay the bills, you may have to sacrifice financially. That's *very* scary, especially if you have children to support.

Here's an example from my own life. A few years back I began a job search. I'd been free-lancing as a writer for several years, but I needed a more steady income. Three job opportunities came my way. The first was a stable corporate job, where I'd be writing summary statements for employee benefit plans. The second was another corporate job, where I'd be responsible for all internal employee communications. Salary and benefits were comparable at the first two. Both were equidistant from my home. The third job, however, was the risky one. It paid less and it had no benefits, but it was working part time for a Baja travel club. I'd worked on contract with these people before, and I adored them. I love Mexico and have traveled there since I was a kid. Furthermore, I'D written a Baja cookbook, which the travel club could help promote.

So what am I going to do? I asked myself. Go with one of the secure jobs, or go with my heart, having faith that, because this club is growing quickly, the money (and benefits) will follow? I've read Marsha Sinetar's book, *Do What You Love, the Money Will Follow,* and I nodded my head, yes, yes, yes, all the way through it. But somehow, as I faced my own risk-taking crisis, my fears rose up to caution me, no, no, no!

So what would you do? Take the safe path (even at the risk of being bored to death?), or jump out there and take a risk?

Father, when I'm faced with choosing between the secure path
and a new, riskier path, please lead me to the right one, so that I
can do good works for you. Give me discernment, Lord.
Amen

WEEK TWENTY-THREE: SATURDAY
SEEING THINGS GOD'S WAY

Turn to me and be saved, all you ends of the earth; for I am God,
and there is no other. By myself I have sworn, my mouth has
uttered in all integrity a word that will not be revoked: Before me
every knee will bow; by me every tongue will swear. They will say
of me, "In the Lord alone are righteousness and strength."

Isaiah 45:22-24

I was at a woman's retreat several years ago where the keynote
speaker, Christian author Sandra Wilson, made the following poignant
remark: "I always thought I believed that God was in control, but in
reality, the credo I lived my life by was: 'Hello everyone! Does Sandy
ever have a plan for you!'"

Everyone laughed. Her words touched a chord in all of us, but I can't
help but wondering, how many of us have forgotten that remark? How
many of us continue to try to force our agenda on the world, just sure
that we know what's best for everyone, and then finding ourselves
disappointed over and over again because *no one appreciates our*
wisdom and insightful plans?

Why do we insist on this being a perfect world where everything runs
smoothly, on our timetable and with our (as we see it) best interests in
mind?

The answer to that question is in the scripture above. God's
perspective is way different from yours and mine. He's the only One

who really sees the big picture. And he does. He sees it all, past, present, future. There isn't anything that ever did or ever will happen that he doesn't already know all about. And although he definitely has a plan for each of our lives, he's given us not only free will, but also tons of wobble space. He knows we're going to struggle, to stumble, to fall down. He wants us to. He wants us to learn from our struggles, our stumbles, and our falls, and to get up and go on, discerning the lessons. He wants us to grow! To become more like his son, Jesus Christ.

How have you tried to inflict your will over God's will? How do you try to play God in your life? In what ways can you lighten up, let go, and give the reins back over to God? How do those words make you feel?

> *Lord, the thought of giving up control scares me more than about anything. Help me to understand that you do have a plan for me, and that suffering and growth is part of that plan. I want to grow, Father. Help me to seek you.*   *Amen*

WEEK TWENTY-FOUR

WEEK TWENTY-FOUR: SUNDAY
LOVE HUNGER

> Single moms are sacred, man. A real man doesn't shoplift the
> pooty from (take advantage of) a single mom.
> Cuba Gooding in Jerry Maguire

One of the biggest challenges I've faced in my years as a single-again adult has been dealing with that yearning, burning, gnawing longing for intense connection with another. Intimacy. The spiritual, emotional, intellectual and sexual sharing between a man and a woman who are committed to each other at the deepest level. The easiest and most obvious antidote for this love hunger is to go out and find someone to fall in love with, right? That's what it says to do in all the magazines I see when I'm in line at the supermarket. That's what they say on TV and in the movies. And let's not forget all those love songs, particularly if you happen to be a fan of country music! Whew! We're inundated with those images.

Yet the movie, *Jerry Maguire,* while inappropriate in some spots, had an underlying message that struck my heart. Here is a hotshot sports agent who, in an attack of conscience writes a mission statement berating the dishonesty and lack of moral fiber in his business. While his dissertation is passionate and from his heart, it is grossly incompatible with the operating philosophy of the company he works for. So he's out on his tail, so to speak, with only a couple of fancy fish for company.

Enter a vulnerable, sweet, idealistic single mom. She falls in love with the man he "almost is." Jerry Maguire falls in love with her little boy. Somehow, in an attempt to outrun their fears, they get married. But the love hunger isn't satisfied. The love both of them ache for eludes them. Why? Jerry asks his friend, the pro football player played so poignantly by Cuba Gooding, after he's just witness Cuba and his wife nuzzling and giggling together at dinner.

At the end of what is my favorite dialog in the movie, Jerry stands firmly convicted. In his own desperation and neediness, he took advantage of a single mom. He failed to see her extreme vulnerability. He was blind to the fact that her circumstances required extra thought and consideration. He failed to see that he was stepping in as more than a husband—he was feeding way more than one person's love hunger. The child loved him, needed him, craved a father figure. The woman loved him, needed him, craved a mate and a father for her son. It was a very complex situation. Not one to be taken lightly or selfishly—by any of us.

If you haven't seen the movie, I highly recommend that you rent it. After you've watched it, write down some of your thoughts and feelings. What are some ways you can assuage your love hunger without letting desperation and neediness cloud solid judgement?

Father, help me not to take advantage of others, to use them to meet my needs for love. Help me to look to you, to Jesus as the lover of my soul right now. Let me take this time for healing, for growth and to get to know you better.

WEEK TWENTY-FOUR: MONDAY
FORGIVENESS—THE MOUNTAIN MOVER

> I tell you the truth, if anyone says to this mountain, "Go, throw yourself into the sea," and does not doubt in his heart but believes that what he says will happen, it will be done for him.
>
> Mark 11:23

Unresolved pain and conflict builds walls between people. As time goes on, those walls get thicker and thicker, taller and taller. Pretty soon the wall has become a mountain, too immense to climb over, too broad to tunnel under and too wide to walk around. We feel ourselves trapped behind it, imprisoned by it. We are.

We know that fear, anger, resentment, bitterness, self-righteousness, agony and desperate self-sabotaging behavior patterns build the mountain, but what keeps it in place? A lack of forgiveness. The only thing that moves that mountain out of the way and slides it right down into the sea (where it drowns, I hope!) is forgiveness. You know what? You can't live if you can't forgive! Pretty soon that mountain gets so monstrous that it buries you alive. And smothers your spirit.

The truth of the matter is that if you don't go through the entire recovery process, if you try to take a short cut around the difficult task of forgiveness, then you will lug that mountain of emotional baggage into your next relationship. And, chances are, if your new love is also hiding behind a mountain of unforgiveness, both of you will be squashed by the unresolved, ugly "stuff" in your lives. Not a pretty picture, huh?

Do you know people, particularly older people who've allowed themselves to be buried mountains of unforgiveness? People who hate life, fear death and live out their days seething with negativity? I do. But I also know the other kind of people. The people who see, accept and make a conscious choice to love and forgive.

Recently my favorite uncle died of lung cancer. He suffered greatly and could only breathe through a hole in his throat the last year of his life. Yet he never complained. He accepted people and made them feel special, even though it was obvious he saw more clearly than most of us did. He could have focused on our shortcomings and nastiness. But he didn't. He chose instead to make his peace with God. He had forgiven everyone and was free to celebrate the goodness in life. In doing so, he encouraged those around him to look up and out instead of down and in.

When you look back over your life, weigh the positive energy associated with forgiveness against the negative energy associated with unforgiveness? Is there a mountain or two in your life that needs to be eradicated?

> *Lord, today I make a conscious choice to be loving and forgiving. Please move the mountains of unforgiveness and bitterness from my life. Clear the path for me to healing. Let me be Your person, reflecting Your qualities. Lift me up and out, Lord. Amen*

WEEK TWENTY-FOUR: TUESDAY
IF GOD FORGIVES ME, I CAN FORGIVE MYSELF!

> "Come now, let us argue this out," says the Lord. "No matter how deep the stain of your sins, I can remove it. I can make you as clean as freshly fallen snow. Even if you are stained as red as crimson, I can make you as white as wool."
>
> Isaiah 1:18, NLT

Are you one of those folks who beat themselves up a lot when they mess up? I am! As difficult as it was for me to believe that God would really forgive me for getting divorced (among other things), it was even harder for me to forgive myself. Something I read in a book finally convinced me that I could, should, and would accept his forgiveness and forgive myself. The author told me that if God forgave me and I refused to forgive myself, I was putting myself ahead of God. I was telling God that I was smarter than he was. Pretty arrogant, huh?

I decided right then and there that if God loved me enough to wash me clean and change me from crimson to pure white, then I better accept that as the gift of grace that it is: undeserved mercy and favor. Accepting that gift freed me from self-indictment. It enabled me to forgive myself, finally. What did forgiving myself do for me? It let me accept myself as fully human. It gave and still gives me the freedom to fail and to make mistakes, while holding myself accountable for taking responsibility for those failures and mistakes. It let (and still lets) me accept and feel the glory of God's forgiveness, which gives me a clean slate and enables me to start over!

After my divorce, I developed a weird behavior pattern. When a man got too close to me, I would become cold, aloof and withdrawn. Into my heart would creep insidious tendrils of disgust and mistrust. Those feelings made intimacy and vulnerability impossible. I ended up chasing men away and sabotaging the closeness I thought I truly desired.

As I reflected upon this behavior, my first reaction was to get down on myself. Yet, as I prayed for understanding, I realized that even though I had accepted God's forgiveness for getting divorced and believed that I had forgiven myself as well, I was still subconsciously punishing myself. Therefore, I had to go back to the place of forgiveness once again and immerse myself in God's truth, his grace, his mercy and, above all, his abiding love. I began to see that I still hadn't let go of the past. As I cried for all the love that had been lost and all the misunderstandings over the years, I felt God's hand reach down into the depths of my heart and gently knit its broken pieces back together.

I forgave myself finally because I truly knew that he had forgiven me. Once I did, the healing came. Have you asked for God's forgiveness yet?

Have you accepted it, or are you still beating yourself up? Have you forgiven yourself?

Father, please help me to own and accept what I did to contribute to the death of my marriage. Help me to feel your love washing me clean. When I am clean, Lord, knit the broken pieces of my heart back together so that I may forgive myself and move forward. Amen

WEEK TWENTY-FOUR: WEDNESDAY
ASKING MY EX TO FORGIVE ME

But you are a forgiving God, gracious and compassionate, slow to anger and abounding in love. Therefore you did not desert them, even when they cast for themselves an image of a calf.

Nehemiah 9:17-18

"I don't get it," he said. "I have read and studied about forgiveness for six months now. I pray about it every day. The last time I went to pick up my sons, I told my ex-wife I wanted to talk with her privately. We went out into the patio and I asked her to forgive me for everything I'd done, knowingly and unknowingly to end our marriage. Do you know what she said?"

No. I shook my head.

"Well, she went into this half an hour tirade against me. Boy, she really hated those words 'knowingly and unknowingly!' She said that if I didn't know what I'd done wrong, well then, she'd be more than happy to fill me in! And boy, did she ever," he finished with a weak semi-grin.

I understood. "You know," I told him, "These things take time. Our timetables and God's timetable are not in sync so much of the time. It may take her 10 years to forgive you. Then again, she may never be able to forgive you. You can't force it. It's between her and God. You just have to keep doing your own part. Every time you find yourself beating your head against a wall, craving her forgiveness, turn it over to God. Keep on praying. Keep on owning your own stuff and turning that cheek. God's love will sustain you, I promise."

This conversation took place several years ago. The last time I talked to this man, he'd gone back his ex-wife three or four more times and asked for her forgiveness. The first couple of times, she ripped his head off. Then she began verbally forgiving him, only to retract her words later. Finally, after the last time she did this, he accepted the fact that she simply wasn't ready to forgive. Maybe she'd never be ready. But he was finally able to stop blaming himself for her ongoing bitterness. He was also able to stop pushing her.

Have you asked your ex for forgiveness? If so, what happened? Do you believe that true healing has taken place between you, or do acknowledge the need for more time to pass?

> *O Lord, teach me how to forgive. Help me not to try to rush it, but to give you the time to work in my life, in my ex's life. Give me a humble heart, Lord.*   *Amen*

WEEK TWENTY-FOUR: THURSDAY
FORGIVING MY EX

> He was punished enough when most of you were united in your judgment against him. Now it is time to forgive him and comfort him. Otherwise he may become so discouraged that he won't be able to recover.   2 Corinthians 2:6-7, NLT

Forgiving one's ex-spouse can be the most difficult part of the entire divorce recovery process. How could this person who swore in front of God and everyone else to love, honor, and cherish you *forever* bail on you? How could this person come to treat you with disgust, bitterness, animosity? How could something that started out so beautiful, hopeful, and tender end up so ugly and cruel?

Wherever you are in your journey, remember one thing. By the time you've completed your journey through divorce country, I trust you will have made it a personal goal to make peace with your ex. It's of paramount importance to your own healing and to your children's. The part of the journey that's full of anger, bitterness, and hatred isn't the end of the story. You don't have to get stuck there. Many people do. It takes hard work and lots of openness to God's grace to get out of the war zone, but it's more than worth the effort, I promise you.

Forgiving your ex-spouse is a major key. How do you do it? What if he or she is still doing things to push your buttons on a regular basis? What if you feel as if you've forgiven that person, only to be assaulted by cruelty, days, weeks, or months later? Do you have to forgive again? Yes. Jesus told Peter in Matthew 18:22 that he should forgive someone seventy times seven. Does that mean a literal 490 times? No. It means more times than any of us can keep track of. We're commanded to keep on keeping on! Forgiveness is a mountain we have to climb many times, in every relationship in our lives if we're living in honesty and brotherly love with one another.

If you've asked your ex for forgiveness and he or she hasn't come to you and asked back, this will likely be an exercise you'll go through on your own. Even though this person won't or can't yet forgive you, you still need to forgive.

Try to remember your ex as he or she was when you first met. List all the qualities that attracted you, that made you even consider this person as a lifetime mate. List three or four of your most special times together. How did you feel then? How do you feel now? Compare and contrast. Now try looking at everything from a different perspective. God's perspective. Try to look at your former spouse through God's eyes. Where is he or she wounded? What is his or her deepest need? How can you be more empathic toward this man or woman whom God loves?

*God, I don't want to keep punishing my ex, in thought and deed.
I want to break the cycle of pain. Help me to remember the good
things and to see this person through your eyes. Thank you, Lord.
Amen*

WEEK TWENTY-FOUR: FRIDAY
A WOLF IN SHEEP'S CLOTHING

> Woe to you, teachers of the law and Pharisees, you hypocrites!
> You are like whitewashed tombs, which look beautiful on the
> outside but on the inside are full of dead men's bones and
> everything unclean. In the same way, on the outside you appear
> to people as righteous but on the inside you are full of hypocrisy
> and wickedness.   Matthew 23:27-28

Her fiancé was perceived to be a fine, upstanding Christian man. But
things started to feel wrong. One day he hit her. Then another day. It
was her fault, he told her. She was too emotional. She could be petulant
and demanding. She did too many things to irritate him. She wasn't
nearly submissive enough. She was too pretty and other men at church
noticed her too frequently.

She called me late one night. "I just don't get it," she said. "He loves
the Lord so much, and he's so committed to living a godly life. Why are
things so crazy with us? Why does he love me one minute and act
disgusted with me the next? Why do I keep provoking him when I know
I shouldn't?"

I talked till I was blue in the face, but I couldn't convince her to break
up with him. A month later he dropped her. He returned the diamond
ring to the jeweler for a refund. This man was pious on the outside and
full of dead men's bones on the inside. This woman had fallen in love
with the outer person but couldn't accept the truth about the inner

man. She'd been so lonely and so broke. She so desperately wanted him to be who he said he was that she was willing to blame herself for his cruelty.

The it's-my-fault-I'm-not-good-enough lie sentences us to victimhood. By buying into the story that she was the sinner and he the saint, she tied her heart and soul up in knots. And allowed herself to be punished and demeaned by this man.

This woman wanted desperately to believe that her former fiance was the man he said he was, the man she wished him to be. Yet as I tried to tell her, his words spoke one way and his actions another. He spoke reverently and intimately of God, but then he'd put her down; he'd tap into her feelings of unworthiness and feed off her low self-esteem. She'd feel broken and blame herself. Then he'd flip back into "love mode," rationalize the ugliness away, and she'd be right there, believing him.

Abuse is crazy making. Have you ever blamed yourself for being treated badly or been disappointed by someone who turned out to be a hypocrite? Have you behaved like a hypocrite? If so, what did this person do to show you he or she was unclean on the inside? Have you behaved like a hypocrite? How?

> *Heavenly Father, thank you for sending your Son, Jesus, to show us what perfection really looks like. Please teach me discernment, Lord, to protect me from the craziness and abuse that hypocrites bring.   Amen*

WEEK TWENTY-FOUR: SATURDAY
GROWING IN LOVE

God is love. When we take up permanent residence in a life of love, we live in God and God lives in us. This way, love has the run of the house, becomes at home and mature in us.

From 1 John 4, The Message

Divorce is love that went bad. Divorce is love that was abandoned. Divorce is love that was tormented and abused. What God brought together in blissful, hopeful, abundant delight has been ripped to shreds. The broken pieces of your heart lie in a heap on the floor, like the shells of Humpty Dumpty's egg. How in the world do you put it all back together again? How in the world do you get past all the nasty, painful, ugly, scary feelings that have invaded your heart and replace them somehow with *love* again? Is it even possible?!

I've known plenty of people who felt so battered after their divorces that they swore up and down they'd *never, ever, ever* love again. Not only do they avoid members of the opposite sex, but they aren't even very kind to their families or friends. Their trust in humanity has been shattered. Their trust in their own judgment has been ruined. And, ultimately, their trust in God has been demolished.

After this kind of devastation, rebuilding love takes time. It takes tons of courage. After all, you may not be sure love even exists at this point in your life. When someone tells you that you need to learn to *trust and love again* or someone tells you not to lose sight of *faith and hope,* chances are you feel as if they're playing a profane joke on you. Cynicism and bitterness, frosted over with fear, can wipe out our memories of all the good that God is and wants for us.

Read today's scripture again. It says that once we take up permanent residence in a life of love, *we live in God and he lives in us.* But how do we do it? How do we leave our brokenness behind and grow in love? First of all, you need to work on your relationship with God. Is it dead, is it barely breathing, or is it growing and flourishing? Seek your heavenly Father, through prayer, worship, Bible study, and fellowship. Next, you need to work on loving yourself. This may take awhile if you have been badly stomped on. Be gentle and patient with yourself. Last, you need to reach out to others in love, even if they don't respond in kind. We've all learned that love is risky. But we all know, deep in our hearts, that because *God is love,* love is worth a risk.

What goals can you set for yourself to help ensure that you grow in love?

> *God, I want to take up permanent residence in a life of love. Help me, Father, to heal from the hurts of my divorce so that I can grow in love.*   *Amen*

WEEK TWENTY-FIVE

WEEK TWENTY-FIVE: SUNDAY
SHOULD I STAY OR SHOULD I GO?

Then you will know the truth, and the truth will set you free.

John 8:32

Several years ago I awoke one night, troubled about a man I was seeing. I saw much goodness and potential in him. Yet in many ways he walked in darkness. He trusted God, but he disliked most people. He showed me how I did things to sabotage intimacy, yet he couldn't risk being vulnerable himself.

I prayed to God: "Should I stay in this relationship or should I leave?"

The clear answer came to me: "*You will know the truth, and the truth will set you free.*" I knew this was a quote from the Bible, but I then didn't know the scriptural address or context. I didn't know what it meant, and I pondered on it in the months to come. Deep in my heart I knew I should end the relationship, but it took me a couple of years to do it.

The truth came to me in little flashes. Eventually I saw that I couldn't fix him. I was getting between him and God, and that was not my place to be! I needed to focus on fixing myself. As I recognized bits of truth, I became more free, less bound up by the darkness, and more understanding of the entirety of Jesus' words in John 8:31-32: "If you hold to my teaching, you are really my disciples. Then you will know the truth, and the truth will set you free."

How does this passage touch you? What have you learned the truth about recently? Are there areas of your life where you need to see God's truth? What are they?

O heavenly Father, thank you for bringing the truth to us. Please help me to hold to your teaching, so that I may be truly set free. Amen

WEEK TWENTY-FIVE: MONDAY
FORGIVING EVEN WHEN IT ISN'T SAFE TO TRUST

Father, forgive them, for they do not know what they are doing.

Luke 23:34

In one workshop I led participants got into a gnarly debate on the issue of forgiveness. "How could someone forgive a murderer?" one man asked. Particularly an unrepentant murderer? Or a rapist? A stalker? The conversation spun from there. Was repentance a necessary ingredient in forgiveness? How could someone be expected to forgive another who was hell-bent on hurting her, again and again? It seemed unjust.

That's one of those paradoxes in life. As Lewis Smedes says in his book *Forgive and Forget,* "When you forgive the person who hurt you deeply and unfairly, you perform a miracle that has no equal."

Forgiveness is for us. It isn't for them. When we forgive, we don't necessarily sentence ourselves to entering into another toxic or dangerous relationship with the person. Sometimes it isn't safe. Sometimes it would be suicidal. We have to discern that. In certain cases it's OK to be restored without reconciling.

Look at today's scripture. Jesus said this when he was hanging on the cross, dying. He knew that the people responsible for his arrest, torture, and impending death had plotted laboriously to get rid of him. He knew why they wanted him dead. He was a threat to the Pharisees' way of life. He scorned their legalism and mocked their pseudo purity.

He knew also that they were incapable of seeing him for who he really was, God incarnate. *He saw. He understood. He asked God to forgive them.*

Did they acknowledge their wrongdoing? No. Did they stop persecuting his followers? No. But he forgave them anyway, because he was incapable of hating them. He hated their actions. Yes. But he didn't hate them.

God reserves the right to avenge. It's his job, not ours. He commands us repeatedly to forgive one another if we expect him to forgive us. Why? Because forgiving frees us from the shackles of bitterness that imprison us and keep us from fulfilling our purposes here on earth. That is the truth.

Is there someone in your life whom you need to forgive, but with whom it isn't safe to resume a relationship? Why? Is the relationship really toxic to you, or are you choosing to see it that way?

> *Lord, so often in a divorce, people make someone they once loved into a monster. If I've done that, please let me know. And to those who've hurt me and lack the awareness to see it, forgive them. They don't know what they're doing.*   *Amen*

WEEK TWENTY-FIVE: TUESDAY
ACCEPTING THE GIFT OF RESTORATION

> ...Thou preparest a table before me in the presence of mine enemies: thou anointest my head with oil; my cup runneth over.... Psalm 23:5, KJV

At a church woman's conference, the pastor's wife gave us all a challenge: "If you will recite Psalm 23 every day, at least once for thirty days, it will change your life." Stop right now and read the whole psalm.

I don't know about you, but I memorized this psalm in the King James Version when I was a kid. I always loved it. The images are soothing. The leading of the Shepherd is gentle, but firm. The skittish sheep feels safe and secure in the Shepherd's care, even when traveling through the really scary places where death looms behind every boulder. The promise of abundance to the point of overflowing in the face of one's enemies always amazed me. The promise that God's goodness and mercy would follow me every day of my life and that I could dwell in his house always amazed me even more.

For Job, restoration came after he shifted his gaze upward and began to praise God, even in the midst of the most painful circumstances. God wants us to acknowledge that he knows what he's doing, always. If we can stop focusing on all that's missing in our lives, drop to our knees, and thank him for all the good, all the abundant blessings that he has, in fact, showered upon us, then we're on the road to restoration.

It starts with praise. It starts with a conscious choice to thank God for the gifts he's given us: his love, our friendships, our families, our health, our talents, gifts and personality, the work we do, and the hobbies and interests we have. List yours today. And recite the twenty-third Psalm. Today. Tomorrow. The next day....

> *Father, I want to begin focusing my energy on the abundant blessings in my life, rather than the painful, difficult circumstances. Thank you so much for all that you have given me. I praise you for that! Amen*

WEEK TWENTY-FIVE: WEDNESDAY
HOW CAN I EVER TRUST AGAIN?

> Our wounds drive us to Christ. Our wounds drive us to each
> other. Our wounds make us more sensitive to other wounded
> people. Our wounds glorify God. We may not understand the
> whys of our wounds, but we know that the God who
> understands the whys loves us and invites us to keep seeking
> Him and His ways.
>
> Dick Purnell, Free to Love Again

"How am I ever going to get up the guts to go out with him?" she
asked me.

"What's the big deal?" I asked back.

"I'm not ready."

"You know what?" I told her. "You remind me of a baby bird. I guess
I get to be your mommy and give you that gentle nudge to get you out
of your nest and fly. You have wings, you know."

She smiled. "I do?"

"Yeah. You do. And he's a nice guy. He's not going to do anything
bizarre like take you to a drive-in movie and try to get fresh with you!"

She finally laughed. An old image from high school didn't make the
prospect of spending an evening with a man seem quite so scary. "I
guess if I could do it back then, I can do it now. What do I tell my kids?"

"Don't. Try saving your dates for the weekends they're at their dad's.
That way you can keep things separate. It's easier on everyone that way,
until you're in a relationship that seems like it's getting serious."

This woman from one of my divorce recovery groups had a typical
case of the dating jitters. At nearly forty, she felt like a teenager with
wrinkles. And kids. And an ex-spouse who was always nosing around.
She wasn't footloose and fancy free as she'd been in high school and

college. Oh no! This time around she had lots of baggage. And it scared her.

Getting ready to "date" after a divorce takes time. And courage. And sometimes a little push out of the nest by a loving friend is necessary if a year or two has gone by and you find yourself still wanting to hide from the world.

Have you ventured out yet? Still feeling pretty gun-shy? Perhaps, rather than rush out to go on a dating spree, it's time to consider giving up your wounds to God, to use as he chooses, for his own glory.

> *God, I understand that all of us who've gone through divorces are left with wounds. It's hard to trust again. Please nudge me out of my nest. Even if I'm not ready to date, use my wounds to help others who are hurting and in need.* *Amen*

WEEK TWENTY-FIVE: THURSDAY
LOVE AND THE EX-SPOUSE

Among the attributes of God, although they are all equal, mercy shines with even more brilliance than justice.

Miguel de Cervantes

He has kids who live with him every other week. She has kids. They go to their dad's on Wednesday nights and every other weekend. They'd met in a single parents group and had been dating for over a year. They'd recently become engaged and wanted their relationship to go the distance. However, both often felt pulled in too many directions. Too often their schedules with the kids didn't jive. Too often one of their exes would pull a fast one and throw everyone into an uproar. How does one navigate the turbulent seas of dating and remarriage after a divorce? Why is it so complicated?

As long as there is chaos and animosity between one member of the "new" couple and his or her ex-spouse, there will be chaos. The sea will be stormy. There's nothing that kills a new relationship faster than toxic waste left over from a prior marriage. And if both partners have it, they're in for a really rough ride.

"So what do we do?" the woman asked me when I ran into her at the grocery store one day. "I keep expecting my fiancé to step in, like some proverbial knight in shining armor and deliver me from my ex-husband. I know it's unrealistic, but my ex is so mean to me!"

"What's he doing that makes you want to be rescued?" I asked her.

Her ex had been telling her and their mutual friends how irresponsible she'd become since she met this new man. When her fiancé stepped in and tried to defend her, the ex began calling and writing him at his place of employment, threatening him and further slandering his ex-wife. It had created a furor in his workplace. This new man loved her and wanted to protect her from being hurt by her former spouse. But it seemed that the more involved he got, the more the fires of acrimony were flamed. To top things off, her fiancé's ex-wife was threatening to take him back to court to sue for more child support as soon as he remarried.

"We're on the verge of blowing this whole thing off," she finished.

My advice to her was that she immediately take steps to separate her relationship with her ex-husband from her new relationship, and that her fiancé do the same. "Your relationships with your exes are your own distinct responsibilities," I explained. "You need to learn to deal with these people yourselves so you can protect what you have together. Otherwise the toxicity will eat your relationship alive."

I didn't know if I got through to her or not, but when I ran into her a few months later, she had wedding band on her left hand.

"After I saw you the last time," she said, "I couldn't stop thinking about what you told me. I talked it over with my fiancé and we decided you were right. I stopped obsessing on my ex. As my heart softened some, I was able to admit that he would always be the father of my children. And, you know, I was married to him for over 10 years. We had some good times. We did. After a while my animosity towards him began to dissolve and I made a lunch date with him. We had a good talk."

Out of a bad situation came much healing. She and her ex were able, over time, to forge a new, healthier relationship. Her fiancé's relationship with his ex-wife improved too. Once again, I will ask you, how is your relationship with your ex? How has it influenced your new relationships?

> *Heavenly Father, if there's still some toxic waste left over from my former marriage, please help me to see it. Help me to see what I'm doing to keep the battle fires raging. I want to be a peacemaker, Lord, not a warmonger.   Amen*

WEEK TWENTY-FIVE: FRIDAY
WHAT'S A HEALTHY RELATIONSHIP ANYWAY?

> Experience teaches us that love does not consist of two people looking at each other, but of looking together in the same direction.   Antoine de Saint-Exupery

In one of our single-again groups a few years ago, the subject of a healthy relationship came up. What was one, anyway? Because we were all divorced and none of us was in a serious relationship, we didn't consider ourselves experts on the subject. But we decided that collectively we might be able to come up with some characteristics of healthy relationships so we'd have something to steer by as we navigated our ways through the unfamiliar seas of post divorce life. While the list applied to serious relationships, we all realized it could equally apply to friendships with people of both sexes, which was a safer place for all of us to start. You may want to make a copy of the list we came up with to remind yourself what your goals are with regard to relationships. Here's the list:

1. A healthy relationship operates on the basic premise that I am seen and see the other person realistically.
2. In a healthy relationship I am free to let down my barriers. It's safe for me to be vulnerable.
3. In a healthy relationship there is understanding, empathy, and compassion for each other.
4. In a healthy relationship we are able to communicate openly and honestly, respecting each other's value as a human being.
5. In a healthy relationship we trust one another to do what we've said we'll do.
6. In a healthy relationship we have compatible personalities, values, morals. We enjoy doing things together and function well as a team.
7. A healthy relationship allows both of us to nurture and maintain our separate selves as well as to celebrate each other.
8. In a healthy relationship there is consideration for the other.
9. In a healthy relationship we are attuned to each other's inner rhythms and committed to each other's personal and spiritual growth.
10. In a healthy relationship God comes first.

    Father, I want to learn from this divorce, so that al my relationships will be healthier. I want to honor you first, and someday, if I marry again, my spouse second. Thank you for allowing me this season of learning. May I keep on growing and learning through the rest of my life.   Amen

WEEK TWENTY-FIVE: SATURDAY
MAKING FORGIVENESS A DAILY PRACTICE

> Therefore, as God's chosen people, holy and dearly loved, clothe yourselves with compassion, kindness, humility, gentleness and patience. Bear with each other and forgive whatever grievances you may have against one another. Forgive as the Lord forgave you.   Colossians 3:12-13

"I want to reconcile with my husband," she told me. "He asked for a separation. Even though we married as Christians and I knew divorce shouldn't be an option, I was so hurt that I rushed right out and hired a lawyer. I filed. Now I've told him I'm sorry, that I was wrong. He doesn't believe me. He doesn't trust me. He's already involved with someone else!"

She dissolved into tears. As I listened to her, I realized that she and her husband had married before they were both fully recovered from their past divorces. Neither was fully able to give him- or herself to the other, because neither was capable of trusting the other. Within weeks of their marriage, they were up to their eyeballs in blaming. And, as she admitted to me, much of what they were upset about was unresolved "old stuff." By the time they separated, they hadn't made love in two months, and they were newlyweds!

I encouraged this woman to ask her estranged husband if he'd be willing to go into counseling with her. That had to be their first step. They hadn't been able to get past the stuff left over from the past by themselves. They needed help.

I saw her six months later at the movie theater, giggling and holding hands with her husband. They were beaming. "Wow," I said. "What happened here?"

They took turns telling me their story. It was all about those three steps: "I was wrong. I'm sorry. Please forgive me." It took a lot of digging, a lot of humility, and a lot of courage, but they did it. They owned their stuff, they repented, and they asked for forgiveness, from God, from each other. They accepted God's forgiveness. They forgave each other, and they forgave themselves. And their divorce was averted. Instead, they accepted the gift of a beautiful marriage, rooted in truth and love.

What does this story say to me? *Forgiveness needs to become a daily discipline.* Without it relationships won't survive. How do you integrate forgiveness into your life—into any relationship you're part of?

Lord, I want to get rid of my baggage from the past so I can move forward in truth and love. Teach me to forgive, God. I can't do it myself. Amen

WEEK TWENTY-SIX

WEEK TWENTY-SIX: SUNDAY
CHOOSING TO COPE WITH YOUR EX

> But the fruit of the Spirit is love, joy, peace, patience, kindness, goodness, faithfulness, gentleness and self-control. Against such things there is no law. Galatians 5:22-23

You can decide right now that you want to deactivate those buttons that keep you emotionally tied (read that *married)* to your ex-spouse. You can decide to make coping with him or her a personal goal. Here are steps to help you set and achieve this goal:

1. Determine what kind of ongoing relationship, if any, you will have with your ex-spouse.
2. Recognize the challenge of constructing a new relationship from the ashes of your marriage. It won't be easy!
3. Consciously choose to have a better relationship with your ex.
4. Set the goal. Write it down, and post it where you'll see it every day.
5. Begin listening to the things you say to yourself (inside your own head) throughout the day, particularly when thinking about or communicating with your ex-spouse. Write them down on a pad of paper or in a notebook. This is crucial! Take note of the way you talk to yourself. Do you beat yourself up a

lot? Do you tend to point fingers at everyone but yourself? Are you kind or unkind?

6. Pray about it every day. Ask God to help you behave more kindly, to yourself and to others.

7. Ask the Lord to reveal your emotional buttons to you. Write them down as you become aware of them. Pray about them. Discuss them with people you trust.

8. Stay on top of it. Remember, this is a goal you want to achieve and achieving it is a process, not an overnight event. Go easy on yourself. Don't forget the adage "Two steps forward, one step back."

9. Keep on praying. Use the fruit of the Spirit as your guideline for coping, not only with your ex-spouse, but also with the deactivation of your emotional buttons.

10. Reward yourself when you catch yourself "acting and not reacting." Remind yourself that you're doing this to improve your own life and your children's lives and to get yourself an emotional divorce.

Lord, I really want to get an emotional divorce. I want to stop reacting when my ex pushes my buttons. Strengthen me, Father, and help me to become free of the ties from the past.
Amen

WEEK TWENTY-SIX: MONDAY
FRIENDSHIPS—FORUM FOR GIFT SHARING

Remember this: Whoever sows sparingly will also reap sparingly, and whoever sows generously will also reap generously.

2 Corinthians 9:6

If we plant the seeds of friendship carefully yet generously and nurture those friendships with reverence, we will reap great gifts from them. It's inevitable.

One of my friends is a talented interior designer. When I moved recently she came and helped me hang pictures on the wall. I wanted the same things to look different somehow and she did it for me! Every time I walk into my living room I am reminded of that gift she gave me. Another friend, a skilled seamstress, sewed new seat covers for the dinette and fold-out couch in a trailer I used to own in Mexico. She made curtains too. And refused payment! What a gift!

Another friend is an incredible listener and the greatest encourager I've ever known. When I was going through some really tough times not so long ago, she was there for me. Whenever I needed her. Without fail. Unconditionally loving and supporting me in my painful growth. I am grateful to her to this day. Still another friend has the gift of discernment. I turn to him when I need to bounce things off someone I consider well grounded and wise. He helps me listen to myself and sets me straight when I veer off course.

I could go on, but I think you get my drift. Our friendships are gifts of incomprehensible value, given to us by God to cherish and nurture. We need to care for them lovingly, and they will help us to bloom abundantly as we help our friends to bloom abundantly as well.

Write down the names of your four closest friends. How did you meet? How did the relationships grow from acquaintances to casual friends to close friends? What special gifts do each of them have? What special gift(s) do you offer to each of them? What kind of harvest has your relationship yielded? Are you satisfied with the yields of your efforts? Are the rewards of those friendships generous or are they spare?

God, thank you for my friendships. Please help me to plant good seeds and take tender care of them so that my friends and I can enjoy an abundance of joy in each other's company.
Amen

WEEK TWENTY-SIX: TUESDAY
THE SIX-HUNDRED-DOLLAR TABLE

> Contrary to the prevailing message of our culture that free sex
> will make us feel good, it actually causes us to feel bad about
> ourselves. What's worse, the feelings of regret sometimes last a
> lifetime and actually inhibit sexual enjoyment later in marriage.
> Rick Stedman, *Pure Joy: The Positive Side of Single Sexuality*

In his book, *Pure Joy: The Positive Side of Single Sexuality*, Rick
Stedman tells a story about a table: A woman who owned an antique
store had some merchandise she wanted to get rid of, so she marked a
table tagged at five hundred dollars down to four hundred. Soon a man
came into the store and inquired about the table. He offered to buy it
for three hundred dollars. The woman was appalled. She told him the
table was worth more than a thousand dollars. Buying it for four
hundred was a great deal. They went back and forth as he kept trying to
get her to lower the price, and she kept giving reasons why it was so
valuable.

Finally, he asked her to change the price. She did. She raised it to six
hundred. He really kicked and screamed, but, as she told him, he'd done
a good job of reminding her just how valuable that table was. She said
that if she sold it for four hundred, she'd be cheating herself. It was a
lovely table and quite a bargain anyway at six hundred. Eventually he
bought the table, for six hundred dollars.

We can see that if we view that table as a highly valuable antique,
we'll take extra-special good care of it. If, however, we see it as a bargain
table, full of scratches and all dinged up, we won't care if the kids leave
water glasses on it, damaging its finish. After all, what's another ring on
an already beat-up table?

The moral to this story is fairly obvious. So is the parallel to our lives. If we give ourselves away too cheaply, we'll be treated with less consideration, respect and dignity than we deserve.

Biblically we know that we are people of incredible, inestimable value to God. He wants us to treat ourselves as his expensive, cherished children, not as beat-up bargain-basement junk. Anyway, how can we feel that our innermost beings, our most sacred, vulnerable, and intimate selves are revered, respected, and affirmed by someone we give ourselves to if we barely know that person? How can casual sex be more than a cheap thrill?

Time increases value in a relationship. Explore that concept in your journal. What feelings does the story about the six-hundred-dollar table bring up in you? Explore them too.

> *God, I don't want to sell myself cheaply. Help me to remember that I am a person of infinite value to you and to treat myself accordingly.*   *Amen*

WEEK TWENTY-SIX: WEDNESDAY
ALLOWING MY FAITH TO GROW

> The kingdom of heaven is like a mustard seed, which a man took and planted in his field. Though it is the smallest of all your seeds, yet when it grows, it is the largest of garden plants and becomes a tree.   Matthew 13:31-32

How does faith grow? What fertilizes it, waters it, makes those cells expand, divide, and multiply as it transforms itself from a tiny seed to a huge tree? How has your faith grown through this season of challenge, change, and even craziness? Have you allowed God to work in your life? Have you turned toward or away from him in your journey through divorce country?

How can we nourish our faith, so that it in turn nourishes us? There are the obvious ways: studying the Bible, hanging out with God's people, going to church. Doing good deeds; getting involved in ministry. Praying. I diligently pursued all these activities. Yet for the longest time I found it hard to feel God's love. I couldn't see God as my "Abba," my daddy. I didn't feel I deserved to approach the throne of grace with confidence, even though the Bible said that I could. That it was my right, my privilege, my pleasure. Even though I read how Jesus responded to pain and suffering with loud cries and tears, I still didn't get it. I still felt I continually had to prove my worth to God. I felt I had to earn his love over and over again. I couldn't believe that he wouldn't turn on me and punish me if I let him down, even if I didn't do it on purpose.

Because of this inability to open myself up to receive his love, when trials came my way, I panicked. Whenever I was on the firing line, I doubted God. I was afraid he'd let me down, and, in the struggles that followed, I was tempted repeatedly to give up on him and walk away. But somehow I didn't. I guess it was because in my heart I knew I had nowhere else to turn.

My faith grew slowly at first. But, over time, I came to see that God really is faithful. I realized that although I may have felt abandoned for a while, God didn't ever, wouldn't ever, abandon me. He never stopped loving me or working on me or believing I'd pull through. Finally, I was able to *feel* His love and *believe in it*. We had a track record, God and I. We became partners in this game of life. I now had someone there for me who always wanted the very best for me and kept nudging me in that direction no matter how much I wanted to do things my way.

How has your faith grown since you started reading this book? Can you describe your faith's odyssey? How has God surprised you, disciplined you, shown you his faithfulness again and again?

O Lord, you are too awesome for words, too magnificent to comprehend! Thank you for choosing me to be in your forever family. Thank you for loving me every single second of every single day.   Amen

WEEK TWENTY-SIX: THURSDAY
GROWTH INVENTORY

Then Peace [who had before been Suffering] said quietly, "I have noticed that when people are brought into sorrow and suffering, or loss, or humiliation, or grief, or into some place of great need, they sometimes become ready to know the Shepherd and to seek his help."   Hannah Hurnard, *Hinds' Feet on High Places*

Go to your favorite quiet place today and answer these questions:

1. Who hung in there with you through the gnarly parts of this divorce?
2. Who did the most wonderful, unexpected thing for you when you needed it the most? What was it?
3. Who abandoned you because your suffering was too much to bear?
4. What issues have you faced head-on and worked through this year?
5. How would you describe your wilderness experience?
6. Which six Bible passages have given you the most hope?
7. What has been your biggest challenge on this journey?
8. How has your relationship with you ex-spouse evolved since the separation? Has it gotten better or worse?
9. How are your kids doing today ? How were they three months ago? Six months ago? At the time of separation? Before that?
10. What tools did you use to help you get through this divorce?
11. How are you doing regarding forgiveness? What have you learned this year about forgiveness?

12. What has helped you the most, day in and day out?
13. What has grief taught you?
14. What is your greatest challenge right now, today?
15. Which goals have you achieved? What are you working on now?
    Father, I thank you for everything you've taught me this year. I thank you for walking with me through the wilderness. Help me to keep moving forward and growing into the person you want me to be.   *Amen*

WEEK TWENTY-SIX: SATURDAY
MAKE ME AN INSTRUMENT

Lord, make me an instrument of your peace. Where there is hatred, let me sow love; where there is injury, pardon; where there is doubt, faith; where there is despair, hope; where there is darkness, light; where there is sadness, joy.

O Divine Master, grant that I may seek not so much to be consoled as to console; not to be understood as to understand; not to be loved as to love; for it is in giving that we receive; it is in pardoning that we are pardoned; and it is in dying that we are born to eternal life.   Saint Francis of Assisi

A friend gave me this prayer on a little plaque several years ago. I always keep near me when I'm working. It reminds me of how and who I want to be. It reminds me of how people behave when the fruit of the Spirit is revealed in their lives, when they're mirroring the actions and attitudes of Jesus.

I've heard countless times that five percent of our happiness is determined by what happens to us. The other 95 percent of our happiness is determined by our attitude! We can't control events, but we can sure control our attitudes. Paul learned the secret of being content in any situation (which is a *great* attitude) in a prison cell in Rome. His comment? "I can do everything through him who gives me strength" (Philippians 4:13).

We have it in us to radiate the servant's heart demonstrated by Saint Francis. We have it in us to avoid the despair that comes from hard times described by Paul. We have it in us through the grace and goodness of the Holy Spirit who lives in our hearts. Take your Bible and journal and go off by yourself. List the opposing traits in Saint Francis' prayer and find a passage in one of the opposites that illustrates how Jesus manifested the positive qualities in his life while overcoming the negative.

> *Dear Lord, I want to be your instrument and to help bring your light into the world. Help me to develop an attitude like Saint Francis, Father. Amen*

WEEK TWENTY-SIX: SATURDAY
GOD IS IN THIS PLACE

> When Jacob awoke from his sleep, he thought, "Surely the Lord is in this place, and I was not aware of it." He was afraid and said, "How awesome is this place! This is none other than the house of God; this is the gate of heaven." Genesis 28:16-17

Have you ever come to the end of a particularly perilous journey and heaved a gigantic sigh of relief, thinking to yourself, *Wow! God's been here with me the whole time. It didn't feel like it, but now that I'm having this Kodak Moment, now that I can flash back over all that's happened and see it in the light of today, I know he was. I know he still is. Look what God taught me! Look at how I've grown! Look at how I've healed! I'm wiser now! I'm kinder now! I'm not so hard-headed. I'm not so hell-bent on revenge anymore. I don't beat myself up for not being perfect. I've learned something about forgiveness. You know, I think I'm seeing a lot more clearly than I used to. And you know what else? I think I actually feel blessed! I hate to say it, but I think I've really grown from this crisis.*

No matter where we go, God is always there. Whether we're hiding out in the bowels of the earth or soaring through the heavens, he's with us. Loving us, protecting us, encouraging us, steering us toward that path of righteousness.

Today is our last day together. It is truly a day for gratitude. Pull out your journal and turn to the Thank-You Notes to God section. Before you begin a full-blown letter, just jot down some ideas. What have you learned? How have you grown? How was God faithful to you even in the depths of despair? How are you different because of the things you've gone through this past six months? What are some of the areas where you know you still need to work? What are some of the places where you still feel that confusing, spinning, don't-know-which-end-is-up vertigo?

> *O Father, thank you for always being there and never letting go of me. Help me to continue on this journey, wherever it is that you would have me go next. I put my trust in you, and I promise to stay close to you for the rest of my life.*   *Amen*

AFTERWARD

We've just traveled together on a six-month journey, you and I—and of course, God. Not a single one of us would have gotten this far without his constant love, care, and ever-present mercy! This may be the last page of the book, but that does not mean that the journey is over, or that you should feel as if you're supposed to be completely healed.

Here are a few thoughts to ponder. The average number of time people go through recovery is three. It may be that you want to read this book and do the exercises again. If you do, start another journal. I bet you'll amaze yourself when you compare the things you write this next time around and what you thought and felt the first time through! Going around more than once helps us to gain perspective. Growth isn't linear. It's more like a roller coaster. We go up and we feel great, we hit those hair-pin turns and we're scared out of our wits. Then we go down and hit those obnoxious lows, and it feels as if pain and despair are going to be our forever companions. And as I've said over and over again, we often go "three steps forward, two steps back."

It takes a while to get through this. Remember? Six months is a start, but the process truly takes a minimum of two years—and that's if you're working hard at it! Most often it takes longer, especially if you have children and ongoing hostile relations with your ex-spouse. Remember, my friend, that when you started this book, you agreed to give yourself the gift of time. Keep on doing it! Allow yourself the luxury of going through this book again. Twice, three times, as many times as you need to. Maybe you'll want to pick it up again tomorrow. Maybe it will be next month. Or in six months. Just keep it handy—next to your bed where you can grab it if those 3:00 A.M. anxiety attacks come roaring back at you.

One last thing: No matter where you are in this journey, God is with you. Every single breath of the way! Consider these words a parting message from me to you:

> *God's unconditional love flows through me, lifts me up*
> *to the place of peace, joy and truth. It enfolds me*
> *in ever-loving, ever-present arms*
> *and soothes the deepest recesses of my soul.*
> *From me it flows outward,*
> *accepting, understanding.*
> *Serene. Steadfast.*
>
> *Amen*

SUGGESTED READING LIST

Christian Books and Magazines

Arterburn, Steve. *Addicted to Love.* Ann Arbor, MI: Servant, 1991. This title may jar you, but our society encourages us to become romance, love, and sex junkies. If you've ever found yourself craving love, affection, or sex like a drug, if you've consistently fallen for people who aren't good for you (or vice versa), this book could turn your life around.

Barr, Debbie. *Children of Divorce.* Grand Rapids: Zondervan, MI: 1992. Sheds a compassionate light on how divorce can influence and often devastate our kids. Practical, tangible ways to help your hurting children.

Burns, Bob. *Recovery from Divorce.* Nashville, TN: Thomas Nelson, 1992. Offers much-needed comfort as it helps us confront and understand the challenging aspects of divorce while moving toward recovery and wholeness.

Burns, Bob, and Whiteman, Tom. *The Fresh Start Divorce Recovery Workbook.* Nashville, TN: Thomas Nelson, 1993. A total recovery program offering practical tools, such as questions, self-tests, exercises, and actual divorce stories to help us regain self-esteem and faith in God, gain strength, rebuild family life, and discover important keys to developing balanced relationships in the future.

Cloud, Henry, and Townsend, John. *Boundaries.* Grand Rapids, MI: Zondervan, 1992. Have you ever had problems saying no? Have you ever felt overwhelmed and underappreciated in your relationships? This wonderfully insightful book can help you learn what boundaries are and how to add them to your life.

Hemfelt, Robert; Minirth, Frank; and Meier, Paul. *Love Is a Choice.* Nashville, TN: Thomas Nelson, 1989. "Codependents usually cannot see things as they are, will not evaluate circumstances as being as bad as they are, pretend bad things aren't happening, find introspection too painful." If these words ring true to you, get this book.

Hunter, Lynda. *Single Moments.* Colorado Springs, CO: Focus on the Family, 1997. If getting to know God intimately is a priority for you, get this book by the editor of *Single Parent Family Magazine.*

Purnell, Dick. *Free to Love Again: Coming to Terms with Sexual Regret.* San Bernardino, CA: Here's Life, 1989. An inspiring look at overcoming destructive behaviors, understanding God's intentions regarding sexuality, marriage, overcoming past shame by experiencing God's forgiveness, learning to forgive ourselves, enjoying healing, and discovering how to have a healthy relationship.

Single-Parent Family Magazine. Published by Focus on the Family, this incredible magazine offers practical help, insight, and healing to people who have gone through a divorce and are now trying to raise their kids, as custodial or noncustodial parents.

Smedes, Lewis. *Forgive and Forget.* San Francisco, CA: Harper, 1984. Shows you how to move from hurting and hating to healing and reconciliation. With the lessons of forgiveness, you can establish healthier relationships, reclaim the happiness that should be yours, and achieve lasting peace of mind.

Smoke, Jim. *Growing through Divorce.* Eugene, OR: Harvest House, 1995. Smoke has spent the more than two decades ministering to those going through the agony of divorce. Offers hope, understanding, and practical guidance for those in the midst of this crisis.

Smoke, Jim. *Turning Your World Right Side Up.* Colorado Springs, CO: Focus on the Family, 1995. Adjusting to being single-again is traumatic. Here is help for developing the courage and strength to move on with your life and tools to get going.

Sprague, Gary. *Kids Caught in the Middle.* Nashville, TN: Thomas Nelson, 1993. An interactive workbook designed to help kids break out of the cycle of divorce and dysfunction by allowing gentle communication with a parent on tough subjects. Offers much-needed support and encouragement.

Sprague, Gary. *My Parents Got a Divorce.* Colorado Springs, CO: Chariot Books, 1992. Boys and girls from divorced families share their feelings so that other kids experiencing divorce can see the healing God has provided in their lives. A great book for kids and for parents.

Stoop, David. *Self-Talk: Key to Personal Growth.* Grand Rapids, MI: Fleming H. Revell, 1996. Practical and easy-to-read. Help for using biblical truths to gain control of your emotions and thoughts while reducing stress, anxiety, guilt, and anger. You will learn to act, rather than react to circumstances.

Whiteman, Thomas. *Innocent Victims: Understanding the Needs and Fears of Your Children.* Nashville, TN: Thomas Nelson, 1992. Will help you see divorce through your children's eyes. Help for developing and maintaining a positive attitude and sense of direction for your kids.

Yancey, Philip. *Disappointment with God.* Grand Rapids, MI: Zondervan, 1988. Is God unfair? Silent? Hidden? If your divorce has almost shattered your faith, this book can offer you solace and direction as you inch your way back to trusting God.

Secular Books

Berger, Stuart. *Divorce Without Victims.* New York, NY: Signet, 1983. A warmly understanding survival manual for parents, with step-by-step instructions for helping a child through divorce with a minimum of stress and turmoil. The full spectrum of issues is examined, from explaining divorce, to games parents play, to stepfamilies.

Brown, Laurene Krasny, and Brown Marc Toby. *The Dinosaur's Divorce: A Guide for Changing Families.* Boston, MA: Little, Brown, 1988. A picture book for kids five and up that deals with the difficult issues surrounding divorce and split households.

Gardner, Richard A. *The Boys and Girls Book about Divorce.* New York, NY: Bantam, 1971. This warm and honest book gives reassuring answers to the questions children are so often afraid to ask during and after a divorce. Written so you can either read it to your children or they can read it themselves.

Sinetar, Marsha. *Do What You Love, the Money Will Follow.* New York, NY: Dell, 1987. Awesome for anyone who's burned out careerwise and wondering what the true life's work should be. How to tune into your inner world and discover your unique talents, improve self-esteem, banish your outdated "should" tapes, and push through the resistance barrier to fulfillment.

Trafford, Abigail. *Crazy Time: Surviving Divorce, and Building a New Life.* New York, NY: Harper, 1993. A compassionate book that charts the milestones from separation to recovery, from the insanity of separation to a new chance for happiness and emotional fulfillment. Outlines the critical emotional passages that every divorcing person confronts and has the opportunity to survive. Provides a good tool to help avoid common pitfalls by recognizing and illustrating their consequences.

Wallerstein, Judith, and Blakeslee, Sandra. *Second Chances: Men, Women, and Children a Decade after Divorce, Who Wins, Who Loses—And Why.* New York, NY: Ticknor and Fields, 1989. The first book to provide a comprehensive account of the long-term emotional, economic, and psychological effects of divorce—on adults and especially on children. A must read.

ABOUT THE AUTHOR

Ann Hazard lives in Cardiff-by-the-Sea, California. She has been a single mother since 1990, when her children were three and five years old. A graduate of U.S. International University in San Diego, CA, Ann spent the first two decades of her career in construction project administration, human resources and corporate communications. In addition to *Rise Up and Walk—A Journey Through Divorce,* she has written two other books: *Cooking With Baja Magic—Mouth-Watering Meals from the Kitchens and Campfires of Baja* and *Cartwheels in the Sand—Baja California, Four Women and a Motor Home.* She has a deep affinity for the people, culture and landscapes of Mexico, and spends as much time there as possible, in her second home in La Bufadora, just south of Ensenada, Baja California. She has worked extensively in Divorce Recovery and as a free-lance writer, specializing in Mexico. Her next book, *Agave Sunsets—Baja Loves Stories* will be released in 2002.

Ann currently writes a column for the San Diego newspaper, *The Coast News,* called "Baja Memories." Prior to that, she wrote a weekly column for the same paper, entitled "Living the Teenage Tango," which dealt with the ups and downs of single parenting. She does a weekly cooking feature, MexCocina for MexGrocer.com, writes monthly for *The Baja Tourist Guide,* has a quarterly cooking column in *Discover Baja Travel Club Newsletter* and has written articles for *Baja Traveler Magazine, Cedros Review Magazine, The North County Times, The Los Angeles Times,* Viajo.com, Recreate.com, BajaPortal.com, EnsenadaGazette.com, Mexonline.com and BajaNomad.com. Ann did all promotional writing for Foxploration, the movie-making park at

Fox Studios Baja. She has also done promotional writing for the famous Rosarito Beach Hotel and the Rosarito Convention and Visitors Bureau.

Ann is committed to pursuing a path of love, awareness, healing and peace for all the people of this world ... on a personal, communal, national and global level. That is the guiding purpose behind this book.

www.ingramcontent.com/pod-product-compliance
Lightning Source LLC
Chambersburg PA
CBHW061338280526
45784CB00001B/55